Life and Death in Mohawk Country

Other books by Bruce E. Johansen:

Wasi'chu: The Continuing Indian Wars, with Roberto F. Maestas

Forgotten Founders: Benjamin Franklin, the Iroquois and the Rationale for the American Revolution

El Pueblo: The Gallegos Family's American Journey, 1503–1980, with Roberto F. Maestas

Exemplar of Liberty: Native America and the Evolution of Democracy, with Donald A. Grinde., Jr.

Life and Death in Mohawk Country

Bruce E. Johansen
Professor of Communication and Native American Studies
University of Nebraska at Omaha

Original Artwork
John Kahionhes Fadden

North American Press
Golden, Colorado

Cover design by Robert B. Phillips
Cover photograph courtesy of *Akwesasne Notes*
Maps by John Kahionhes Fadden

Library of Congress Cataloging-in-Publication Data
Johansen, Bruce E. (Bruce Elliott)
Life and death in Mohawk country / Bruce E. Johansen.
p. cm.
Includes bibliographical references and index.
ISBN 1-55591-906-5 (cloth)
1. Mohawk Indians—Gambling. 2. Mohawk Indians—Politics and government. 3. Mohawk Indians—Government relations. 4. Gambling—Akwesasne Indian Reserve (Québec and Ont.) 5. Gambling—(State)—Saint Regis Mohawk Indian Reservation. 6. Akwesasne Indian Reserve (Québec and Ont.)—Social conditions. 7. Saint Regis Mohawk Indian Reservation (N.Y.)—Social conditions. I. Title.
E99. M8J65 1993
971.4 ' 34—dc20 92-43430
CIP

Printed in the United States of America

0 9 8 7 6 5 4 3 2 1

North American Press
350 Indiana Street, Suite 350
Golden, Colorado 80401-5093

To those who have lived and died in Akwesasne's struggle to preserve life for coming generations: Jake Fire, Mathew Pyke, "Junior" Edwards, and many others.

▼▼▼

Contents

▼▼▼

Foreword

Life in Indian country has taken a most interesting turn over the past five years. From the 1960's Native American movements have been characterized by efforts to retain a distinct native society based on the retention of aboriginal culture, the protection of reservation lands, and the preservation of treaty rights.

Since the Reagan administration the principles for which Native people fought so long and hard have changed. From cultural revival and preservation of the land, native governments have turned to commercial gaming as a primary source of economic development—but not without resistance and often heated internal debate.

In Iroquois country there are very specific traditional laws that prohibit commercial gaming. The Iroquois Confederacy has time and again issued statements substantiating this position. The Mohawk Nation is one of six members of this ancient Confederacy. The problem with the Mohawks was that the United States and Canada imposed colonial governments upon its territory at Akwesasne resulting in three Indian councils vying for power over 8,000 people on 28,000 acres of heavily polluted lands astride the St. Lawrence River. This small reservation is also split in half by the international border, making it a jurisdictional nightmare.

Given this unstable environment, gambling was bound to produce friction. The supporters of the Mohawk Nation (and hence the Iroquois Confederacy) opposed using hard fought for, and hard won, native rights to make money from an activity the elders deemed inconsistent with Iroquois culture. This did not stop individual Mohawks from exercising an entrepreneurial spirit by defying their leaders and opening bingo halls and casinos.

How does a community with such a widely respected history of positive political and cultural activism such as Akwesasne fall apart? What are the factors in the destruction of a people so many had looked to as leaders in the Indian movement? Why did the Mohawk people turn on each other in a great orgy of violence and hate? What are the consequences for Indians as a whole and can we extract lessons from the trauma suffered by the Mohawk Nation?

Professor Johansen has provided much of the answers in his book *Life and Death in Mohawk Country*. He has for the first time given careful analysis to the many factors that caused the death and destruction of 1989–90. He brings to the story a strong background in Mohawk history, having already been author of two books about the Iroquois. In addition, he has had a unique relationship with many of the people mentioned in this book, one based on trust and respect. Professor Johansen was given exclusive access to primary records and first account testimony in the belief he would write an objective analysis of what happened and why. In this, he has succeeded.

Other books have been written about the Mohawk gambling wars of 1989–90 and how the violence at Akwesasne was grafted onto its sister communities of Oka and Kahnawake, but no volume, until this one, has given the reader the necessary background essential to understand why things happened as they did. Without knowing the elements that characterized the fight at Akwesasne, one cannot fathom the events at Oka and the subsequent effects on Native people throughout North America. What was sorely lacking in previous books was a command of the facts as the Mohawk people saw them. Until Professor Johansen began his research, no author had the trust and confidence of the Mohawk people necessary to write about events that are as sensitive as they are terrifying.

As one who was deeply involved in the defense of the Mohawk Nation and the Iroquois Confederacy during this time of troubles, I can say, with confidence and enthusiasm, Professor Johansen has compiled the definitive work on this subject. I was a witness to most of the events in *Life and Death in Mohawk Country* and am pleased with Johansen's exceptional analysis of the many complicated factors that resulted in the breakdown of our community in 1990. He tells the story clearly, accurately, and in a style that is both visual and dramatic. This book is more than highly recommended, it is essential to anyone with an interest in the Mohawks–Iroquois specifically and native people as a whole. *Life and Death in Mohawk Country* would serve as caution to all communities considering commercial gambling as a means to easy wealth.

February 1, 1993
Douglas M. George-Kanentiio
Editor, Akwesasne Notes *and* Indian Time

▼▼▼

Preface

This book was first conceived by Mark Narsisian and John Kahionhes Fadden, both Akwesasne Mohawks. John is a teacher, artist, and associate curator of the Six Nations Indian Museum at Onchiota, New York. Mark has been active in publication of *Akwesasne Notes* and *Indian Time* at Akwesasne. I got to know John during the course of my work on an earlier book. We had become friends through correspondence in 1988; in late May and early June 1990, we met for the first time at his home.

Our original meeting was to consider ideas for sketches that John was contributing to my book. As we talked about historical artwork, the crisis at Akwesasne had reached fever pitch following the shooting deaths of two Mohawk men on May 1, 1990. John suggested that there was a book in it and that I ought to write it. We visited the reservation on June 2, 1990, one day after a tribal election. Two days later, John convened a meeting of Mohawk activists and journalists to talk about the book idea.

I agreed with John that a book ought to be written after hearing what Mohawk people had to say and reading a smattering of news clips from the local newspapers on events that had already occurred at Akwesasne. John and his father Ray Fadden had already clipped articles from many of the newspapers in upstate New York on the rising tension, the blockades, and the shooting deaths of "Junior" Edwards and Mathew Pyke. After looking at a fraction of them, I asked John to funnel source material my way in Omaha. John and Ray parted with a large collection of videotapes, newspaper clippings, and other documents.

Along the way, John also convinced many other people to trust me with their files, including Mark Narsisian, Chief Tom Porter, and the staff of the North American Indian Traveling College. Konwawihon Fox must have gotten rather tired of standing over a photocopying machine.

Thanks also are due the Mohawk Council of Akwesasne (the tribal government that Canada recognizes), especially Salli Benedict, who did much to correct misimpressions and errors in early drafts of this book. Mrs. Paul Herne, Sue Ellen Herne, and Terry Peters also provided critiques. At Akwesasne, Glen Lazore helped with the factual background of the book and provided lodging during my second research trip in August 1991. Doug George and other staff at *Akwesasne Notes* and *Indian Time* allowed me generous access to their clippings, photo, and artwork files. Darren Bonaparte loaned me his cartoons from both newspapers. Allen Gabriel from Kanesatake and Eileen Patton from Kahnawake provided invaluable aid in correcting mistakes I had picked up from newspaper accounts about events in and around Oka.

Much of the material in this book was drawn from newspaper clippings, diaries, and other contemporary reports. Sources are identified in the notes section at the end of each chapter. Usually I found that the reporters and eyewitnesses closest to the scene were the most consistently reliable. These included the Mohawk people themselves and reporters who covered the reservation on a regular basis for U.S. daily newspapers in Watertown, Albany, and Syracuse, as well as Cornwall, Ottawa, Montreal, and Toronto in Canada. Names that stand out as I reviewed thousands of news clips and videotapes sent by Mohawk people include: Paul Warloski of the Malone *Telegram*, Alexander Norris of the Montreal *Gazette*, Alison Calkins of the Plattsburgh *Press-Republican*, Robert Whitaker and Michael Gormley of the Albany *Times-Union*, Barbara Stith and Tom Foster of the Syracuse *Post-Standard*, M.C. Burns of the Syracuse *Herald-American*, Timothy Cornell of the Watertown *Daily Times*, and Doug George, editor of *Indian Time* and *Akwesasne Notes*. I also owe a debt of gratitude to the staff at the two Mohawk papers for information, advice, and companionship. Other material was gathered through personal interviews and correspondence.

The most helpful single document about the crisis at Akwesasne was the transcript of the New York State Assembly hearings, which recorded two days of testimony, July 24, 1990, at Fort Covington and August 2, 1990, at Albany. Many of the personal statements cited in the book were drawn from this 1,300-page manuscript. Gerald Alfred, a Kahnawake resident and doctoral candidate in government studies at Cornell University, published a highly useful account "From Bad to Worse: Internal Politics in the 1990 Crisis at Kahnawake" in *Northeast Indian Quarterly* (Spring 1991). The Iroquois Confederacy's negotiating team's reports provided invaluable detail and insight that helped me develop the sequence of events at Kanesatake and Kahnawake.

Toni Truesdale of Philadelphia provided copies of videotaped news broadcasts recorded by John Kahionhes Fadden. Nathan Koenig, director of White Buffalo Multi-Media of Woodstock, New York, also generously shared videotaped materials with me. The American Indian Program at

Cornell University supplied access to its detailed reports on the environmental situation at Akwesasne.

I also would like to thank my wife, Patricia Keiffer, who showed her love by putting up with my author's habits. I tell her that writing a book is as close as a man can come to having a child. I'd also like to thank the professors, students, and staff of the University of Nebraska at Omaha Department of Communication, especially Don Wright and Dave Manning, who kept the office Macintoshes operating as I pounded the life out of their keyboards and ran reams of paper through our laser printers.

Additional gratitude is due the Freedom Forum, which supplied a grant that helped support research expenses for this work, as well as for articles drawn from it. Dr. Felix Gutierrez of the Freedom Forum and Dr. James Carey of the University of Illinois were especially helpful. Editors Shirley Lambert and Tammy Ferris of North American Press/Fulcrum also contributed immeasurably to the coherence and scope of the final product.

▼▼▼

Table of Relevant Persons, Places, and Terms

Nonviolent observers at barricades

- Linda Champagne, Martin Luther King, Jr., Institute for Nonviolence
- Horace Cook, Iroquois Confederacy
- Charlotte Debbane, Canadian citizen
- Margaret Weitzman, Potsdam, New York

Iroquois observers and negotiators

- John Mohawk (Seneca)
- Oren Lyons (Onondaga)
- Leon Shenandoah, speaker, Iroquois Confederacy (Onondaga)

Mohawk settlements (see map on page xv)

- Akwesasne
- Ganienkeh
- Kahnawake
- Kanesatake

Structure of Iroquois Confederacy

- Note: Haudenosaunee, meaning "people of the Longhouse" is an indigenous term for the Iroquois Confederacy. Iroquois is a French name; Six Nations is English and refers to the six Iroquois tribes (see list under "Nation councils")
- Haudenosaunee Grand Council, at Onondaga, south of Syracuse (United States)
- Haudenosaunee Grand Council, Grand River (Canada)
- Kahnawake Longhouse

Nation councils
- Mohawk or Mohawk Nation Council, "keepers of the eastern door"
- Oneida
- Onondaga, "firekeepers"
- Tuscarora, adopted into confederacy ca. 1710
- Cayuga
- Seneca, "keepers of the western door"

Reservation governing bodies created by non-Iroquois law
- Kahnawake band council
- Mohawk Council of Akwesasne: Canada, Québec, Ontario; Akwesasne Mohawk Police
- St. Regis Tribal Council: United States, New York state

Akwesasne or the St. Regis Mohawk Indian Reservation (see maps on page 29)
- Cornwall Island
- Hogansburg
- Route 37 (gambling strip)
- St. Regis Village
- Snye

Environmental advocates
- Henry Lickers, Mohawk Council of Akwesasne
- James Ransom, St. Regis Tribal Council
- Ward Stone, New York Department of Environmental Conservation

Gambling opponents
- Barbara Barnes
- Salli Benedict
- Darren Bonaparte
- Rosemary Bonaparte, former chief on St. Regis Tribal Council
- Brian Cole, economic planner, St. Regis Tribal Council
- Dave "Davey" George, brother of Doug George
- Doug George (Kanentiio), editor of *Akwesasne Notes* and *Indian Time*
- Lee Ann (or Leanne) Jock
- Ernest King, chief, Akwesasne Mohawk Police
- Brenda LaFrance
- Ron LaFrance, subchief, Mohawk Nation Council; director, American Indian Program, Cornell University
- Jerry McDonald
- Mike Mitchell, grand chief, Mohawk Council of Akwesasne
- Barry Montour (son of Art Kakwirakeron Montour)

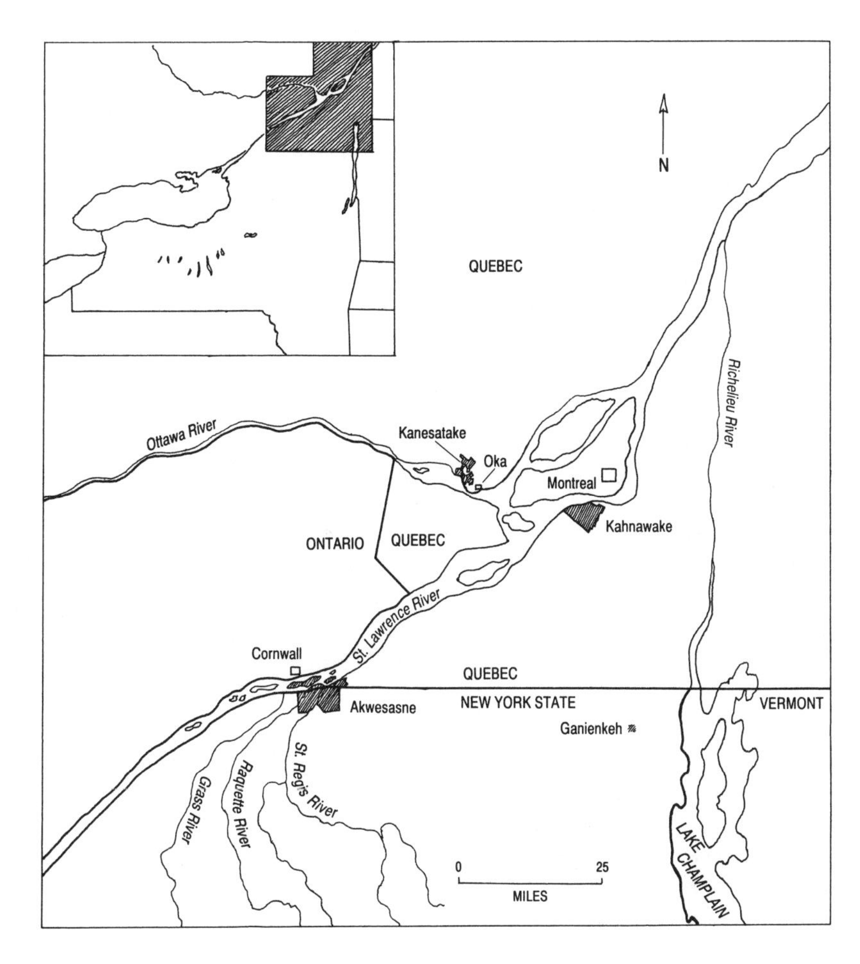

Barbara Montour, wife of Barry Montour
Margaret Peters
Tom Porter, subchief, Mohawk Nation Council
Mathew John Wenhiesseriio Pyke, killed May 1, 1990, with J. R. "Junior" Edwards, who was not clearly identified with either side
Andrea Swamp
Jake Swamp, subchief, Mohawk Nation Council
Harold Tarbell, head chief, St. Regis Tribal Council, until June 1990

Warrior Society (Mohawk Sovereignty Security Force)
Francis Boots
John Boots
Stanley Cohen, attorney
Minnie Garrow
Louis Karoniaktajeh Hall, ideological founder
Mark Maracle

Art Kakwirakeron Montour
Lorraine Montour
Verna Montour
Mike Myers
Onkwe Bingo Jack (headquarters)
Seth Shapiro, attorney
Tommy Square
Loran Thompson, "dehorned," or impeached, subchief, Mohawk Nation Council
Warrior Longhouse, Kahnawake

Gambling supporters
Julius D. "Speed" Herne
Leo David Jacobs, chief, St. Regis Tribal Council
Tony Laughing, Tony Vegas International
William (Bill) "Wild Bill" Sears, Wild Bill's Grocery
Norman "Nummie" Tarbell, chief, St. Regis Tribal Council
Cindy Terrance, editor, *The People's Voice*
Guilford D. White, Mohawk Bingo Palace
Lincoln White, chief, St. Regis Tribal Council

Laws, court decisions, and treaties
(chronological order)
Treaty of Canandaigua (1794) allows Iroquois to request U.S. aid to remove non-Indians or halt criminal activity.
Jay Treaty (1794) defines Mohawks' border crossing rights.
Worchester v. Georgia (1832) U.S. Supreme Court ruling establishing native reservations as "dependent domestic nations."
Dawes (Allotment) Acts (1880s) U.S. Supreme Court ruling that split Indian reservations held in common into individual land holdings.
Indian Advancement Act (1884), Canada
Seminole Tribe of Florida v. Butterworth (1980) U.S. Fifth Circuit Court *PL-280* (last amended, 1968) U.S. federal law regarding state jurisdiction on Indian reservations.
Indian Gaming Regulatory Act (1988) Public Law 100-497, implements Indian Gaming Regulatory Act

Non-Mohawk political figures and public officials
George Bush, U.S. president, 1988–1992
John Ciaccia, Indian affairs minister, Québec
Thomas Constantine, superintendent, New York state police
Mario Cuomo, governor, New York
Arthur O. Eve, New York State Assembly
Maurice Hinchey, New York State Assembly

Leigh F. Hunt, Syracuse police chief; director, New York native-relations office (created 1991)
Senator Daniel Inouye, chairman, U.S. Senate Select Committee on Indian Affairs, United States
Marcel Lemay, Sureté du Québec officer killed at Oka
Manuel Lujan, secretary, U.S. Department of Interior
Brian Mulroney, Canadian prime minister
Chris Ortloff, New York State Assembly
Ronald Reagan, U.S. president, 1980–1988
Steven Sanders, New York State Assembly
Thomas Siddon, Indian-affairs minister, Canada

Law-enforcement agencies
- United States
  - Federal Bureau of Investigation (FBI)
  - New York state police
- Canada
  - Army
  - Ontario provincial police
  - Royal Canadian Mounted Police (RCMP)
  - Sureté du Québec (SQ)

Historical personages
- Deganawidah, founder of the Iroquois Confederacy, establishing the Great Law of Peace (referred to as the "Peacemaker" in all oral discourse)
- Jake Fire, Mohawk martyr, killed May 1, 1899
- Handsome Lake, prophet, Code of Handsome Lake, ca. 1800
- Hiawatha (Aiowantha), speaker for Deganawidah

▼▼▼

Introduction

It isn't often that the Omaha *World-Herald* serves up a photo of an acquaintance hitting the ground with a large-caliber rifle in hand. On May 2, 1990, however, over cold cereal, I surveyed with disbelief a four-column photo of Doug George clutching a rifle atop an article reporting that two Mohawks had died in violence over reservation gambling. Was this man in Vietnam-era battle fatigues also the soft-spoken editor of *Akwesasne Notes*, with whom I had talked a year earlier?

That a newspaper editor would take up a rifle to defend his brother's house told me a lot about the atmosphere at Akwesasne, where in the spring of 1990, guns and firebombs became part of the debate over gambling on the reservation. A month later, I visited John Kahionhes Fadden, an Akwesasne Mohawk, and we sought out George. He winced as he talked about the moment captured in the photo. "I hardly knew how to use that gun," he said. Nevertheless, during the early morning of May 1, 1990, as George watched Associated Press photographer Ryan Remiorz make his way along the shore of the Saint Lawrence River near his brother Davey's house during a murderous firefight, he had expressed concern for the photographer's safety. "Get down! I'll show you how to crawl," George had shouted at Remiorz, cradling the rifle in his arms. The photographer, who knew a good picture when he saw one, then took the shot that appeared across the United States and Canada the next day.

George played a direct role, as editor and participant, in a conflict that was analyzed in the press mainly as a clash between Mohawks. "Mohawk civil war" was the popular phrase. The conflict was usually characterized as a battle between Mohawk factions over gambling. Although the events that shook the Mohawk reservations of Akwesasne, Kahnawake, and Kanesatake did pit Mohawks against Mohawks (often estranging members of families), and although gambling was a major issue, the root cause was not personal animosity, smuggling, guns, or gambling alone. The events were rooted in the loss of a productive land base and a way of life that was once based on it.

To call the conflict a "civil war" ignores the non-Indian context. Non-Indians polluted the Saint Lawrence River and industrialized its shorelines; non-Indians provided the customer base for casinos and smuggled cigarettes. Non-Indians pushed the Mohawks at Oka, Quebec, onto parcels of land that comprised only a portion of what they once occupied, igniting violent confrontation over centuries-old land claims later in the summer of 1990. To call the conflict a "civil war" does highlight the disagreements between the Mohawks themselves and accentuates the fact that most of the blood spilled was Mohawk blood. In the final analysis, however, calling what erupted in the spring and summer of 1990 a "civil war" ignores centuries of bad faith and broken promises.

The strife that paralyzed Mohawk country in 1990 was not a series of events isolated in time but the violent culmination of many events and issues that grew out of the ruination of the traditional way of life. This attempt at tracing the recent history of Mohawk country is really a case study of how the modern industrial state can crush a native way of life. Without loss of the land and the way of life that Mohawks had based on it, the nationalistic Warrior Society, a Mohawk paramilitary group whose image mesmerized headline writers in the northeastern United States and most of Canada during that violent summer of 1990, might never have arisen. Had the construction of the Saint Lawrence Seaway shortly after World War II and subsequent industrialization of the area not destroyed traditional ways of making a living in Mohawk Country, gambling and smuggling may never have emerged as avenues of economic survival there.

The Saint Lawrence Seaway brought manufacturing plants to Mohawk country that profited from ready access to the ocean and cheap power. This industrial base generated the pollution that ruined the farming, fishing, and hunting economy at Akwesasne and its sister Mohawk reserves. The destruction of the natural world, along with erosion of Mohawk land base, made living by the old ways nearly impossible and prompted many Mohawks to look for other ways to survive in the cash economy. During the first half of the twentieth century, many moved away; some became the legendary "Mohawks in high steel," the men who constructed large parts of the urban skylines from Montreal to New York City. Later some returned home to ply the smuggling trades and build the gaudy "strip" along Highway 37 across Akwesasne, which straddles the U.S. and Canadian border.

A steep rise in Canadian taxes on tobacco opened opportunities in smuggling of cigarettes, which were sold at smokeshops on the Mohawk reserve of Kahnawake, near Montreal. Ancillary smuggling in alcohol, illicit drugs, and weapons followed. The smuggling trade provided the precedent and the seed money for gambling that was never regulated according to U.S. law. Very little of the gambling revenue went to meet tribal needs.

In addition to smuggling, the paramilitary Warrior Society was growing at all three Mohawk reserves. The Warriors fed on the frustrations of Mohawks whose old ways had been destroyed and whose lives were deteriorating day by day as factories poisoned the lands that had not been taken from them. While many Mohawks disparaged the violent tactics of the Warriors that often made them feel like hostages in their own homes, everyone in Mohawk country understood the roots of the problems that had led to the rise of tension and conflict.

As many states set up lotteries to supplement tax revenues, the federal government decided that gaming revenues could "wean" the Indians from the federal "teat." As it sought to deregulate banking, trucking, and other industries, the Reagan administration also set out to privatize native tribes, encouraging private economic development.

The Supreme Court in *Worchester v. Georgia* (1832) declared Native American communities to be "dependent domestic nations." U.S. courts have been wrestling with definitions of sovereignty ever since gambling became the latest governmental answer to Indians' impoverishment. The U.S. federal government was acting in federal tradition when it enacted the Indian Gaming Regulatory Act of 1988. The act said that tribes could begin regulated gaming subject to negotiation of compacts with states that surrounded their reservations. Like most previous grand experiments, this one sometimes fulfilled expectations. Just as often, other realities rudely intervened. At Akwesasne, gambling was already well established, without a state compact or tribal regulation, even before the 1988 act was passed. With the complications of an international border and the smuggling trade, the situation at Akwesasne would become a test of this federal government experiment in economic and social engineering, which would collide with the ambitions of outside investors to turn "Indian country" into islands of hands-off gambling.

Even at the height of the violence in 1990, Mohawks on both sides steadfastly maintained that a solution lay in the rehabilitation of the earth. From this perspective, gambling was more a catalyst than a cause of the violence that reached its peak during one hellish week in late April 1990 at Akwesasne, which culminated in nightly firefights that reminded some observers of Beirut or Northern Ireland.

Similarly, at Kanesatake (Oka), the expansion of a golf course from 9 to 18 holes also was more a catalyst than a cause, although the press quickly dubbed the confrontation at Oka the "Golf-Course War." Land claims, not gambling, was the primary issue. This confrontation with police and Canadian Army troops lasted longer than the 1973 standoff at

Wounded Knee, South Dakota. It touched off native protests across Canada, and helped prompt an intense debate over how that country was treating native people. In Canada, the violence occurred in an atmosphere in which the impetus toward gambling was much more tepid, and not at all encouraged by off-reservation governments. Superficially, the situations at Akwesasne and at Oka seemed to share little, but in reality both stemmed from the loss of a sustainable land base, an issue that Mohawks share with native people across North America.

In 1990 at Akwesasne, however, the violence was most pervasive. It escalated from early protests against gambling in the late 1980s (including the trashing of one casino and the burning of another), to attempts by gambling supporters to brutally repress this resistance, to residents' blockades of the reservation to keep the casinos' customers out, to the violent destruction of the same blockades in late April. By the end of April 1990, the violence spiralled into brutal beatings of antigambling activists, drive-by shootings, and night-long firefights that culminated in two Mohawk deaths during the early morning of May 1. Intervention of several police agencies from the United States and Canada followed the two deaths; outside police presence continued two years later.

Akwesasne struggles daily with a maze of governmental jurisdictions unfamiliar to many North Americans. It shares many economic problems with other native communities such as high unemployment, alcoholism, drug addiction, and a lack of an adequate economic base. Akwesasne's profile of social and economic dysfunction compares unfavorably even with many inner cities in North America. Perhaps worst of all, the air, water, and soil at Akwesasne has been poisoned by upstream industrial plants along the Saint Lawrence to a degree that some of its wildlife could be classified as hazardous waste.

To understand how the crisis at Akwesasne, Kahnawake and Kanesatake took shape, the reader needs to understand the governmental landscape. The land the Mohawks call Akwesasne was separated by the U.S.–Canadian border shortly after the War of 1812. The area under Canadian jurisdiction is also separated by the border of English-speaking Ontario and French-speaking Quebec. The Mohawks who live on the U.S. side of the international border live in New York state. Thus, one community lives under five external governments.

Three bodies govern the reservation itself. The oldest is the Akwesasne Mohawk Nation Council, a council assembled according to the Great Law of Peace, the Iroquois' own governance system. This council predates European settlement and is not recognized by the United States or Canada. Therefore, these two national governments created one governing body for each side of the international boundary: the St. Regis Tribal Council in the United States and the Mohawk Council of Akwesasne in Canada.

The nine men on the Mohawk Nation Council are descended through clan bloodlines from the Mohawk nation council of the ancient

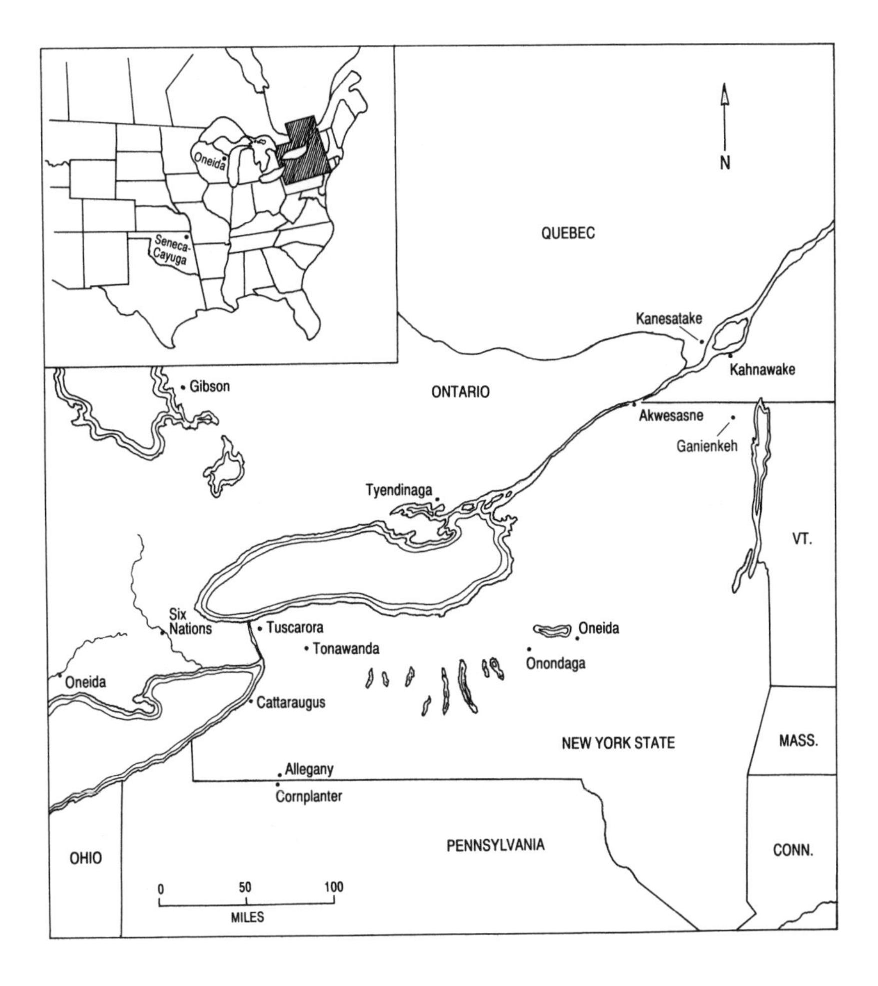

Iroquois Confederacy, which was formed well before contact with Europeans. The nine chiefs are the elected leaders of a participatory democracy, each selected from three clans (bear, wolf, and turtle) by clan mothers charged with polling the consensus of their family members. Treaties negotiated with the Mohawks before 1800 were signed with the Mohawk Nation Council, not the St. Regis Mohawk Council nor the Mohawk Council of Akwesasne. Mohawks from both sides of the international border participate in the Mohawk Nation Council, which comprises one of six national Iroquois councils (Seneca, Tuscarora, Oneida, Cayuga, Onondaga, and Mohawk). Together, the six national councils make up the Iroquois Confederacy, with its central fire, or executive function, exercised by the Onondagas, who coordinate the confederacy from their small reservation in Nedrow, New York, a few miles south of Syracuse.

The Mohawk Nation Council has been an influential force at Akwesasne for centuries. That influence continues today. In 1990, the Mohawk Nation Council was made up of one chief, Ross Tekarihoken David, who has been "condoled" (installed as a chief according to ceremony) and eight subchiefs: Jake Swamp, Tom Porter, Edward Gray, Richard Powless, Richard Mitchell, Richard Cook, Louis Thompson, and Ron LaFrance. (Tom Porter resigned his position in early 1992 for health reasons.)

A chief of the Mohawk Nation Council is appointed for life, unless he is "dehorned" (impeached) or resigns. A chief or subchief is said to assume antlers when he is installed into office; the horns may be removed for impeachable behavior outlined in the Iroquois Great Law of Peace. Because it receives no governmental funding from the United States or Canada, the expenses of the Mohawk Nation Council are met by donations from individual Mohawks and some of Akwesasne's businesses. As one of the original five nations of the Iroquois Confederacy (the sixth nation, the Tuscaroras, were invited into the confederacy about 1710), the Mohawk Nation Council's leaders (as well as other citizens) carry their own passports, which are recognized by several foreign countries, such as Switzerland, but not by the United States or Canada.

The St. Regis Tribal Council, which is recognized by the United States, was created by New York state in 1802. It consists of three trustees, three subchiefs, and a tribal clerk. This council is referred to as the St. Regis Tribal Council, the New York council, or the U.S. elected council. The positions on the council became elective about 1898.

Many Mohawks refuse to participate in a system that they believe has been imposed on them from the outside. Only a small minority of Akwesasne's people participate in most of the elections. The chiefs and subchiefs are elected at large on the part of Akwesasne under U.S. jurisdiction, with elections for each chief's position rotating every three years. For example, Norman Tarbell finishes his three-year term in June 1993, and Leo David Jacobs' term expires in June 1994. Subchief James Ransom is also a crucial figure as the St. Regis Tribal Council's most knowledgeable environmental advocate in a land ravaged by pollution.

Canada recognizes the Mohawk Council of Akwesasne, which consists of 12 chiefs and one grand chief. The chiefs are presently elected in groups of four, representing three districts within the portions of Akwesasne that lie within Canadian jurisdiction. The grand chief is elected at large. All 13 are elected on the same ballot every three years. The Mohawk Council of Akwesasne, established in 1899 by Canada's Department of Indian Affairs, is sometimes informally referred to as the Canadian-side council, the Canadian band council, or by the initials comprising its proper name, MCA. Its operations are funded by Canadian government. The present grand chief, Mike Mitchell, has been an important opponent of high-stakes casino gambling at Akwesasne, along with chiefs Lynn Roundpoint and Lloyd Benedict.

In one way or another, Akwesasne Mohawks in the course of their everyday business deal with eight different governments, not including counties and off-reservation municipalities. To many Akwesasne Mohawks, these overlapping boundaries have played a very large role in creating an atmosphere of anarchy that has allowed the development of the large-scale cigarette, liquor, drug, and weapons smuggling as well as unregulated casino gambling. The international boundary (as well as those of states and provinces) create so many governmental units that the reservation, especially the parts under U.S. jurisdiction, has become a legal no-man's land with no police force of its own. The rationale for the casinos had already been tested in smuggling: they called it "sovereignty." In native law and tradition, the issues of sovereignty ensures native peoples' rights to chart their own path. Some of the smugglers who formed the nucleus of the progambling forces took the concept of native sovereignty and turned it into a legal and public-relations tool to further their business interests.

To describe the situation in a nutshell, I will borrow from the words of Darren Bonaparte, a Mohawk writer and artist who experienced much of it firsthand:

> If one were to generalize the pattern of intimidation and violence that plagued Akwesasne for the past two years [1989–1990], the result would read an awful lot like the packaging of a B-grade movie for videocassette. It was almost as if some sleazy Hollywood film producer sat down and wrote a script about what it would be like if the *Godfather, Scarface*, and the *Untouchables* took place on an Indian reservation and proceeded to act out that script with real guns and real ammunition.[1]

Akwesasne is an important place in the recent history of native America. It hosted the White Roots of Peace, a traveling group that carried the message of the Great Peace around the United States, beginning in the 1960s. For centuries the Iroquois Confederacy has been among the most influential political organizations in native America, a continuation of its pivotal role in native affairs predating the "discovery" of America by Europeans. The Iroquois, especially the Mohawks, also have been major figures in American history, literature, and lore; the patriots who dumped tea in Boston Harbor dressed as Mohawks; *Drums Along the Mohawk* has been a classic in American literature for centuries. For more than two decades Akwesasne also has served as home base for *Akwesasne Notes*, the only native-produced newspaper distributed nationally during most of that period.

People on both sides of the feud over gambling sometimes refer to themselves as traditional Mohawks. The term can mean a person or a family who chooses to live outside the "mainstream" life imposed on Native Americans by the European or white culture and governments. Traditional may refer to a person or group of people who chooses to live without modern conveniences such as electricity and running water that many in North America take for granted. They often support themselves to a great degree, as their circumstances allow, outside of the cash economy. The traditional way of life has become nearly impossible at Akwesasne in recent years due to such environmental degradation that many Mohawks can no longer eat the fruits of the earth and rivers without poisoning themselves. Traditional also may mean a person or group of people who reserve their political participation for the Iroquois system that predated European contact; they choose not to participate in provincial, state, or federal elections. Often such people also mesh their everyday lives with a degree of spirituality and respect for the earth that may be difficult for many non-Indians in the late twentieth century to comprehend. A significant proportion of Akwesasne's Mohawks do this today.

Many Mohawks do not imply that they have been wholly untouched by European cultures and technologies; the description means that a person observes Mohawk traditions, including the ability to speak the native language. Just as no Mohawk today lives as his or her ancestors did in the days of the Iroquois League's founding, every non-Indian today has been shaped by the many contributions that native cultures have made to our material and intellectual lives, from the food we eat, to the language we use (*blizzard*, for example, is a Native American term), to our custom of taking daily baths.

Proponents of high-stakes commercial gambling at Akwesasne also sometimes call themselves traditionals, on the premise that such enterprises are creating an independent economic base for a sovereign nation. While the gaming trade has, indeed, supported itself outside of U.S. law, it is constructed to profit from a nonnative clientele. It is also a trade that defines success in terms of the dollar, an "imported" currency. Many Mohawks who oppose commercial gaming believe not only that the dollar is an imported currency but also that the whole concept of profit has been imposed upon them.

The term traditional is used to mean different things by all factions in this dispute. I have tried to remove it from the pages that follow, preferring instead to describe events and people involved in them by more specific references. Having decided to omit references to people who call themselves traditional while trying to describe a society that vests great importance in tradition, I hope I will not create even more confusion. The Mohawks of Akwesasne, Kahnawake, and Kanesatake, like many other Native Americans across North America, have struggled with great vigor, against mighty odds, to maintain the integrity of their cultures. All sides in the recent disputes in Mohawk Country call upon the past to justify their vision of the future.

The current flap over reservation gambling begins in 1979 when the Seminoles became the first Indian tribe to enter the bingo industry. The state of Florida challenged the legality of the games, only to have the Fifth Circuit Court of Appeals rule that Seminole bingo could continue because the federal government had never transferred to Florida jurisdiction that would have allowed the state to enforce its civil laws on Indian lands. The Seminole decision hinged on a finding of the court that Indian bingo in Florida fell under civil not criminal jurisdiction. If the Fifth Circuit had ruled that the bingo games fell under criminal law, the state's jurisdiction that would have applied because of federal law PL-280, which allowed states to extend criminal jurisdiction over Indian reservations. However, in 1968, the PL-280 law was amended to require tribal consent before the state could assume jurisdiction. Only those states that had taken jurisdiction before 1968 were allowed to keep it.

By early 1985, approximately 80 of the nearly 300 recognized American Indian tribes in the United States were conducting some sort of game of chance.[2] By the fall of 1988, more than 100 Indian tribes participated in some form of gambling, which grossed as much as $255 million a year. The proliferation of gambling on native reservations came at a time that gambling was moving from a few enclaves, such as Reno and Las Vegas, Nevada, to become a more broadly accepted feature on the social landscape across the United States. Reservations, many of them within an hours' drive of major metropolitan areas, became small islands where many state prohibitions on gambling did not apply. As early as 1985 the Congressional Research Service (CRS) warned of infiltration of Indian gaming by organized crime.[3]

Individual prizes in some reservation bingo games were reported to be as high as $100,000, while bingo stakes in surrounding areas under state jurisdiction were sometimes limited to $100. Marion Blank Horn, principal deputy solicitor of the Interior Department, described the fertile ground gambling enterprises had found in Indian country.

> The reasons for growth in gambling on Indian land are readily apparent. The Indian tribal governments see an opportunity for income that can make a substantial improvement in the tribe's [economic] conditions. The lack of any state or Federal regulation results in a competitive advantage over gambling regulated by the states. These advantages include no state-imposed limits on the size of pots or prizes, no restrictions by the states on days or hours of operations, no costs for licenses or compliance with state requirements, and no state taxes on gambling operations.[4]

By the early 1990s, gambling had helped bring death to Akwesasne, but on other reservations it had provided a small galaxy of material benefits for formerly impoverished native people. A half-hour drive from the Twin Cities in Minnesota, blackjack players crowded 41 tables, while 450 other players stared into video slot machines inside the tipi-shaped

Little Six Casino, operated by the 103 members of the Shakopee Mdewakanton Sioux. By 1991, each member of the tribe was getting monthly dividend checks averaging $2,000 as shareholders in the casino. In addition to monthly dividends, members became eligible for homes (if they lacked them), guaranteed jobs (if they were unemployed), and full college scholarships. The tribe had taken out health insurance policies for everyone on the reservation and established day care for children of working parents. The Little Six Casino has been such a financial success that it has spilled out of its original "tipi" into 11 double-wide trailers. Although Minnesota prohibits organized gambling, it does allow social gaming. A judge has ruled that the games inside the tipi and double-wide trailers are social in nature, possibly because profits go to benefit tribal members on an egalitarian basis.

Very few tribal gambling ventures ran as smoothly as the Little Six Casino, however. As soon as profit-minded business interests (native or not) began exporting gambling enterprises, trouble invariably followed. In July 1991 dozens of police officers quelled a tense standoff between two factions at a bingo hall in Baraboo, Wisconsin. One of the factions alleged misuse of tribal funds in the bingo hall; the other defended its operation. The "Winn-a-Bingo" hall was operated by the Winnebago tribe, which maintains several gambling-related business ventures on reservation lands in Iowa, Wisconsin, and Nebraska. A few days earlier, a similar confrontation had occurred outside a closed bingo hall near Black River Falls, Wisconsin.

Nevertheless, by late 1991, 11 Wisconsin Indian tribes were negotiating gambling compacts with that state. The Potawatomi had opened a 48,000-square foot bingo parlor in Milwaukee's graying industrial district, on urban trust land. The Potawatomi Bingo's sleek green-and-red structure stood out like a giant Christmas ornament amidst ranks of factories and warehouses and was making plans to expand into blackjack and video slot machines. At the same time, Wisconsin Governor Tommy Thompson filed suit in Chicago's federal circuit court to stem the spread of Indian gambling. The governor said that Indian-sponsored gaming had initiated demands by non-Indians for a piece of the action, turning Wisconsin into a wide-open gambling state.

Wisconsin filed suit with friend-of-the-court support from 17 other states: Alabama, Arizona, California, Connecticut, Florida, Michigan, Minnesota, Mississippi, Montana, Nebraska, Nevada, North Dakota, Oregon, South Dakota, Washington, and Wyoming, all states in which various forms of gambling were mushrooming, and not only on Indian reservations.

By 1991, 150 of 278 native reservations recognized by non-Indian governmental bodies had some form of gambling. According to the Interior Department, gross revenue from such operations was expected to pass $1 billion that year.

One of these reservations was Akwesasne, where gambling had arrived illegally. What happened at Akwesasne had its own special characteristics, but Mohawk country also has often experienced the special agonies of Native America before other Indian peoples. Akwesasne is not, for example, the only native community where the environment that once formed the basis of native economies has been all but destroyed. Environmentally, Akwesasne has been the canary in the coal mine for the rest of Native America. It is a story worth weighing.

All sides at Akwesasne agree that the degradation of the environment and the loss of a sustaining land base are at the bottom of present-day problems.

The destruction of the land is the central issue to all the events of 1988–1991. An account of this environmental crisis begins in chapter 1 ("The Toxic Turtle"). I then describe the consequences of this destruction, along with the rise of smuggling and gambling, in chapter 2 ("The Gambling War: Beginnings"), which brings this narrative to the end of 1989. Chapter 3 ("A Community Under Siege") covers a period of rising tension in the first four months of 1990, including the erection of blockades, and their final destruction during the third week of April. Chapter 4 ("Downslide to Death") covers only one week, April 25 through May 2, 1990. It was the most violent week in the history of the community, culminating with the deaths of two Mohawks on May 1. Chapter 5 ("Law of Peace, or Law of Power?") takes the narrative to the end of 1990, and is intended to be reflective in nature because this was a time of debate within the Mohawk communities and the broader Iroquois Confederacy. This debate centered on the ideology of the Warrior Society, as developed by founding ideologue Louis Hall. The historical dimensions of this ideological struggle are developed toward the end of that chapter, as the Iroquois debate what has become of their legendary Great Law of Peace. Chapter 6 ("The Cultural Anatomy of a Golf Course") describes events in Canada, centering on the Kanesatake Mohawk reserve in Oka, Quebec, where violence peaked after the deaths at Akwesasne. The narrative also includes related events at another Mohawk reserve, Kahnawake, near Montreal, birthplace of the Warrior Society, including the blockade of the Mercier Bridge and some of the largest racial riots in Canada's history. In chapter 7 ("A Time for Healing"), the setting returns to Akwesasne, during 1991, during the aftermath of the previous year's crisis. This story is not complete, of course. Many questions were left unresolved as this book was being readied for the press.

Notes

[1] New York State Assembly Hearings. Transcript, *The Crisis at Akwesasne,* Albany, August 2, 1990, p.557.

[2] *Christian Science Monitor,* March 25, 1985.

[3] M. Maureen Murphy, "Gambling on Indian Reservations," Congressional Research Service, Library of Congress (April 26, 1985): 11.

[4] Roger Walke, "Gambling on Indian Reservations: Updated October 17, 1988," Congressional Research Service, Library of Congress: 3.

There is big money at stake at Akwesasne. Illegal gambling, gun smuggling, cocaine, and other drug smuggling is worth several million dollars each week. Control of the reservation—a government illegally placed or legitimately selected by the people—means a way of life, or living. And now, of course, a way of dying.

Linda Champagne,
Martin Luther King, Jr.,
Institute for Nonviolence,
observer at Akwesasne,
March and April 1990

Through all this time I've been pistol-whipped. I've … had daily and nightly phone calls saying they're going to kill me. I've identified a lot of those people who called me. They're my friends. People I grew up with. I've been beaten half to death. … Am I full of hate? I'm full of bitterness. But the teachings of my people are strong in me. And right now, there are many of us who are going through this internal battle. Because of my teachings, we say that people who have strayed and do damage to their own people, we are supposed to pick them up and support them, and bring them back to … reason.

Brian Cole,
Akwesasne resident,
New York State Assembly hearings,
The Crisis at Akwesasne,
Albany, August 2, 1990

CHAPTER 1

▼▼▼

The Toxic Turtle

For three millennia of human occupancy, the site the Mohawks call Akwesasne was a natural wonderland: well watered; thickly forested with white pine, oak, elm, hickory, and ash; home to deer, elk, and other game animals. The rich soil of the bottomlands allowed farming to flourish. The very name that the Akwesasne Mohawks gave their land when permanent occupancy began about 1755, near the site of a Jesuit mission, testifies to the richness of game there. In Mohawk "Akwesasne" means "land where the partridge drums," after the distinctive sound that a male ruffled grouse (partridge) makes during its spring courtship rituals. Lying at the confluence of the Saint Lawrence, St. Regis, Raquette, Grass, and Salmon rivers, the area once had some of the largest runs of sturgeon, bass, walleye, and pike in eastern North America.

In the space of two generations, this land of natural wonders has become a place where you cannot eat the fish or game. In some places, you cannot drink the water, and in others people have been told not to till the soil. In place of a sustaining river to which Mohawks still offer thanksgiving prayers, late twentieth-century capitalism has offered them incinerators and dumps for medical waste, all free from state and federal law. Akwesasne has become the most polluted native reserve in Canada, and one of the worst-poisoned patches of earth in the United States.

Within the living memory of a middle-aged person, the land where the partridge drums has become a toxic dumping ground riskier to health than many urban areas, the kind of place where any partridge left alive is more likely to be worrying about its heartbeat rather than its drumbeat. These environmental circumstances have, in two generations, descended on a people whose whole way of life had been enmeshed with the natural world, a place where the story of Iroquois origin says the world took shape on a gigantic turtle's back. Today, environmental pathologists are finding turtles at Akwesasne that qualify as toxic waste.

The speed with which Akwesasne has descended from near heaven to an environmental hell makes it a metaphor for environmental degradation. A once pristine landscape of rivers and forests has been turned into a chemical dump where unsuspecting children played on piles of dirt laced with polychlorinated biphenyls (PCBs) dumped by a nearby General Motors foundry. The PCBs are highly stable molecules of two conjoined hexagonal rings of varying numbers of chlorine atoms. The number of such atoms determines the degree of toxicity. In some of its forms, PCBs cause liver damage and several forms of cancer. The chemicals were used to insulate electrical equipment before they were banned by the federal government during the 1970s.

The Mohawks of Akwesasne are not "new age" converts to environmental consciousness. For many generations, they have watched and protested against what has become of their homeland. As early as 1834, their chiefs told Canadian officials that control structures built to channel the flow of the Saint Lawrence River near Barnhart Island were destroying important fish spawning grounds. Environmental degradation at Akwesasne took a quantum leap after the late 1950s, however, when the Saint Lawrence Seaway opened access to bountiful, cheap power. Access to power drew heavy industry that soon turned large segments of this magnificent river into open sewers.

Mohawk Nation Council subchief Tom Porter offered a traditional thanksgiving prayer to open the New York Assembly hearings into the crisis at Akwesasne in 1990. He asked how humans could have forgotten our place in the intricate order of nature. Translated here by Jim Ransom, the thanksgiving prayer itself illustrates how intricately love and respect for the earth are woven into Mohawk culture, and how deeply the pollution has wounded the traditional way of life.

> [Before] our great-great grandfathers were first born and given the breath of life, our creator at that time said the earth will be your mother. And the creator said to the deer and the animals and the birds, "the earth will be your mother, too. And I have instructed the earth to give food and nourishment and medicine and quenching of thirst to all life." ... We, the people, humbly thank you today, mother earth.
>
> Our creator spoke to the rivers and our creator made the rivers not just as water, but he made the rivers a living entity. ... You must have a reverence and great respect for your mother the earth. ... You must each day say "thank you" [for] every gift that contributes to your life. If you follow this pattern, it will be like a circle with no end. Your life will be as everlasting as your children, who will carry on your flesh, your blood, and your heartbeat.[1]

Ward Stone, a wildlife pathologist for the New York State Department of Environmental Conservation (DEC) believes that Akwesasne is "the worst place in the world to be a duck."[2] He may be guilty of hyperbole, but not much. That duck may have been as bad off in certain areas of the Mediterranean Sea where the Cetacean Society, a group of Italian scientists, has found dolphins contaminated by up to 1,400 times the amounts of DDT and PCBs considered safe. Perhaps a duck sitting downwind of Union Carbide's Bhopal plant in India might have wished he was swimming around Mohawk country during a couple of days in early December 1984, when a chemical leak killed a least 2,500 people and injured 200,000 others. Otherwise, the environment of Akwesasne today punishes any living system. It is very difficult to be a duck, turtle, fish, shrew, or even a human being.

When Stone began examining animals at Akwesasne, he found that the PCBs, insecticides, and other toxins were not being contained in designated dumps. After years of use, the dump sites had leaked, and the toxins had gotten into the food chain of human beings and nearly every other species of animal in the area. The Mohawks' traditional economy, based on hunting, fishing, and agriculture, had been literally poisoned out of existence.

Pollution in Iroquois country is not limited to Akwesasne, but it is most acute there. For example, Onondaga Lake is so polluted that its fish are inedible. The lake that once supplied the firekeepers of the Iroquois Confederacy with food is today dominated by the skyline of Syracuse. Even without an urban landscape, the waters of Akwesasne are so laced with PCBs that people whose ancestors subsisted on fish for thousands of years can no longer eat them. "We are still lonesome for those fish," says Tom Sakowkenonkwas Porter, one of nine Akwesasne Mohawk Nation Council chiefs.[3] Porter's family lives at Raquette point with his Choctaw wife and six children in a house that Porter, a carpenter by trade, built by hand many years ago. Until 15 years ago, when they were warned against eating fish from the waters around Akwesasne, Porter's family, like many Mohawks, took sturgeon, bullhead, bass, trout, and other fish from nearby rivers in their nets, eating what they needed and keeping extra fish for visitors in submerged boxes. The Porters now worry not only about the fish but also the produce they raise in gardens around their house. Even the health of the Belgian horses that Porter raises is at risk.

The nets have since rotted, symbolic of the destruction of a way of life by PCBs, Mirex, mercury, and other contaminants. The rivers of Akwesasne, once a center of the traditional economy and culture, did more than provide fish for eating. As with the native harvesters of salmon in the Pacific Northwest, the people of Akwesasne did not just catch and eat fish. They gave thanks to the fish for allowing itself to be caught and eaten and to nature for providing the catch. The rivers and the fish were the center of a way of life being destroyed.

The pollution at Akwesasne (and at other points along the Saint Lawrence River) has affected the food chain into the Atlantic Ocean. Sea life feeding on fish from the Saint Lawrence River, such as Beluga whales, suffer from various forms of cancer, reproductive problems, and immune-system deficiencies. More than 500 environmental contaminants have been measured in autopsies of the wildlife in and near Akwesasne, 125 of them in the fish, with PCBs being the most prominent. Industrial plants, including the General Motors foundry, give the area a skyline of spewing smokestacks that popular imagery might associate with New Jersey or Delaware, not upstate New York. Popular imagery did not matter as much to the locators of industrial plants as access to international shipping facilities and cheap hydroelectric power.

The scope of the environmental disaster at Akwesasne began to unfold in the early 1980s as environmental scientists began progressively more intensive testing of the area. While environmental scientists were just discovering Akwesasne's problems, farmers in the area had been suffering for years. Lloyd Benedict, a former chief on the Mohawk Council of Akwesasne, living on Cornwall Island, said that the number of cattle on the island fell from about 500 to less than 200 during the 1960s because of fluoride poisoning. "That was because the cattle were dying and the farmers just couldn't keep up with replacing [them] all the time."[4]

A study by Cornell University indicated that smokestack effluvia from a Reynolds metals factory also was killing once profitable cattle and dairy farms in Cornwall, on the Ontario side of Akwesasne. The study linked the fluorides to the demise of cattle as early as 1978. Many of the cattle suffered from fluoride poisoning that weakened their bones and decayed their teeth. Ernest Benedict's Herefords died while giving birth, and Noah Point's cattle lost their teeth. Mohawk fishermen landed perch and bass with deformed spines and large ulcers on their skins. The fluoride was a byproduct of a large aluminum smelter in Massena, New York, that routinely filled the air with yellowish-gray fumes smelling of acid and metal.

At about the same time, Dr. William Burns, a federal dental officer, said he believed that fluoride exposure was causing an abnormally large number of children at Akwesasne to have brittle and deformed teeth. A subsequent study failed to find a direct connection between flouride exposure and dental problems in people there. The problem might not have been lack of evidence, but the small size of Akwesasne's population, which prevented scientists from getting a large enough sample to establish statistically valid epidemiological results.[5]

The Cornell study provided an early glimpse of PCB poisoning at Akwesasne. The Mohawk Council of Akwesasne filed a $150 million lawsuit against Alcoa, but settled for $650,000. The council spent so much on lawyers' fees that it nearly went bankrupt. Reynolds Metals, owner of the aluminum smelter, cut its fluoride emissions from 300 pounds an hour in 1959 to 75 pounds per hour in 1980, but the few cattle still feeding in the area continued to die of fluoride poisoning.

The pollution of Akwesasne is accentuated by the fact that most of the plants emitting toxins are located west of there, upstream, and often upwind. The Saint Lawrence at Akwesasne also carries pollutants dumped into the Great Lakes system as it moves downstream toward the Atlantic Ocean. Akwesasne lies downstream not only from the General Motors foundry and other polluters but also from some of what could be a hall of infamy for toxic wastedom, including the notorious Love Canal.

In 1981, the Mohawk Council of Akwesasne and the Canadian Ministry of Health requested a study of exposure to fluorides, mercury, Mirex, and PCBs by the Environmental Sciences Laboratory at the Mt. Sinai School of Medicine. By December 1981, brief reports alleged the presence of PCBs around the General Motors foundry. The reports were practically on the rumor level at the time. There was no precise information on the degree of PCB contamination or its location. This information was vital to Mohawks in Raquette, some of whom lived less than 1,000 yards from General Motors' dump site, as well as people whose water intake from the Saint Lawrence River was only a half mile from the plant.

At about the same time, almost two years before General Motors officially acknowledged that a problem existed, the New York DEC rejected the company's cleanup plan, which would have merely closed and capped the waste sites with none of the expensive but environmentally necessary remedial work that would stop the deadly spread of PCBs that already had leached out of the foundry's dump.

By the early 1980s, John Wilson of the New York DEC indicated that the department had learned of possible PCB contamination at Akwesasne. Preliminary tests had shown the area to be the worst PCB-contaminated site in Franklin County, with "widespread contamination of groundwater."[6]

Wilson then made a comment that sent shivers through Akwesasne. He said that some of the groundwater had been contaminated, and that "there was no reversal practical."[7] Wilson also angered many Mohawks, stating that the Indians had not been notified in spite of their many shallow wells that might suffer from groundwater seepage. Robert Hendrichs, manager of the General Motors foundry, said that the company was preparing its final cleanup proposal and that General Motors was working harmoniously with state environmental officials. Hendrichs also said that PCB-laden materials had been used at the foundry since 1972, when such use became illegal, and that other toxic wastes were being shipped to a federally approved waste disposal site. He left a few questions unanswered. When did the contamination begin? How many PCBs had been released? How far into the environment had it spread? With what effects?

Akwesasne had now been so "notified" through the Massena newspaper. A people who are environmentalists by tradition and inclination began to learn how governmental and government bureaucracies deal with the poisoning of the air, water, and soil.

For a time early in 1982, it seemed as if concern over PCB contamination at Akwesasne had been one of the shortest pollution scares on record, as General Motors and DEC assured the Mohawks that there was little to worry about. As the New York Department of Health began testing wells in the Raquette Point area, a DEC water-quality expert "explained that the hazardous waste dumps on the General Motors property were separated from the reservation by geographical and geological barriers unlikely to permit the spread of the pollutants."[8] No PCBs were found in the first well-water sample at Racquette.[9]

When researchers tested the water itself, they were unable to find traces of PCB because it is not water soluble. By the middle of January, however, body-fat analyses were beginning to come in from Mt. Sinai, and they told another story. Traces of PCBs had been found in the bodies of several St. Regis residents. While the Mt. Sinai study did not link the PCB contamination directly to General Motors' dump, Dr. Stephen Levin, an environmental specialist at the hospital, said that "the initial results suggest there is a local source of PCB contamination."[10] A week later, a test was reported that had found PCBs in one well at St. Regis. The well was not close to the General Motors plant, however, and no connection was suggested.[11]

Little seems to have been done to act on early reports of scattered PCB contamination at Akwesasne. In April 1982, DEC criticized a General Motors plan to use "scavenger wells" meant to keep groundwater below the level of lagoons tainted with waste from the dump. In March 1983, the state health department and St. Regis Tribal Council set up a well-sampling schedule. In July, the tests produced indications of cancer-causing pollutants such as benzene and trichloroethylene in groundwater below homes at Akwesasne. A public relations spokesman for General Motors said that neither chemical was being used at the foundry.[12]

In mid-July 1983, St. Regis Tribal Council environmental technician Jim Ransom complained that General Motors was being less than forthcoming with information. "We don't know exactly what's in the dump," he said.[13] In August, General Motors officials declined to attend a meeting of New York state, Canadian, and tribal environmental officials. General Motors said it knew of no evidence showing that its landfill was causing health problems. At the meeting, DEC officials disclosed that they had asked the Environmental Protection Agency (EPA) to put the General Motors dumps on the Superfund list. The EPA at that time estimated that the area contained 800,000 cubic yards of sediments contaminated with PCBs. Residents were warned not to eat vegetables from their own gardens.

Despite General Motors' attempts to downplay the problem, Berton Mead, a DEC engineer, said on August 18, "there are a number of areas ... with high levels of PCB-contaminated groundwater. ... It does violate the groundwater standards."[14] At the time, however, General Motors had done no testing off its own property. The company said it did not have enough information to develop a remedial plan. Berton also said that DEC did not have enough information "to make an intelligent decision" about how the PCB problem at Akwesasne should be corrected.[15]

In October 1983, the EPA fined General Motors $507,000, charging the company with 17 counts of illegal PCB disposal. At that time the fine was the largest the agency had levied in a PCB-related case. The EPA also made Superfund money available to help dredge sediments laced with PCBs from the bed of the Saint Lawrence and other waterways. During the same month, the United Auto Workers disclosed that in 1982 it had threatened a strike at the foundry over PCB exposure on the job. To avoid the strike, the company complied with union demands to clean the interior of the plant. The Mohawks outside, with no such leverage, were not so lucky.

In November 1983 the Watertown *Daily Times* obtained internal DEC memos dated 1981 to 1983 that revealed that there may have been PCB contamination in the area during that period. There may also have been PCB leakage at General Motors in addition to those instances disclosed by the company for the Superfund list. The newspaper also reported that General Motors had not complied with DEC requests for information. While many Mohawks and other local people had criticized DEC for foot-dragging on the issue, the internal memos indicated that the agency had tried to do its job while General Motors did its best to stall.

The memos obtained by the newspaper indicated that Robert McCarty, a site investigation supervisor, suggested possible contamination of the reservation and the Saint Lawrence River. Darrell Sweredoski, a DEC engineer, commented, "Groundwater contamination is evident in all wells and at all elevations along the eastern boundary with the reservation. ... I can only conclude from this information that contamination from one or both of the sludge deposits has indeed migrated off-site to the east."[16] Apparently unaware of Sweredoski's findings, J. L. Jeffrey of General Motors wrote to DEC the following May 6: "Since there is no proof that the Indians are affected by the sludge deposits, there is no purpose to involving them in the closure planning."[17]

By 1983, *Indian Time*, a newspaper published for Akwesasne residents, was carrying detailed reports on the effects of PCB contamination as far away as Japan. One article, published in early July, focused on the chemistry and industrial uses of the chemicals. The July 27 issue of *Indian Time* described the effects of PCB poisoning based on exposure in Yusho, Japan, where a heat exchanger leaked PCBs that contaminated a shipment of rice oil during 1968. "Toxic effects in human beings include an acnelike skin eruption called chloracne, pigmentation of the skin and nails, distinctive hair follicles, excessive eye discharge, swelling of the eyelids, headache, fatigue, nausea and vomiting, digestive disorders, and liver dysfunction."[18] Symptoms persisted in some cases for several months after workers left the source of contamination, which also caused some cases of impotence and hematuria (blood in the urine).

More than 1,000 Japanese who consumed some of the contaminated rice oil were tested afterwards. The concentration of toxicity in the rice oil was 2,000 to 3,000 parts per million, a level of contamination that would become very familiar to environmental scientists testing animals at Akwesasne during the next few years. Of 13 Japanese women who were pregnant when they consumed the toxic rice oil, 2 had still births. Live births were characterized by grayish-brown skin pigmentation, discolored nails, and abnormally large amounts of eye discharge. Some of the babies had abnormally shaped skulls and protruding eyeballs. Such evidence convinced researchers that "PCBs were transferred to the fetus through the placenta."[19] Some babies seemed to be getting a double dose because PCBs also had contaminated their mothers' milk.

In January 1984 *Indian Time* reported that Environment Canada was preparing to test for mercury, PCBs, and Mirex contamination on Cornwall Island. The article reported that Akwesasne had been accorded an "A-1" rating by Canadian environmental officials because of a history of open dumping on the island. In February 1985 *Indian Time* began publishing acid-rain readings indicating that precipitation falling on the reservation had an average acidity (pH) ranging from 4.06 to 5.11, considerably more acid than the 5.6 considered the usual minimum pH factor of natural precipitation.

In July 1984 General Motors disclosed in a report required by the EPA that PCBs and other toxic wastes such as solvents, degreasers, trichloroethylene, and formaldehyde had been dumped in the Akwesasne area since 1959, when the plant opened. From 1968 through 1973, PCBs were used inside the foundry to protect against fire and thermal degradation in the searing heat of its die-casting machines. The company at that time had no idea how much had been disposed of over the years (that figure was later estimated to be 823,000 cubic yards). In the sanitized language of the corporation, some of that waste was "not containerized." In plain English, the toxins were dumped on the open ground in a number of sites, the North Disposal Area, the East Disposal Area, the Industrial Landfill, and four sludge lagoons, most of which were close enough to both Akwesasne and the Saint Lawrence River for contamination.

The company also admitted that its dumping grounds were unlined and uncapped. General Motors also disclosed that the sludge lagoons had overflowed into the Saint Lawrence at least seven times between January and September 1982. As a result, the Saint Lawrence now contained "hot spots" of PCB contamination more than 50 parts per million.

Hugh Kaufman, assistant director of EPA's Hazardous Waste Site Control Division, said in October 1983 that General Motors could easily have contained toxic leakage from its dumps. The toxic plague that scientists were beginning to piece together at Akwesasne also could have been contained if the Reagan administration had been more interested in prosecuting violations of environmental laws, according to Kaufman.

His remarks were recorded at a Clarkson University conference on "Managing Environmental Risk," on October 2 and 3. Kaufman said that while technology existed to avoid many toxic-dump problems, the government and industry were not putting in the necessary time and money to use it.

Kaufman said that of 18,000 "candidate sites" around the United States, only 8,000 had been subject to inspection. Of those, 800 had been "identified for national action," of which the Superfund at present had funds to clean up only 115—less than 1 percent of the toxic-waste sites that might need it. Kaufman said, "We don't have the resources. It's a brand new program. The EPA lost three years thanks to Mrs. Buford, thanks to Rita Lavell [agency supervisors appointed by President Reagan]. ... You are talking about a situation that will take you through the next century just to stabilize."[20]

According to Kaufman, special-interest groups were preventing the government from issuing effective regulations to prevent the creation of new waste dumps, as the EPA struggled to deal with decades of neglected effluvia. He also said that lobbyists had been very effective on Capitol Hill in delaying the cleanup of existing sites, so costly and embarrassing to companies such as General Motors that for so long had disposed of their toxic wastes the easiest and least expensive way possible without regard for environmental consequences.

Referring specifically to the General Motors dumps near Akwesasne, Kaufman said that General Motors did not have to dump its toxic waste in lagoons. "If it's PCB-contaminated waste oils, a mobile incinerator can be set up at the site. Those materials can be destroyed by the company tomorrow, no problem. ... PCB-contaminated waste oils are one of the easiest waste streams to destroy." Kaufman indicated that perhaps General Motors was more willing to pay fines than to install costly new technology. If that was the case, he said, the EPA should install the technology and charge the company three times the damages. "Certainly," Kaufman said, "General Motors cannot complain that they cannot afford a half-million dollars to set up an incinerator there." Kaufman then implied that the company was using its inability to come to an agreement on cleanup with the state as a delaying tactic:

> Have they [General Motors], in their plan, requested a mobile incinerator to destroy those materials, or have they just said they are going to dump some kitty litter in it and put a clay cap on it?[21]

> The longer that those waste materials remain in that lagoon, the more toxic material is going to continue to leak into the groundwater. ... Under immediate removal or emergency action, [EPA] can go in and

> destroy those waste oils and PCBs. ... It's a simple case, but there are two different issues. One issue is dealing with stopping the leak. ... [The] second issue is the long-term issue of documenting the movement of contamination from the site.[22]

General Motors spokesman Bill O'Neill replied that the company "has been working with state and federal agencies to remedy that situation." O'Neill reiterated the company's position that the EPA should not be involved in the "site solution." O'Neill said: "The site is ours, and ... if there is any action that is necessary ... we will be responsible for it and we will take care of it." He said the company "had a method" to deal with the problem, but didn't specify what it was.[23]

At Akwesasne, environmental bills were coming due with amazing swiftness. The degree of crisis at Akwesasne seemed to expand with the number and intensity of studies conducted to measure it. As Kaufman spoke, only the bare outline of the problem at Akwesasne had become officially visible. By the middle 1980s, Ward Stone had begun to piece together evidence indicating that Akwesasne had become one of the worst pollution sites in New York state and possibly one of the worst in North America.

The Mohawks started Stone's environmental tour of Akwesasne with a visit to one of the General Motors waste lagoons, a place called "unnamed tributary cove" on some maps. Stone gave it the name "Contaminant Cove" because of the amount of toxic pollution in it. "When I first went there in 1985, there were Indian children playing barefoot [in the cove]. They were walking in hazardous waste. There was so much PCBs and other contaminants in the sediment of that cove, that the cove bottom was actually hazardous waste."[24]

One day in 1985, at Contaminant Cove, the environmental crisis at Akwesasne assumed a whole new foreboding shape. The New York State Department of Conservation caught a female snapping turtle that contained 835 parts per million of PCBs. While no federal standards exist for PCBs in turtles, the federal standard for edible poultry is three parts per million, or about one-third of 1 percent the concentration in that snapping turtle. The federal standard for edible fish is two parts per million. In soil, on a dry-weight basis, 50 parts per million is considered hazardous waste, so that turtle contained roughly 15 times the concentration of PCBs necessary, by federal standards, to qualify its body as toxic waste. In the fall of 1987, Stone found another snapping turtle, a male, containing 3,067 parts per million in its body fat—1,000 times the concentration allowed in domestic chicken, and 60 times the minimum standard for hazardous waste. Contamination was lower in female turtles because they shed some of their PCB's by laying eggs, while the males stored more of what they ingested.

In 1985 Stone, working in close cooperation with the Mohawks, found a masked shrew that somehow had managed to survive in spite of a PCB level of 11,522 parts per million in its body, the highest concentration that Stone had ever seen in a living creature, 250 times the minimum standard to qualify as hazardous waste! Using these samples and others, Stone and the Mohawks established Akwesasne as one of the worst PCB-polluted sites in North America. The animals tested by Stone contained not only alarming levels of PCBs but other toxins as well, including the insecticide Dieldrin and the most toxic form of dioxin (2,3,7.8-TCDD).

The turtle carries a special significance among the Iroquois, whose creation story describes how the world took shape on a turtle's back. To this day, many Iroquois call North America "Turtle Island." Stone commented, "To the Mohawks, and to me, it appeared that if turtles were being sickened by pollutants, it might indicate that the very underpinnings of the earth were coming apart."[25] Now, at Akwesasne, the turtle had assumed a new status as harbinger of death by pollution. Pollution also threatened a struggling caviar industry in the area, and shut down many fishing camps that used to draw anglers from around the northeastern United States and Canada. One fishing camp operator, Tony Barnes, was forced to leave his nets to rot in 1985. His only remaining livelihood, and the only use for his boats, became ferrying environmental investigators across the river. Other former fishermen got occasional work collecting water and soil samples.

The Mohawks and Stone continued to find contaminated animals at Akwesasne. In the fall of 1987, they found young ducks in an area once called Reynolds Cove that contained PCBs in their body fat at 300 parts per million. The ducks were too young to fly, so environmental inspectors could be sure that the PCBs had been ingested locally. Stone reported:

> In the fall of 1987, Mohawk biologist Ken Jock and I went to that cove and there was a ravine with a stream coming down with a lot of white, foamy water on it, and a strong, chemical odor coming off of that water. We sampled the stream for several thousand feet up to the fence line of Reynolds. And I found that it had high levels of PCBs in the water and high levels in the sediment, for a depth of about eight inches. So they had been going in there and layering [waste] for many years.[26]

After these initial discoveries, Stone had trouble getting others to investigate Reynolds, which used PCBs in a heat transfer system that was used to heat pitch. According to Stone, the system experienced explosions, as well as fires, and leaked thousands of gallons of PCBs, especially when it was being refilled.

As he compiled data at Akwesasne, Stone also became a subject of investigation himself.

> I got investigated for about six months as to whether my science was correct. Reynolds said the river was polluting them, [that] the river was

> putting pollutants into their plant in coolant water, and [that] they were not polluting the river. That ... was garbage. Our data has held up. They are not only polluting the Saint Lawrence River, but the Raquette River as well. And it's going to cost tens of millions of dollars to clean the river and to control the pollutants from Reynolds.[27]

Stone, an employee of New York's state environmental agency for 22 years, said that some of the delay in diagnosing the scope of the environmental disaster at Akwesasne came from DEC itself.

> I counted thirteen people from DEC who went to study that plant [Reynolds] looking for PCBs. No one made a diagnosis. It was about a one-and-a-half hour situation for me, taking samples to make the diagnosis. A couple thousand dollars worth of chemistry. It was mere child's play. If pollution can be missed at Reynolds, it can be missed anywhere. ... This should have been detected and cut off at least a decade ago.[28]

The Akwesasne area also was home to many trappers before construction of the Saint Lawrence Seaway devastated the trapping areas and wetlands. To speed the melting of ice in the spring, the level of the river is raised and dropped very quickly so that air pockets caught in the water will pulverize the ice. The swirling, crushing action of water, ice, and air also floods muskrat and beaver hutches, killing their occupants. The animals drowned en masse, destroying the traditional trapping industry in the area. In a similar vein, logging and acid rain have destroyed many stands of the black asp that Mohawk people use to make baskets and other crafts. Chief Benedict, representing the MCA (Mohawk Council of Akwesasne) testified:

> A lot of these things all contributed to a community that was sensitive to its natural surroundings and depending on its natural surroundings. Then, all of a sudden, the rug is pulled out from under you. Then we're expected to survive. But we don't have the tools to survive in this contemporary time.[29]

Jim Ransom outlined his own proposal for cleanup of the General Motors waste sites.

> The contaminated sediments need to be excavated and treated on site. The reservation soils need to be removed and treated on-site. Clean soils should be brought in to replace the soils taken out. The [General Motors] industrial landfill needs to be permanently treated by excavating and treating the contaminated soils. General Motors could be given time to find an in-place treatment technology for the landfill. An interim cap should be placed on the landfill immediately to isolate it, as it is still an active source of PCBs [leaking] into the Saint Lawrence River. Other permanent treatment technologies need to be looked at in addition to incineration and biological treatment. The risks of incineration are potentially high, and biological treatment is not proven for a site this size.[30]

Studies also found that drinking water at Raquette, directly downstream from the General Motors plant, was contaminated with PCBs. The main intake for the tribe's community water system was 2 miles downstream from the foundry and its gaggle of waste sites. General Motors then began supplying people in the area with bottled water, including students at the Akwesasne Freedom School.

In 1986 pregnant women were advised not to eat fish from the Saint Lawrence, historically the Mohawks' main source of protein. Until the 1950s, Akwesasne had been home to more than 100 commercial fishermen, and about 120 farmers. By 1990, less than 10 commercial fishermen and 20 farmers remained. The rest had been put out of business by pollution, which has devastated the Mohawks' traditional economy, sending many of them to search for employment in casinos and cigarette stores, or off the reservation, to survive. Other people were advised to limit their consumption of Saint Lawrence fish to half a pound a week.

By 1990 the state was warning residents not to eat any fish at all if they had been caught in certain areas of the reservation. Tony Barnes ran a fishing camp for 40 years that helped to put five of his children through college and built his house. By the late 1980s fish caught at his camp were deformed and could not even be sold as fertilizer.

> You see big sores on them, and their gills are all red. Their mouths are all rotting, and their tails are deformed. Nobody even wants them for fertilizer because you will just be contaminating your garden. Sure, [the fish] make great fertilizer, but they will kill you.[31]

In place of the native economy, the government offered food stamps, just enough to buy a fatty diet of macaroni and potatoes. The few Mohawks who could afford fish were buying them from New England vendors who visited the reservation in refrigerated trucks. After the Mohawks' intake of native fish was restricted by pollution, the rate of adult-onset diabetes—a problem afflicting many Native American communities—began to soar at Akwesasne. By 1990 half the people living at Akwesasne over the age of 40 were diabetic. Health problems developed hand in hand with destruction of the traditional economic base. By 1990 80 percent of the adults on the reservation were unemployed or underemployed, and 70 percent were drawing public assistance. This was the environmental context in which gambling and smuggling developed as Akwesasne's main industries.

In early October 1989 the Environmental Protection Agency ordered the Alcoa and Reynolds plants, whose 2,500 employees form the economic backbone of Massena, New York, to determine the degree to which their effluent (especially PCBs, organic toxins, and metals) had polluted the rivers around Akwesasne. The two companies also were instructed to design a system to clean up the river sediments containing pollutants, including possible dredging, along with other, more sophisticated alternatives. As a final step, the EPA ordered implementation of that system. The order did not give a final deadline for completion nor estimate a final cost, but the companies could be fined $25,000 a day if the EPA thought they were stalling. In early January 1991 Alcoa announced that it would take a $90 million charge against earnings to settle its environmental obligations at the plant in Massena.

The EPA released its Superfund cleanup plan for the General Motors foundry during March 1990. The cleanup was estimated to cost $138 million, making the General Motors dumps near Akwesasne the costliest Superfund cleanup job in the United States, number one on the EPA's "most-wanted" list as the worst toxic dump in the United States. By 1991 the cost was scaled down to $78 million, but the General Motors dumps were still ranked as the most expensive toxic cleanup. The plan covered much of the PCB cleanup from the plant but not the industrial landfill. Cleanup of that area could cost an additional $202 million, according to the EPA report. The EPA was proposing first to dredge and clean the Saint Lawrence River, then to excavate, incinerate or biologically treat polluted soil at the plant and some of its dump sites, as well as on some areas of Akwesasne. The EPA estimated that the whole process would take 7 to 10 years. General Motors' counterproposal, estimated to cost $37 million, would have encapsulated the waste sites and monitored them to assure that toxic wastes were not migrating.[32]

Pollution also may be related to an increase in birth defects among Akwesasne Mohawks. Katsi Cook, a Mohawk midwife on the reservation, said that she never wanted to become an environmental activist, but the role was forced on her as she found more and more infants at Akwesasne being born with cleft palates, deafness, and intestinal abnormalities. She then began to study PCB contamination in mothers' milk at Akwesasne.

One mother at Akwesasne, Sheree Skidders, began to cry as she described how she, her husband Richard, and their seven children learned that they and their land were being poisoned. One day, a man showed up to test the water. Another day, Stone took one of their ducks to test the level of PCBs in its body fat. A little later, another environmental scientist noted that she was breast-feeding her youngest child and suggested that she have her milk tested. Sherree was repelled by the thought, but she had her breast milk tested anyway. It was laced with PCBs. She had been poisoning her own children. "Now, you have to wonder every time you take a breath," she said.[33] From the Skidders' farm, the family can see the large water tower that stands atop the General Motors plant. The setting sun sometimes throws the stark shadow of General Motors' water tower across the land that used to sustain the Skidders and other Mohawks, a visual reminder of responsibility for the land's demise.

As the people of Akwesasne learned the scope of their poisoning, other corporate "suitors" appeared on the reservation with proposals for municipal waste and medical incinerators, among other things. Terry Peterson, owner of the now defunct United Scientific Associates of Nashua, New Hampshire, told the Mohawks that "they're sitting on a gold mine for themselves up there."[34] The "gold mine" he referred to was his proposal to build a large complex to gasify municipal solid waste, a medical-waste incinerator, and a huge landfill. One purveyor of waste-plant-fueled dreams treated Ron LaFrance to a very expensive lunch. LaFrance, a Mohawk Nation Council subchief, director of Cornell University's American Indian Program, and a man widely known around Mohawk country for his love of a good meal, sarcastically asked him, "Why do you want to go into an Indian community? Is there some sort of compassion from your company to 'save' the Indian?"[35] The Mohawks' response to nearly all these self-described "friends of the Indian" was a swift and emphatic "no."

In December 1989, however, Mohawk Nation Council subchief Edward Gray was given permission by the Mohawk Nation Council to build a recycling plant for construction debris on the advice of a New Hampshire "waste broker." The new plant was called C & D Recycling. After heavy trucks invaded the reservation, a popular outcry caused cancellation of the plan. The Akwesasne Task Force on the Environment asked that the plant be terminated after Warriors, with broad community support, refused to let waste-laden trucks pass onto the site of the proposed dump in February 1990.

Residents had learned that some of the trucks were hauling debris contaminated with PCBs, the very carcinogens that had done so much to debase their land and water during the previous four decades. Some of the construction waste also contained lead-based paint, asbestos, wood preservatives, and insecticides. Some of the debris caught fire before it was even unloaded. Dana Leigh, one opponent of the new recycling operation, said it was hypocritical for the Mohawks to allow dumping of potentially hazardous waste on the reservation while they criticized local industrial plants for fouling their land, water, and air.

Gray also learned that the trucking firm hauling debris to his recycling plant was under investigation in Massachusetts for illegal dumping. This might be one reason it decided to buddy up with the Mohawks, who quickly unified to fight a new environmental threat at the same time that factional violence related to gambling divided the tribe. Even in this time of profound division, both supporters and opponents of commercial gaming heeded Ward Stone's warning that as environmental laws tightened outside native lands, promoters would be seeking new dumping grounds. As had happened so often in the past, Akwesasne got it first. All Mohawks did not speak with the same voice on the pollution front, however. After the Warriors' outcry against the proposed dump, some Akwesasne residents also asked when they would raise similar protests against sewage seepage from some of the casinos.

As the people of Akwesasne turned thumbs down on a stream of new disposal proposals, in March 1991 the EPA filed complaints seeking $35.4 million in fines not only from General Motors, but also against the two largest U.S. waste management companies. Both had helped General Motors dispose of its PCB-laden wastes on and near the reservation. By making haulers of toxic waste liable for their cargo, the EPA was attempting to force them to police their loads more strictly. This was the first time that EPA had extended liability to haulers of toxic wastes. "We're insisting they look beyond just the truck that appears on their doorstep, so they don't become an active party in circumventing the law," said Michael J. Walker, EPA associate counsel for toxic substances.[36] Environmental spokesmen for the two hauling companies, Browning-Ferris Industries and Waste Management, complained that the EPA placed an unfair burden on them. "They're asking a disposal company to become an arm of law enforcement," said Peter Tarnawskyj, manager of environmental compliance at Niagara Falls–based Browning-Ferris.[37]

The EPA's case contended that both hauling companies illegally diluted PCBs dumped near the General Motors foundry, a move that the auto maker had believed would excuse it from having to incinerate, rather than bury, its effluent. Incineration is environmentally more sound but up to 10 times more expensive than the burial of wastes. The EPA contended that at least 31,000 tons of PCB-contaminated waste was diluted in order to avoid the standard requiring incineration. The two hauling companies said that by the time the waste in question arrived at their dumps it was solid, not liquid. This is one way to get around the indictment that applies only to liquid wastes. General Motors reduced the case to a dispute over semantics, "a disagreement over sampling and analysis." The EPA was seeking $14.2 million from General Motors, the same amount from Browning-Ferris, and $7.1 million from Waste Management.

In August 1990 Stone said that enforcing agencies were dealing with environmental problems at Akwesasne too slowly, as if they were engaging the offending corporations in a sort of bureaucratic pantomime.

> As I speak, Alcoa is still putting PCBs into the Grass River. And they are going into the nearby Saint Lawrence into Indian waters adjacent to Cornwall Island, a main part of the fishing and hunting area of Akwesasne. ... Reynolds Metals is heavily hitting the [Saint Lawrence] River with PCBs, fluorides, aluminum, a wide variety of pollutants right now. It's ongoing. The water is still being degraded.
>
> When I arrived in June 1985, the United States Environmental Protection Agency was involved at General Motors. ... We still have a pollution problem more than five years later. The river is not cleaned up. [The EPA] didn't identify Reynolds. It was pathology DEC that identified that, and the Mohawks. And so, the EPA is involved, but exceedingly slowly. And it's quite questionable whether or not their standards of cleanup will be sufficient to bring the river back—we think that it won't—to a place

> where the Mohawks will once again be able to utilize the fish and wildlife for food.[38]

By December 20, 1990, General Motors officials were complaining they could not meet the 1-part-per-million standard for PCBs in river sediment, nor even the 10 parts per million required by the EPA on the plant grounds itself. "It's going to be hard for us to agree to a standard we don't think is technically possible," said David L. Lippert, media manager for General Motors' automotive components group in Detroit.[39] The EPA estimated that its cleanup plan for the foundry would cost $78 million and would include removal of soil contaminated with PCBs from the reservation, dredging and treatment of contaminated sediments from the river beds of the Saint Lawrence and Raquette, removal of polluted soils from two General Motors disposal sites, and treatment of waste water before it was released into the Saint Lawrence River. The company also threatened to close its foundry if the EPA forced it to close down and clean up its active waste lagoons. Additionally, General Motors argued that to dredge the river would stir up more PCB residue than would be released if the area was simply left alone. For the seventh year since the General Motors site had been placed on the EPA Superfund list, the company and the government continued to dicker over just how to clean up this corner of Mohawk country. As they did, the PCBs continued to spread. Such was the nature of natural life, and death, as 1991 opened in the land of the toxic turtle.

Six months later, in July 1991, Alcoa suddenly agreed to pay $7.5 million in civil and criminal penalties in connection with dumping of PCBs and other pollutants at its Massena plant. The $3.75 million criminal penalty alone was the largest ever assessed in U.S. history for a hazardous-waste violation. After the company pled guilty to state pollution charges, its chairman Paul O'Neill said, "Alcoa has a clear environmental policy which was not followed in this instance."[40] More bluntly, the company had continued to dump PCBs and other hazardous wastes long after they became illegal. A state investigation had found that during 1989 the company had excavated 33 railroad carloads of PCB-contaminated soil while it prepared to install a drainage system. The soil was left piled for more than 90 days, after which some of it was hauled away by train. The company also pled guilty to illegally dumping caustic and acidic waste down manholes at its plant in Massena. Alcoa pleaded guilty to four very expensive misdemeanors. The $3.75 million in additional civil penalties were levied because the company failed to report (or underreported) unauthorized discharges of hazardous wastes on approximately 2,000 occasions since 1985.

Alcoa's guilty plea was hailed as an environmental victory. After the euphoria faded, many at Akwesasne remembered that it was only one small step in the long road to restoring an environment that could once again sustain life in their homeland. The size of the fines merely indicated how great the damage had been and continues to be. Mark Narsisian, a resident near the General Motors foundry, said, "People have the false sense that money will even things out. If I can't plant in the ground anymore, what good is it? If I plant my coins in the ground, [will] corn grow?"[41] Narsisian's comments underline a timeless dilemma for American Indians who have exchanged their land and resources for money: Without land and a healthy environment, money is worthless.

The people at Akwesasne have disagreed vehemently on whether their homeland should be opened to gambling, but nearly everyone living there deplores the environmental degradation of the area. Loran Thompson, a spokesman for the Warriors supporting gambling, sounding a lot like Tom Porter, an opponent of commercial gambling, said that he had to plow under his garden because pollution from the General Motors foundry had poisoned its soil. He described a lagoon near the Saint Lawrence where he remembered that, in his youth, one could practically walk on the back of the fish. Now, there are no fish. The lagoon is a backwash of thick, black sludge.

> The family lived off that pond. Muskrat, ducks, geese, fish. We used to swim there, too. I get so depressed just to think about it. ... You should have seen it here when I was a kid—beautiful, clean, crystal-clear water. We used to come here for our drinking water.[42]

"Now," says Thompson, who lives an eighth of a mile from one of General Motors' dumps, "I have a hard time explaining to people why I live here. Some days you can hardly breathe, from the stryene that comes out of their [General Motors'] smokestack. It's all gone now. Progress took it all away. Progress? We go backwards."[43]

Thompson's wife died of cancer a few years ago, just as he discovered that his dream of having a farm had died in the PCB-laced soil.

"My father raised us with gardens and animals. That's what I was going to do. I had two beautiful gardens. I was raising pigs; [I] was going to get horses and cows. ... I got rid of the pigs. I got rid of the gardens. People are afraid to start anything here."[44]

Thompson's family was the fourth generation to farm land now unsuitable for raising food. They could not raise crops on it, hunt animals that fed on it, nor fish from water bordering it without poisoning themselves. Despite this, Thompson says he will never move. By his reasoning, he and the rest of the Mohawks were on this land first, before industry spoiled it. "I've lived here all my life," said Thompson, "and I'm going to stay here, even if it kills me."[45]

The environmental crisis at Akwesasne had become so acute by mid-1990 that in the midst of the violence over gambling, Mohawk leaders called a press conference to remind people that the biggest problem they faced was environmental pollution, not the gambling feud. The press conference convened at New York's Five Rivers wildlife preserve, in a joint presentation with Greenpeace, the Sierra Club, New York Public Interest Research Group, and other environmental advocacy groups.

"If we are to heal the divisions and the crisis at Akwesasne, we first must deal with the environment," elected chief Harold Tarbell said May 30, three days before his opposition to gambling cost him his seat on the St. Regis Tribal Council.[46] Ward Stone said that General Motors, Reynolds, and Alcoa had polluted the area for decades. "The PCBs are flowing out of the General Motors plant right now," he said, contradicting company assertions that direct pollution had stopped.[47]

"We can't try to meet the challenges with the meager resources we have," said Henry Lickers, a Seneca employed by the Mohawk Council of Akwesasne. Lickers has also been a leader in the fight against fluoride emissions from the Reynolds plant. "The next 10 years will be a cleanup time for us, even without the money."[48]

The destruction of Akwesasne's environment is credited by Lickers, the Mohawk who has been a mentor to today's younger environmentalists at Akwesasne, with being the catalyst that spawned the Mohawks' deadly battle over high-stakes gambling and smuggling. "A desperation sets in when year after year you see the decimation of the philosophical center of your society," he said.[49] Many of gambling's most ardent supporters assert that the contamination of Akwesasne made gaming necessary for economic survival, since people there can no longer live off the land. The destruction of a natural world that once fed, housed, and clothed the Mohawks closed off other ways of making a living.

Maurice Hinchey, chairman of the New York Assembly's Environmental Conservation Committee, said that he would continue to press in Albany for action on Akwesasne's environmental crisis. He said that there are few places where all these destructive forces have had a much impact as Akwesasne. The Mohawks are not alone, however. Increasingly, restrictive environmental regulations enacted by states and cities are bringing polluters to native reservations. "Indian tribes across America are grappling with some of the worst of its pollution: uranium tailings, chemical lagoons and illegal dumps. Nowhere has it been more troublesome than at ... Akwesasne," wrote one observer.[50]

If there was one front on which all sides at Akwesasne could unite and provide a national example, it was the environment. On this issue all Mohawks find themselves on the same side, calling for restoration of the ability of the earth to sustain them, and generations to come.

Notes

[1] New York State Assembly Hearings, Transcript, *The Crisis at Akwesasne,* Ft. Covington, July 24, 1990, pp. 24–28.
[2] *Wall Street Journal* (New York, NY), November 29, 1990.
[3] Associated Press, *Herald-American* (Syracuse, NY), July 15, 1990.
[4] New York. State Assembly Hearings, Transcript, *The Crisis at Akwesasne,* Ft. Covington, July 24, 1990, pp. 289–92.
[5] *Indian Time* (Akwesasne), August 16, 1991.
[6] *Observer* (Massena, NY), December 8, 1981. Cited in Cornell University American Indian Program, "Significant Dates, Events, and Findings in the Akwesasne-General Motors Environmental Situation," n.d., p. 5. Typescript in Cornell AIP files.
[7] Ibid.
[8] *Post-Standard* (Syracuse, NY), December 21, 1981.
[9] *Standard-Freeholder* (Cornwall, NY), January 7, 1982.
[10] *Daily Times* (Watertown, NY), January 12, 1982.
[11] *Post-Standard* (Syracuse, NY), January 19, 1982.
[12] *Observer* (Massena, NY), July 21, 1983.
[13] *Advance News* (Ogdensburg, NY), July 17, 1983.
[14] *Observer* (Massena, NY), August 18, 1983.
[15] Ibid.
[16] *Daily Times* (Watertown, NY), November 28, 1983. The memo was dated February 2, 1982.
[17] Ibid.
[18] *Indian Time* (Akwesasne), July 27, 1983.
[19] Ibid.
[20] WSLU-FM (Canton, NY), public radio broadcast report, St. Lawrence University, October 10, 1984. Typescript in Cornell AIP files.
[21] Ibid.
[22] Ibid.
[23] Ibid.
[24] *Wall Street Journal* (New York, NY), November 29, 1990.
[25] New York State Assembly Hearings, Transcript, *The Crisis at Akwesasne,* Albany, August 2, 1990, p. 295.
[26] Ibid., 288.
[27] Ibid., 289.
[28] Ibid.
[29] New York. State Assembly Hearings, Transcript, *The Crisis at Akwesasne,* Ft. Covington, July 24, 1990, p. 289.
[30] Jim Ransom, Letter to the Editor, *Courier-Observer* (Massena, NY), November 3, 1990.
[31] *Indian Time* (Akwesasne), August 16, 1991.
[32] The General Motors ruling was mentioned in context of a hearing being held December 13 in Saratoga Springs, New York to determine whether GE would be forced to spend $270 million cleaning up PCBs along the Hudson River north of Albany, near Fort Edward. GE claimed that the cleanup was unnecessary because a specialized group of microorganisms in the river bed could degrade the PCBs. This form of "bioremediation," said to be under development by GE and biotechnology concerns, employs cylinders 6 feet across and 16 feet long, which are sunk into river bottoms containing some of the 209 varieties of PCBs. The cylinders release bacteria related to those commonly used in sewage-treatment plants and to clean up oil spills.

The *Wall Street Journal* also reported that the hearing would have a bearing on PCB cleanups in rivers and streams of upstate New York by Reynolds Metals Co. and Aluminum Company of America. While GE said it is spending $50 million on bioremediation technology, some environmental advocates believe that the research is a public-relations stunt designed to get the company out from under more costly dredging to clean up PCB-laden river bottoms.

[33] Jeff Jones, "A Nation Divided." *Metroland*, June 7–13, 1990, 1.

[34] *Wall Street Journal* (New York, NY), November 29, 1990.

[35] Ron LaFrance interview with author. Akwesasne, August 4, 1991.

[36] *Wall Street Journal* (New York, NY), April 8, 1991.

[37] Ibid.

[38] New York State Assembly Hearings, Transcript, *The Crisis at Akwesasne*, Albany, August 2, 1990, p. 288.

[39] *Post-Standard* (Syracuse, NY), December 20, 1990.

[40] *Democrat and Chronicle* (Rochester, NY), July 12, 1991.

[41] *Wall Street Journal* (New York, NY), November 29, 1990.

[42] *Herald-American* (Syracuse, NY), June 30, 1990.

[43] Ibid.

[44] Ibid.

[45] Ibid.

[46] *Post-Standard* (Syracuse, NY), May 31, 1990.

[47] New York State Assembly Hearings, Transcript, *The Crisis at Akwesasne*, Albany, August 2, 1990, p. 288.

[48] *Post-Standard* (Syracuse, NY), May 31, 1990.

[49] Associated Press, *Herald-American* (Syracuse, NY), July 15, 1990.

[50] Rupert Tomsho, *Wall Street Journal* (New York, NY), November 29, 1990.

CHAPTER 2

▼▼▼

The Gambling War: Beginnings

At Akwesasne, the only American Indian reservation split by the U.S.–Canadian border, gambling grew from illicit roots in smuggling. During the 1970s, when gasoline prices soared in the United States, various profiteers opened pump stations at Akwesasne where New York motorists could fill up with cheaper fuel produced under Canadian government price controls. The "buttlegging" (cigarette smuggling) trade followed, beginning in the early 1980s, as Canada's national government imposed high luxury taxes on tobacco products, making untaxed cigarettes purchased on U.S. or Canadian Indian reservations much cheaper. In the pipeline, Canadian cigarettes were shipped first into the United States as exports, thus escaping Canadian taxes. Once over the border, the cigarettes were smuggled back across, usually through Akwesasne, where they were sold without taxes in several dozen smoke shops on the Kahnawake reserve outside Montreal. Cigarettes smuggled directly from the United States would have borne U.S. tax stamps; the Canadian smokes had no tax stamps on them. Once the cigarette pipeline got underway, other illegal or illicit goods were added, such as liquor, drugs, and weapons, including AK-47s and other semiautomatics.

In the early 1980s, bingo first came to Akwesasne at Billy's Bingo Hall, a small operation barely resembling the glitzy strip that would later erupt along Highway 37, the main route through the U.S. side of Akwesasne. Billy's, operated by William Sears, a Mohawk, was set up as an exclusive franchise from the tribe. In return for the franchise, Sears contracted to turn over 49 percent of his profits to the St. Regis Tribal Council. Sears negotiated with this tribal council (rather than with the Mohawk Nation Council) because it is recognized by U.S. and state governments. St. Regis is the name Europeans gave to the area that native people call Akwesasne; it is also the name of a village on the Canadian side of the reservation.

In 1984 Guilford White and his partner Basil "Buddy" Cook, both of Akwesasne, decided they ought to upstage Billy's with a world-class, high-stakes bingo parlor. They pooled funds with several non-Indian investors from Las Vegas and Texas, and in May 1985, the Mohawk Bingo Palace opened to a fanfare of newspaper articles describing how remote Akwesasne had suddenly become a new tourist mecca. It also opened to protests. Some Mohawks thought that high-stakes bingo and other forms of gambling would lure the underworld and rend the cultural fabric of the community. They picketed along Route 37, about 200 yards from the Bingo Palace. Operators of small-stakes charity bingo games in New York communities near the reservation also fretted that the Mohawk Bingo Palace would cut into their businesses. Some Mohawk opponents of bingo attempted to obstruct buses bringing players to the reservation. A few scuffles broke out, and several people were arrested for disorderly conduct and traffic violations.

On May 23, 1985, two days before the palace opened, *Indian Time*, a community newspaper at Akwesasne whose editors opposed commercial gambling, coordinated a referendum on commercial bingo with 380 people from both sides of the reserve voting no and 25 voting yes. Bingo operators rejected the referendum as invalid because it included only a fraction of the 7,000 to 8,000 people living at Akwesasne at the time. The elected chiefs of the St. Regis Tribal Council on the U.S. side urged residents not to vote and declared the referendum invalid. The Mohawk Nation Council (drawing representation from both sides of the border) supported the referendum.

Before confrontations turned violent, a number of community meetings were held in an attempt to peacefully resolve the conflict over gambling. The earliest were held at the Mohawk Bingo Palace, but they broke up after casino employees vented their anger at "antis" for trying to deprive them of their jobs. Opponents of gambling felt intimidated by the accusations at the site. An attempt was then made to move the meetings to a neutral setting at the St. Regis Mohawk Elementary School Gymnasium in Hogansburg. These meetings also turned into shouting matches. At one meeting gambling supporters read letters composed by children that advocated shooting opponents of gaming. At another meeting chiefs from the three councils governing Akwesasne even reached an agreement that gambling should stop, but owners of casino and bingo halls ignored it.

Guilford White described protesters as chronic malcontents while presenting himself as an "angel" of economic salvation. He asserted that the Mohawk Bingo Palace provided 125 jobs, 120 of which he said went to Mohawks. This is a powerful allure on a reservation where, in 1987, 60 percent of the people who had jobs earned less than $7,000 annually, or poverty-level earnings.

As debates among Mohawks continued, bingo players arrived from upstate New York as well as Montreal and other Canadian cities. They paid $25 to $50 for a set of cards and a chance at prizes ranging from a few dollars to almost $100,000. During its first few months in operation, the Mohawk Bingo Palace installed a number of extra attractions such as the Money Machine, a clear plastic cage a little larger than a phone booth, its floor thick with crumpled paper money in denominations up to $100. The lucky occupant of the Money Machine got 60 seconds to grab as much money as possible while an industrial-strength fan swirled the bills around the cage.

The Mohawk Bingo Palace quickly became the most lavish gaming house in the area, its 1,800 seats often brimming with players. One day in 1986 an elderly woman from Ontario walked away with a single prize of $98,000. On another day Robert F. Snyder of Watertown, New York, spent $66 and came away with a new 1986 Chevy Chevette. White advertised ever more lavish prizes: a Cadillac, a dream home in Florida, a round-the-world vacation trip, a million-dollar pot. Meanwhile, the St. Regis Tribal Council complained that the Bingo Palace was not providing records of its operations as stipulated in its contract with the tribal government. The council threatened to close it down in October 1987. "As far as I can see, the only people who are benefitting are the Indian and non-Indian investors," said elected chief Brenda LaFrance.[1]

At about the same time slot machines began to appear in back rooms of restaurants, gas stations, and convenience stores along Highway 37, defying the elected tribal council's objections. Gambling had definitely arrived.

The Mohawk Warrior Society first emerged in the printed record of the gambling dispute at Akwesasne during September 1987. Francis Boots issued a statement prior to a meeting of about 50 gambling supporters at Billy's Bingo Hall: "Any attempt taken by outside police forces will be considered as a military expedition against a people at peace with the United States."[2] The statement asserted that any attempt by the St. Regis Tribal Council to request state police aid to enforce its ban on slot machines would be "unauthorized and unsanctioned by the Mohawk people."[3] This initial press release contained two elements essential to Warrior ideology at Akwesasne from that day forward: an identification of gambling with Mohawk sovereignty and a penchant for identifying the Warriors' interests with those of the Mohawk people. The statement also engaged in a degree of hyperbole that would become familiar in following years; it declared that the threat of outside intervention had placed the Warrior Society "on red alert."[4]

Barbara Barnes, director of the North American Indian Traveling College at Akwesasne and an ardent opponent of gambling, characterized the growth of gambling during the late 1980s:

> The slot machines were brought in slowly and subtly by Mohawk businessman Eli Tarbell. One or 2 machines, and then 50 machines, and finally over 200 machines. Then it was a gold rush, and others were opening casinos and putting in slots, blackjack, roulette, and card games. We were in the midst of a glitter-gulch strip, [with] no community controls, no government approval, no tribal regulations, and no profits to the people.[5]

By late 1987, despite opposition by the St. Regis and Mohawk Nation councils, slot-machine gambling at Akwesasne had grown to the point that New York state police estimated it was providing $7 million a year in tax-free profits to the owners of six establishments. In a predawn raid December 16, 1987, state troopers seized 77 slots at the Bear's Den, 30 at Wild Bill's, 62 at the Night Hawk, 49 at the Silver Dollar, 70 at the Golden Nugget, and 5 at C & R. The casino operators placed orders for new slots the next day.

The 293 machines, costing between $1,000 and $2,000 each, were hauled away in eight U-Haul trucks while gambling-parlor owners Eli Tarbell, William Sears, James Burns, Roderick Cook, Paul Tatlock, and Roger Tarbell looked on. There was no armed resistance; Troop B Commander John Lawliss of the New York state police said that his troopers were met at three of the gaming establishments by lone armed watchmen. Less than three years later, state police would look down the barrel of a private army guarding the gaming establishments that outgunned them.

Doug George, editor of *Akwesasne Notes,* was an outspoken opponent of commercial gambling at Akwesasne. On January 9, 1988, a firebomb razed the newspaper's offices. *Akwesasne Notes* has been one of the foremost native-owned editorial voices for Native American rights in the United States and Canada since the late 1960s. The publication has a geographic reach that few newspapers can match, with copies being mailed to indigenous people and their supporters around the world. Usually, when a newspaper is firebombed, losing everything, the story makes the pages of other newspapers. When one of the most influential Native American newspapers in the United States was torched, the mainstream press generally ignored the story. Hogansburg Fire Chief Frank Lacerenza said that the fire was accidental, despite "recent tensions on the reservation." The staff of the newspaper firmly believed that the fire had been set.

The fire gutted the Nation House that had been the newspaper's home for most of the previous two decades. In its first editorial after the fire the editor of *Akwesasne Notes* wrote:

> Our offices were torched by those amongst us here at Akwesasne who oppose our reporting on the conflicts that are plaguing the Haudenosaunee [Iroquois] nations. ... With the gambling, the cigarette smuggling, the violence ... it is understandable why those criminal elements amongst

> us are opposed to a free press disseminating information about the illegal and immoral activities around us. ... They almost succeeded in putting us out of business ... but we will survive.[6]

In Washington, D.C., as the *Akwesasne Notes* office was being firebombed, the Indian Gaming Regulatory Act was making its way through Congress. Introduced by Senator Inouye, chairman of the Senate Select Committee on Indian Affairs, the act became Public Law 100-497 (1988), establishing federal standards for gaming on Indian lands. It was written to allow class III gambling, including casinos. A native nation or tribe must sign a compact with the state that surrounds its territory outlining conditions under which gambling may take place, and the secretary of interior must consent

The 1988 federal law established a five-member board to govern Indian bingo, instructed Indian tribes to pay a 5 percent tax on profits to support the commission, and mandated state approval to operate pari-mutual betting and casinos. Many tribal leaders roundly panned the new law. "It's based on greed, plain and simple," said John Gonzalez, then president of the National Congress of American Indians (NCAI).[7] The 200-member NCAI, the largest and oldest organization of federally recognized Indian tribal governments, complained that the necessity to seek state control for hard-core gaming would seriously erode tribal sovereignty.

Under the 1988 law, reservation gambling was to be regulated, and some of its profits were supposed to go into tribal budgets for the common good of native people. Gambling at Akwesasne (some of which began before the law was passed) was not regulated by anyone, and its profits usually flowed straight into the pockets of its sponsors.[8]

As President Reagan signed the new Indian gambling act, Mohawk Tony Laughing opened the first Las Vegas–style casino at Akwesasne, Tony Vegas International. The new casino opened without state, federal, or tribal approval. Laughing told the press that armed guards would defend it from the police raids that had plagued earlier attempts to install slot machines on the reservation. At one point, the elected St. Regis Tribal Council shut off Tony Vegas' water supply, along with that of Hart's Palace, another casino. The gambling promoters brought in bottled water for their employees and customers. "We want to let people know we're making a distinction between legitimate business and crime," said Harold Tarbell, one of three elected chiefs on the U.S. side.

Laughing opened his casino even as the St. Regis Tribal Council and Mohawk Nation Council chiefs told him it was illegal. According to Harold Tarbell, "These guys have gone too far—they are on the edge of anarchy. Nobody likes to live like that. There are going to be a lot of irate members out in the community. I'm concerned that they may take matters into their own hands."[9] With no police force of its own, however, the St. Regis Tribal Council could put no muscle behind its demands that Laughing close his casino. To Tarbell, the gambling operators were endangering tribal sovereignty because they gave state police an excuse to come on the reservation. In fact, John Lawliss, Troop B Commander of the New York State Police, hinted shortly after Laughing's gaming parlor opened that if the casino wasn't closed by the Mohawks themselves, "the police would be back up there."

The $375,000 building housing Tony Vegas International was constructed with thick brick walls, no windows, and only one entrance, so that it could be easily defended. Laughing began with 24 slot machines, planning to expand to 500, along with blackjack, craps, and other games of chance. Laughing was seen tooling around the reservation in his late-model Cadillac, contacting people on its cellular phone. "Gambling is a viable way of making a living for me and my family. It's a way for us to get into the mainstream of society."[10] At the time, Laughing proposed that slot machine owners pay a monthly royalty of $50 per machine to the St. Regis Tribal Council. The proposal that was not acted on by the council because accepting such a gratuity would give illegal gambling a patina of legality.

Even as the casinos were being built with profits from the smuggling trade, most Akwesasne Mohawks fervently supported the treaty rights that enabled them to cross the international border freely with goods. Treaty rights were not negotiable even though smugglers flaunted them. The people of Akwesasne long asserted the right to use the border freely as an aboriginal right because they had occupied the area long before the border was drawn. The right is also recognized in the 1794 Jay Treaty.

Nevertheless, for many years Canadian customs officials denied free travel to Mohawks passing through their checkpoint at Cornwall Island on the reservation until a series of protests by Mohawks during the 1980s forced customs authorities to respect their rights under the Jay Treaty. On March 22, 1988, about 600 Mohawks accompanied Mohawk Council of Akwesasne Grand Chief Mike Mitchell as he drove across the International Bridge in a blue pickup truck loaded with a washing machine, clothes, motor oil, and bibles. Canadian authorities did not arrest him, even though they maintained that he was engaging in an illegal act. Mitchell said that Canadian authorities restricted border-crossing rights to crimp smuggling and thereby threatened legitimate crossings. The smugglers had tried to stop the march because it would bring attention to them.

Canadian authorities made occasional high-profile raids at Kahnawake, a Mohawk reserve near Montreal, 60 miles east northeast of Akwesasne, to seize smuggled cigarettes and cash, much of which had come over the border through Akwesasne. On June 1, 1988, a force of 200 Royal Canadian Mounted Police seized $450,000 worth of contraband cigarettes and $284,000 in cash as they arrested 17 Mohawks at Kahnawake. The cigarettes were being sold at 32 discount smoke shops on the reserve.

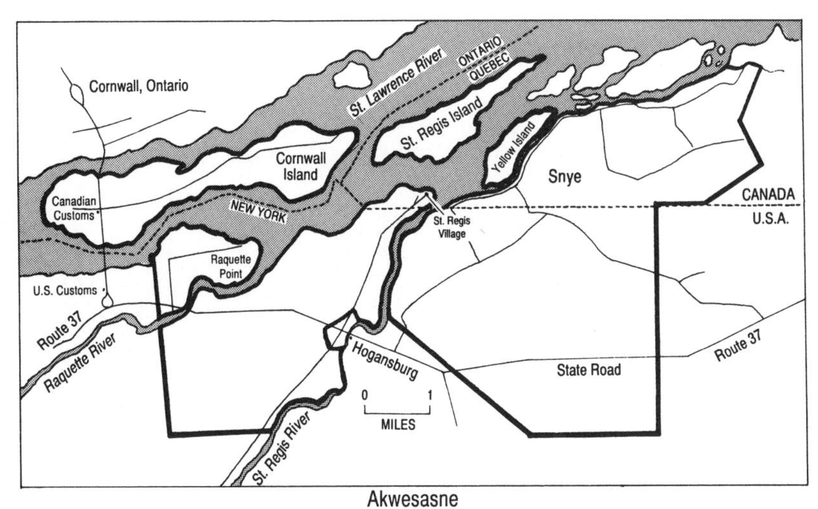

Akwesasne
(St. Regis Mohawk Reservation)

Reservation residents responded by blocking all access to Kahnawake, including the heavily traveled Mercier Bridge on which they erected a blockade of cars, trucks, and piles of gravel. The Mohawks asserted that the police raid was an invasion of their sovereignty. Canadian taxation officials said the cigarette trade was costing Canada $25 million a year in lost revenues.

Despite smuggling, American officials recognized the Jay Treaty and allowed Mohawks to cross the border freely. In practice, this means that Mohawks may pass from one side of the international border to the other without having to follow the usual customs procedures, such as registering one's name, declaring valuables, and submitting to search. The smuggling trade also flourished in no small part because during much of the long winter the Saint Lawrence River often freezes to a depth that allows anyone to drive an automobile across the international boundary in either direction almost anywhere at Akwesasne. It is one of the most permeable borders on earth.

As Akwesasne's casino row grew, so did the influence of the casino owners and their employees on tribal politics. The gambling industry at Akwesasne made good on its pledge to unseat elected chiefs who opposed them. On June 4, 1988, Leo David Jacobs, an advocate of reservation gambling, defeated incumbent St. Regis Tribal Council chief Rosemarie Bonaparte, an opponent of gaming, 445 votes to 440. "It's shocking. Nobody expected this," said Doug George, editor of *Indian Time*. Gaming supporters had labeled Bonaparte a "traitor" to the Mohawk nation following her support (with other antigaming chiefs) for the New York police raid that had resulted in seizure of 293 slot machines at six gambling houses six months earlier. Despite the heated nature of

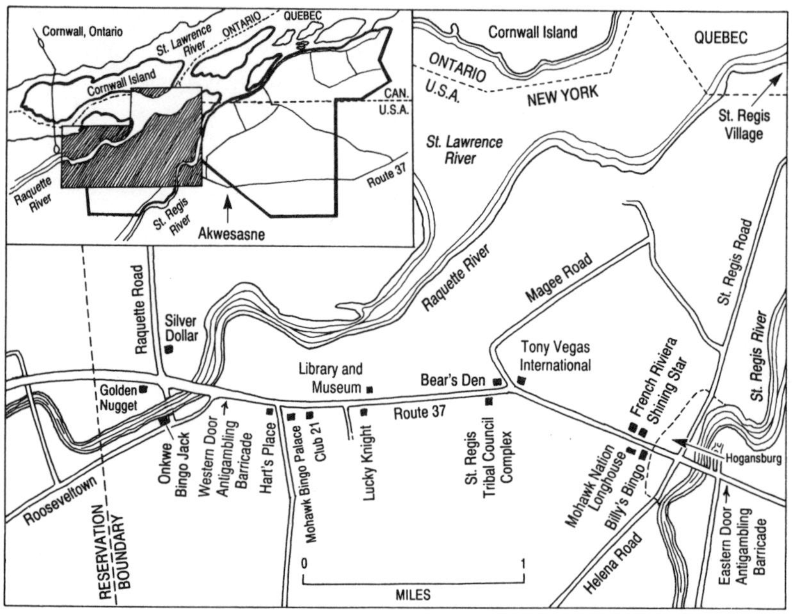

Akwesasne Route 37

the campaign rhetoric, both sides agreed that the election had been conducted fairly. The result withstood a recount.

By early 1989 a 2 1/2-mile stretch of Route 37, bristled with a half-dozen high-stakes bingo halls and casinos, all looking very much like a bargain-basement version of Las Vegas, a glittering strip sparkling with names such as Silver Dollar and Wild Bill's. One sign showed a giant hand clutching a wad of dollar bills as it urged prospective gamblers to "Come into our world."

As the glitter strip grew, the U.S. Department of Interior's inspector general launched an investigation into the activities of Thomas Burden and Emmett Munley, who played key roles in securing early financing for the Mohawk Bingo Palace. The investigation found that Munley twice before had been rejected for a Nevada casino license because of his associations with people of unsavory reputation.[11] Munley, who was said to own an 86 percent stake in the Bingo Palace, tried to wrest control from the two minority shareholders, Basil "Buddy" Cook and Guilford White. Munley claimed that the two Mohawks were using unrest on the reservation as a cover for their seizure of the bingo hall from him. Munley and three other investors had put up more than $2.4 million to open the Mohawk Bingo Palace. Doug George said he had warned White (a first cousin once removed of elected chief Lincoln White) in 1984 that he was getting involved with possible underworld connections. However, White ignored him. News accounts portrayed White, a former Washington, D.C., union agent, as an aficionado of good cigars, who liked to dress in Vegas–

style lime green sports coats, as he described the opposition to gambling as "phoney [*sic*] Indian beads and braids bullshit."[12]

Fire struck the offices of *Akwesasne Notes* for the second time in roughly a year on January 23, 1989. The Hogansburg Fire Department again responded to the blaze and contained the fire after about $10,000 to $15,000 in damages mostly due to smoke and heat. Sheetrock walls inside the newspapers' new offices in St. Regis Village kept the fire from spreading. Akwesasne's radio station CKON, housed in the new office with *Akwesasne Notes*, along with the community newspaper *Indian Time*, reported that the second fire also was arson. A reward of $500 for information leading to the conviction of the purported arsonist was offered. George told off-reservation reporters that a door to the office had been forced at the time of the fire. George said that the fire was probably set not by gambling supporters, but by an individual who was angry about articles the newspapers had published previously. As with the first blaze, Massena state police officials denied George's allegations. Official investigator Hollis Hastings said that the assertions were "garbage." Losses from the second fire were insured.

On June 6, 1989, a brawl between gambling supporters and opponents at Tony Vegas International (TVI) escalated into a fight that injured Mohawk Eric Sunday. At its height, the scuffle involved about 400 people, including gambling opponents, casino employees, and Warriors. After state police waded into the crowd, gambling opponents told them to remove TVI's slot machines, or they would do it on their own. Police seized one machine for evidence and arrested Laughing as the crowd streamed into the casino and wrecked 50 other one-armed bandits.

Shortly after the riot at TVI, New York state police imposed a two-day crackdown on illegal reservation gambling resulting in the arrest of four people. More than 200 slot machines and other gambling devices were confiscated. These machines were added to 400 others in police storage, which had been seized in earlier raids on seven gambling operations at Akwesasne.

Standing in a small sea of more than 150 blackjack tables, under ornate, fake-crystal chandeliers, Tony Laughing's lawyer brokered an agreement that called for the police to charge Laughing with promoting gambling, a misdemeanor. Laughing employed this tactic so that he could get the disturbance over with in time to open for business the same evening. Laughing emphasized that his casino was a business and that every night it stayed closed cost him tens of thousands of dollars in cash flow.

The riot and police seizure of slot machines occurred on a Tuesday. By Friday, Laughing was out on bail and had six new slots in place with more on order in time for the weekend rush. Laughing's parking lot was full of customers and it was business as usual by Saturday. Laughing also had just finished swearing 52 arrest warrants for people he believed had invaded his casino and wrecked slot machines the previous Tuesday.

Responding to charges that he was in business solely to line his own pockets, Laughing wrote, "Did you know that TVI supports various Little League teams and hockey teams, [and] sponsors struggling stock car drivers?" TVI had recently pledged 30 remote-control television sets to a home for elderly Mohawks. "Two television sets are in place for the elderly Mohawk residents, and the rest will follow."[13]

On May 16, 1989, nine chiefs of the Mohawk Nation Council at Akwesasne asked President Bush to intervene and remove gambling devices from Akwesasne, repeating a request made in August 1987. The request was made under the 1794 Treaty of Canandaigua (signed by George Washington) that allows the Iroquois to request federal intervention to remove non-Indians or to halt criminal activity. The request for such intervention was made by the Mohawk Nation Council and not by the St. Regis Tribal Council, because the United States negotiated treaties with its forebears.

Doug George recalled how the Mohawk Nation Council assembled for the agonizing decision to call on the United States to intervene in their homeland. The council discussed requesting removal of gambling devices at several meetings during 1987, 1988, and 1989. In a system that stressed consensus over party rivalry, the Mohawk Nation Council chiefs argued that non-Indians were backing gambling on the reservation and that the gaming was being operated illegally without consent of either the Mohawk Nation Council or the St. Regis Tribal Council. George recalled the momentous decision.

> It is a cool morning at Akwesasne in early May. ... As the chiefs and clan mothers begin driving to the Longhouse, their initial mood changes from quiet pleasure to deep concern. The Longhouse sits on an east-west axis. The building itself is a Quaker [design]: plain, rectangular, white-washed, with shuttered windows, bare of any adornment, except for two iron woodstoves on either end of the house. Built in the 1930s, the structure is 75 feet long and 25 feet wide. There are two entrances: one opens from the east, and is the means of entry for the men, while the door to the west is for the use of women. Inside, there are two tiers of benches along the four walls. The women of the Nation will be seated apart from the men, in the western half of the Longhouse. Only at funerals and weddings are the men joined by the women.
>
> The plain, wooden Longhouse contrasts strongly with the glitzy row of casinos (large sheet-metal sheds that look like warehouses topped by neon signs), smoke shops and gas stations that the chiefs and clan mothers had passed along Route 37, a former cattle trail, on the way to their meeting. They pass the many warehouse casinos, now open 24 hours a day, seven days a week. Gamblers are being bused in from throughout the Northeast, upsetting area residents and making local driving hazardous. The narcotics trade is also thriving, as dope peddlers sell cocaine and crack from their doorsteps. ... This day, a decision would be made by the chiefs that would change the painted face of

Akwesasne, lead to police invasions, beatings, late-night shootings, and the deaths of two Mohawks, as a world of faith and spirit clashed with power and flesh.

[Around the Longhouse] the tall, green cedars swayed gently in a southwesterly breeze, their comforting sighs in rigid contrast to the flashing neon signs of nearby gaming dens. As the "good minds" (*rotiiane,* the Mohawk word for their leaders) got out of their cars, they looked across the highway into a full [casino] parking lot. White-shirted guards leaned against their four-wheel-drive Ford Broncos, their eyes hidden behind opaque sunglasses, arms folded across bloated stomachs. From citizen-band radios mounted on the dashboards of their trucks, the static-filled voice of "casino base" sought information on the movements of the Longhouse chiefs. ... At this hour, the guards are usually asleep in their trucks. ...

The chiefs themselves trade uncertain glances as they file into the Longhouse. Inside the Longhouse, the chiefs sit according to clan: the three male Bear Clan leaders sit against the eastern wall, with the Wolf Clan leaders to their left on the south side, and the Turtles to the north. Across from the men sit the women, ever watchful, ready to interject if political customs are violated. Small talk, quiet and respectful, ends as the chiefs and clan mothers take their seats on the hardwood benches. The day's business begins, as all public events must, [as] one of the chiefs takes hold of a string of sacred wampum beads. ... The chief clears his voice, then begins to recite, from memory, the Thanksgiving Address, using words empowered by a people in desperate need of clear minds. Generation after generation, Iroquois speakers have used the same words to acknowledge the beauties of the natural world. Gratitude is expressed to mother earth, to her medicinal plants, the seeds placed inside her by man, the waters of the planet, and all animals, whether finned, furred, or feathered; to the winds, the thunder, the human beings, their spiritual guides, and, finally, to the Creator. ... The prayer is long, melodious, and comforting. Men and women bow their heads in respect.

With the conclusion of the prayer, the "good minds" review the day's agenda. ... What the Council will do to remove gambling from Mohawk territory. ... Much pressure is being brought on the Council to act swiftly, decisively, before violence erupts. Yet the Council must be ever cautious of endorsing any action that might risk human life, for they are entrusted with upholding the Peacemaker's Great Law.

[Chiefs from each clan state their views, standing, according to George's account, "so their voice will not be lost or their words misunderstood." The Wolf Clan's leaders speak first, then the Turtles, then the Bears. Discussion ranges through recent history, rejecting the use of violence by one Mohawk against another.]

A request is made for someone to go out and find a copy of the Treaty of Canandaigua, [but] the Bear Clan has one handy. It is read aloud, slowly, in Mohawk. ... One concern seems to be on everyone's mind: How will the president [of the United States] enforce the treaty? Does it mean an invasion by FBI agents? Will the mistrusted New York state

> police come in? Will the National Guard be used? Does it mean we lose jurisdiction and sovereignty? How will the chiefs be protected, for surely they will be labelled traitors and threatened by the gamblers?
>
> Hours of discussion pass, as many people arrive at the Longhouse to observe, taking seats in their respective clan areas.
>
> Some leave to have a cigarette outside and keep an eye on the guards across the road. The slow, low talk of the men drifts in from the doorstep; now and then, gentle laughter is heard. The sounds are reassuring.
>
> At midday, a simple meal of sandwiches, fruit juice and coffee is prepared and served. The formal meeting adjourns for a while, as people from the three clans cross the floor to talk about friends, families, and common fears. After lunch and socializing, the formal meeting resumes. After some more discussion, the assembled chiefs come to a meeting of the minds.
>
> [They are] entrusted by the Great Law to pass legislation only when its effect on generations to come has been considered. Gambling is not only illegal, the Turtles say, but it makes a few very rich. When this happens, all people are corrupted. The Turtle chiefs also speak of infiltration by the Mafia, not only upon Akwesasne, but in other Indian communities across the United States. If we don't stop them now, we will be living in a state of fear. Contact the president. The Bears speak last, as they usually do. They have carefully listened to the other clans, to the clan mothers, the faithkeepers, the elders, and the children. The Bears say they accept the consequences of what they are about to do. There is no other way; the Americans must enter Akwesasne to take away the evil which, if allowed to grow, will consume the entire [Mohawk] nation.
>
> Consensus among the clans has been realized. The Nation Council appointed specific people to draft the letter that will be sent to Washington. A battle has been joined. Soon, the world of Akwesasne will face a wave of retaliatory terror.[14]

During the U.S. tribal election in late May 1989, Lincoln White was elected and became the second progambling chief on the St. Regis Council. As controversy and violence related to gambling increased at Akwesasne, gambling's economic clout continued to grow. By mid-1989, roughly 500 people were employed by gambling operations at Akwesasne, the largest source of employment on the reservation. One of every ten Akwesasne Mohawks living on the U.S. side of the border was working in a gambling establishment. "There are going to be a lot of positive economic developments," said Guilford White, manager of the Mohawk Bingo Palace.[15] Like other bingo and casino operators, he said that gambling would be used to jump start the economy of Akwesasne, as other enterprises also developed under a pro-business tribal council. As he was inaugurated White spoke of developing a resort on 185 acres at Raquette Point (on the reservation), as well as luring light industry.

By June 1989 reservation residents were beginning to talk of blockading Route 37 to keep the casinos' clientele away if state police didn't close the gaming houses. Many people saw this action as their only option. Reservation residents had combined their antigambling efforts into a group called Determined Residents United for Mohawk Sovereignty (DRUMS). They planned a blockade for June 9 but abandoned it in favor of a peaceful march.

On July 20, 1989, 200 FBI agents and New York State Troopers raided seven casinos on the reservation, arresting 13 people and seizing cash and financial records. Many of the casinos had been tipped off in advance. Slot machines, craps tables, roulette wheels, and other gambling equipment had been removed the day before the raid. Between 60 and 70 Warriors and other gambling supporters assembled, prepared to defend the casinos and their owners with high-powered weapons. The disturbance closed the international border for six hours. The slots were replaced within hours after the raids.

On July 21, the state police continued to seal off Akwesasne's U.S. side. Gambling supporters set up their own barricades, piling logs and overturning a flatbed trailer and gas tanker truck on Route 37. This barricade was apparently an effort to keep police away from the casinos. The police also established short-lived checkpoints to warn nonresidents of the violence. The gamblers' barricade was dismantled the next day, but 11 people were injured in fights at the state police barricade. Gambling raids continued, as casino owner Peter Burns, a one-legged diabetic in a

Art Montour confronting New York State Police, June 6, 1989. (Photo: Akwesasne Notes)

wheelchair, held police at bay with an unloaded gun before being taken into custody. Burns was held on $100,000 bail. He was charged with using a deadly weapon to impede the execution of a federal search warrant. He also faced federal felony counts involving possession of illegal gambling devices and operating an illegal gambling business.

Also on July 21, police arrested Art Kakwirakeron Montour, a frequent Warrior spokesman, and charged him with using a gun to hold off state troopers and FBI agents during gambling raids the previous day. Montour, a former ironworker and native of the Kahnawake in Quebec residing off the Akwesasne reservation in Bombay, New York, called the raid a declaration of war. "It's upsetting when you're invaded by a foreign nation. You're on our land and our territory. You are the aggressor."[16] Montour was charged with forcibly impeding execution of a search warrant through the use of a deadly weapon. A trooper's arm was broken in the scuffle to arrest him. A three-year-old child also was hurt in the brawl involving about 100 state troopers in riot gear and almost as many casino employees and Warriors.

Within hours after the state police and FBI carted off the slot machines on July 20, St. Regis elected chiefs Jacobs and White penned an angry letter to Governor Mario Cuomo that echoed Montour's words calling the state police gambling raid an invasion and an "act of war against the sovereign Mohawk territory at Akwesasne." The letter held the governor "responsible for any abuse or acts of racism that may occur against any of our people."[17]

Jacobs and White's July 20 letter was sent against the wishes of head chief Tarbell and the tribal council's legal advisors, Pirtle, Morisset, Schlosser & Ayer of Seattle. Pirtle advised the three elected chiefs on August 7 that the firm, which had represented the tribe for two years, was withdrawing its counsel regarding gambling issues. The firm had been criticized by Chief Jacobs after its lawyers refused to tell him what he wanted to hear. Instead, as officers of the courts, Pirtle said it was the firm's responsibility to maintain that casino gambling was illegal on the reservation and that under existing law the raids of July 20 had been carried out legally.

In a press release dated July 24, the Mohawk Nation Council reiterated Tarbell's and Pirtle's points in stronger language:

> The Mohawk Nation Council has determined that high-stakes commercial gambling, uncontrolled and unregulated, has a destructive influence on our people; it leads to political and cultural destruction. ... The Nation Council has not authorized anyone to form a Mohawk Security Force, nor has it appointed Art Montour-Kakwirakeron to represent the traditional Mohawk people in any way or on any issue.[18]

Gambling operators were getting another story from their lawyers. On August 12 John M. Peebles, an attorney with Domina, Gerrard, Copple &

Stratton, P.C., of Omaha, Nebraska, advised Tony Laughing that "electronic or electro-mechanical facsimiles of any games of chance or slot machines may be operated by the St. Regis Mohawk Tribe pursuant to the Indian Gaming Regulatory Act." Peebles constructed his argument based on provisions of a New York state law that permits possession of slot machines manufactured before 1941 as antiques as well as provisions of a state law that allows slot machines to be transported through state territory "in a sealed container to a jurisdiction outside the state of New York for purposes which are lawful in the outside jurisdiction."[19]

What the slot machine operators needed, according to Peebles' analysis, was an agreement with the St. Regis Tribal Council allowing the use of gambling devices as well as a compact with New York state allowing the same. This was a major reason that the advocates of casino gambling were putting so much energy into electing tribal chiefs on the U.S. side of Akwesasne who supported their efforts. As early as November 12, 1988, Chief Jacobs said that he had written to state officials asking for such a compact under the terms of the 1988 Indian Gaming Regulatory Act. On August 14, 1989, two days after attorney Peebles wrote to Tony Laughing, both Chief Jacobs and Chief White reiterated this request in a letter to Ed Brown, assistant secretary for Indian Affairs, Department of the Interior, in Washington, D.C. They requested a meeting with him and the Criminal Division of the Department of Justice on the issue.

After the raids, residents of Akwesasne debated the continuing state police presence on their land. While the Warriors, the casino owners, and their employees maintained that the police had violated Mohawk sovereignty, St. Regis Tribal Council Chief Harold Tarbell said, "If the majority of the community has a choice between the security force [the Warriors] and police patrols, they're going to want the police."[20] Doug George said, "It's kind of like the Gaza Strip. We can't go anywhere. People are staying in their homes. We are in a state of occupation and police have effectively sealed the reservation off."[21] The police later relaxed their blockades, allowing vehicles carrying food, medicine, and other supplies onto the reservation.

Tribal leaders from all three councils governing Akwesasne met daily in long sessions in an unsuccessful attempt to resolve the confrontation. "This will split the community for many years. The division is long and won't mend itself for a long time," said former elected chief Brenda LaFrance.[22] According to Jake Swamp, "We've been asking them [the Warriors] to give up that kind of nonsense and come back with the people, but it seems like they like their new lifestyle, and that involves smuggling and gun-running and anything having to do with making large amounts of money real quickly."[23] Swamp was one of the nine traditional chiefs who had signed the May 16 letter to President Bush requesting federal intervention.

During the July 20 gambling raids Tony Laughing, owner of Tony Vegas International, had eluded police raiding his casino as about 15 armed gambling supporters prevented them from entering the building. On July 29 state police were still searching for him as the seven casinos lining the reservation's main highway remained closed. Police barricades kept their clientele from entering the reservation. David Jacobs, one of the three elected chiefs on the St. Regis Tribal Council, split with head chief Tarbell. Jacobs circulated petitions calling for the police blockades to come down. On July 29 Jacobs planned to deliver the petitions to Cuomo, who initially refused to mediate the dispute saying, "If I sat down with them, what would I do with the hospital workers striking in New York City?"[24]

On July 31 police removed their barricades. Police said that these roadblocks had been erected mainly to keep non-Indians from being injured, not to protect reservation residents. Nine days later, the largest of the seven casinos reopened, a day after gambling advocates claimed victory in a referendum of reservation residents that purportedly approved of gambling at Akwesasne. The referendum drew only 480 votes from the 8,500 reservation residents. Antigambling residents boycotted it. The referendum was an informal poll in which people marked a ballot that asked them to endorse "all of the following: Peachstone [a ceremonial game played to 'please the creator'], bingo, blackjack, and casino games, including slot machines."[25] Mohawk Nation Council Chief Tom Porter said, "The people who are responsible for this election won't last long. They have stomped on the face of the creator."[26] The next day, several residents opposed to gambling "voted" by spraying with bullets the transformers supplying electricity to the casinos.

After the state police and the FBI left Akwesasne, events descended into anarchy once again. Members of the Warrior Society's Mohawk Sovereignty Security Force (MSSF) bragged openly to news media representatives that they were the legal police force on the reservation, even though they held no charter from either the Mohawk Council of Akwesasne, the St. Regis Tribal Council, or the Mohawk Nation Council. The Warrior Society once again called the Mohawk Nation Council chiefs "traitors," and "agents of foreign governments," who were using the "cloak of illegal gambling" to invade Akwesasne with the complicity of the Tricouncil (all three governmental bodies at Akwesasne), "a total dictatorship."[27]

Truckloads of masked men whom Barbara Barnes likened to the Ku Klux Klan cruised at night around homes of people who had spoken out against gambling. The home of Ron LaFrance, Wolf Clan subchief and acting director of Cornell University's American Indian Program, was torched as well as the homes of three other Mohawk Nation Council subchiefs. The windows of Brenda LaFrance's car were shot out by automatic-weapon fire. Jake Swamp said that his family rotated watch all night every night for several weeks in an attempt to assure safety for their home.

Some opponents of gambling maintained that the only way to force the casinos to close was through blockades or sabotage. In August

Akwesasne residents threatened to burn down Laughing's casino, but armed guards deterred them. The Warriors asserted that they were the law on the reservation. In response a crowd of about 350 Mohawks surrounded the Warriors' headquarters in Hogansburg on August 27 and beat up several Warriors. One man, a Warrior spokesman, was forced through a gauntlet of Mohawks, a long-standing and symbolic form of public disapproval at Akwesasne. At times, he was dragged by the hair, then forced through the parallel lines of angry men, who punched and kicked him. Later, the group massed at the Mohawk Bingo Place and blockaded Route 37 for six hours in an attempt to keep customers from patronizing reservation bingo halls and casinos.

Later that day, the same crowd set fire to the Lucky Knight Casino, which was under construction near Route 37. *The People's Voice* called the actions at the Mohawk Bingo Palace and the Lucky Knight "an attack by [a] terrorist mob." The newspaper quoted Veronica Adams, co-owner of the Lucky Knight.

> The people began arriving by car ... at about 10 P.M. that evening. At least 100 people came and parked in the road and at the Akwesasne Library. Then, the people started to run around the building. The group [was] armed with baseball bats and clubs. Once I saw the people go around the building, I went to a home of a friend down the road and tried to call home. I didn't want my children to go there [to the Lucky Knight] because I figured there might be trouble. [Then] I went back and saw the pink in the sky and knew that those people were burning it.[28]

A Warrior Society press release dated August 28 said:

> Last evening, a vigilante group of approximately 50 people, led by Head Chief/Trustee of the Mohawk Council of Akwesasne Mike Mitchell, and traditionals Richard Mitchell, Jake Swamp, Tom Porter, Richard Cook and Idrene Thompson, provoked a mob scene in front of the Mohawk Warriors' Society Headquarters.[29]

The press release described the sequence of events, then concluded:

> The Warriors' Society will continue to maintain and defend the sovereignty and jurisdiction of the Mohawk Nation at Akwesasne according to the Great Law of Peace of the Haudenosaunee. We will continue to promote peace and harmony among the Mohawk people of Akwesasne.[30]

On September 2 another scuffle took place after about 50 gambling opponents tried to enter the Warriors' headquarters at the Onkwe Bingo Jack. When other Warriors arrived at the building to reinforce the 25 who were inside, the two sides engaged in a battle of fists, billy clubs, and baseball bats that lasted about an hour. No one was seriously injured. Two weeks later, violence flared again when Warriors and gambling opponents battled with rocks during an incident that left at least two Warrior vehicles damaged by fire.

On September 6 four burly men paid a visit to Chief Tarbell in his office at the Tribal Community Building in Akwesasne. They presented him with a document indicating approval of gambling by the St. Regis Tribal Council. According to an affidavit sworn by Tarbell, the text of the document he was pressured to sign, but did not, had been prepared by Laughing's attorney John Peebles. The four men—whom Tarbell identified as John Bigtree, Jr., Randy Bigtree, Ray Garrow, and Ricky Tarbell—insisted several times that Tarbell sign it. The short, slight Tarbell called the incident intimidation and told the men, "If you think a bunch of big guys is going to make me sign, forget it."[31]

Two weeks after the gambling advocates' confrontation with Tarbell, Doug George said, "They [gambling interests] are organized and they are criminals and they protect their activities with force and with the threat of violence."[32] Security had become more of a concern at *Akwesasne Notes* and *Indian Time*. Following the earlier firebombings, the newspapers' offices moved to the Canadian side of the reservation, a location thought to be less vulnerable to attack. Even so, they were guarded night and day. "It's very similar to Colombia. ... I see it as a plan to overthrow the governments here and put in their place what they want, and we are going to be living in anarchy. They'll depose anybody in their way," said Barbara Barnes.[33] On any given day, the offices of the newspaper hosted a constant stream of people coming and going, as if from a command center, as they discussed which "front" of the "war" was active at a certain hour. George said, "We are in a state of semi-war, and now the era of diplomacy has ended. It seems inevitable that someone will get killed. The two sides are set."[34]

On September 16, 1989, a vehicle owned by Louie Jackson, a gambling opponent, was torched. Jackson himself had been constantly tailgated by Warriors for several days before his vehicle was set aflame. Late in the evening of the same day, friends gathered at the house to protect the Jacksons from a feared Warrior attack. A group of men opposed to casino gambling had already confiscated an AK-47 and a portable two-way radio from two Warriors.

The same evening, gambling advocates cruised slowly along Route 37 past an antigambling crowd. They turning spotlights and headlights into the eyes of the crowd and yelled profanities at them. Shortly after that, 40 to 50 casino security guards and other gaming advocates armed with baseball bats and plastic riot shields emerged from TVI, a short walk down the highway. The progambling group banged bats on the highway as it advanced slowly on the crowd of gambling opponents.

Soon, the two groups faced each other, lined up on opposite sides of the highway. One man stepped forward from the gambling opponents' line and yelled, "What are you here for, to protect your precious casinos, guns, and drugs? What kind of life is that for my kids? And you want to protect it!"[35] A few of the younger progamblers growled at the man to shut up as people on both sides began yelling. Women standing behind the antigamblers' line recognized the potential for violence and called the New York state police. They did not respond, fearing that they would provoke a violent confrontation with the Warriors. The shouting match lasted for about an hour before both groups slowly dissolved into the night, ending one in a continuing and ever-intensifying series of incidents at Akwesasne during the fall of 1989.

Because state police did not come onto the reservation, Tony Laughing—still officially listed as a fugitive from a federal arrest warrant—frequently used his office at TVI. He even granted interviews against a backdrop of 10 AK-47 rifles lining a wall. He showed a reporter a bullet hole above his desk. Laughing said, "They [opponents of gambling] can picket all they want. But if they attack my property, we will defend it."[36] The casino owner described how he fed the casino's daily transaction records into a paper shredder he called his "Ollie North machine." Laughing estimated that he had recouped his initial $700,000 investment in his casino (earned from smuggling cigarettes) and tripled it for a net profit of about $2.1 million. In another interview, Laughing defended the casinos as a source of jobs. "These are good-paying jobs, and that is clear money. There is no income tax."[37] Laughing said he employed 280 people at Tony Vegas International, 240 of them Mohawks. Security personnel earned $5 to $12 an hour and poker dealers up to $1,200 a week.

Barbara Barnes had a different account of the way the gambling halls handled employment.

> The owners said their places would employ people. With eight casinos ... over 1,000 Mohawks should be employed. Not so. The majority of people employed are non-Indians. The non-Indians have the high-paying jobs and the Mohawks the menial tasks.[38]

When Warriors asserted that they were smuggling cigarettes in defense of Indian sovereignty, Barbara Barnes replied, "The Warriors are smugglers. They are not protecting our sovereignty, and they are not the kind of people who should be patrolling us."[39]

On September 21 Laughing was arrested following a 30-minute, high-speed chase. Laughing had been spotted about 6:20 P.M. in a car driving through Fort Covington, New York, outside reservation borders. State troopers gave chase after the car refused to stop. Police chased the car to the Canadian National Railway tracks in Brasher, where the car stalled. Laughing shoved the front passenger door open and fled into nearby woods where police finally arrested him. The driver, Brenda Jock, was charged with hindering prosecution, reckless endangerment, and several motor-vehicle violations. State police found $87,000 in cash in the car. Laughing said that he was on his way to dinner when police arrested him: "Seriously, I figured that if I did get caught I'd have my bail money."[40]

In September the Warriors issued more press releases speaking for "the Mohawk people." They again declared themselves to be on "red alert" against the intervention of state police on the reservation: "Any action taken by outside police forces will be considered a military expedition against a People at peace with the United States. ... Those involved will be held liable. ... [Such actions would be] unauthorized and unsanctioned by the Mohawk People.[41] Ernest King, chief of the Canadian Mohawk Police, replied, "Their [the MSSF's] plan is to dissolve the [Mohawk police force]."[42] The Mohawk Council of Akwesasne issued a press release backing King's police force.

> The Mohawk Sovereignty Security Force has stepped up its campaign of terrorism with the Mohawk community. The Mohawk Council of Akwesasne will not tolerate these provocations. The MCA will use its [police] powers to protect its citizens from the subversive and illegal activities of the [MSSF].[43]

Thomas Square, a Warrior, said, "We're just for the jobs in the community, so we won't have to take handouts from Canadian and U.S. governments." He asserted that the MSSF was funded by cigarette smuggling linked to Kahnawake. Square continued, "It's just inter-nation commerce. It's like bringing cigarettes from New York to New Jersey. Would you call that smuggling?"[44]

On September 26 and 27 St. Regis Tribal Council Chief David Jacobs appeared as a character witness at Laughing's bail hearing. Jacobs called him "industrious ... a man of high principles." The prosecutor called Laughing "a danger to his community. ... [His] relationship with the armed Warrior Society presents a risk to the community."[45] Federal District Magistrate Gustav DiBianco ruled that Laughing should remain in jail pending the outcome of charges against him. At the bail hearing, Laughing's attorney Michael Vavonese offered to put up TVI as collateral. He said it was worth $1 million. If TVI would not serve as collateral, Vavonese hinted that Laughing could back his bail bond with some of the 280 acres of land that Laughing owned in and near Akwesasne. Magistrate DiBianco ruled on September 28 that Laughing should remain in the Madison county jail pending the outcome of his trial. DiBianco said that experience indicated Laughing might jump bail and hide on the reservation.

With an agreement on bail near, 50 Mohawks traveled 150 miles from the reservation to Syracuse on October 6 and packed Magistrate DiBianco's courtroom during the second round of hearings on Laughing's release. Arguments revolved around the legality of Laughing's gaming operations. New York law requires that anyone freed on bail promise not to engage in illegal activity. Laughing was later released on $300,000 bail, only to be jailed again in late May 1990 after he violated terms of his bail bond by entering his casino at Akwesasne.

Meanwhile in early October, the nightly guerilla raids on the casinos increased. On October 7 rocks and paint were heaved at four buses leaving the Mohawk Bingo Palace; shots were fired at one of the buses as it cleared Canadian customs at Cornwall Island. No one was injured. Another bus, from Syracuse, also was attacked. A large rock crashed through its windshield, but no one was injured. The next night shots were fired at the transformer supplying electricity to the Bear's Den. The same evening several shots were fired at a state patrol car as it made a U-turn on Route 37. State police again threw up blockades on the highway, only to remove them the next day.

Jacobs and White finally met with Ed Brown of the Interior Department October 13. Head Chief Tarbell and subchief Hilda Smoke also attended. Brown said that the two progambling chiefs had never requested a gaming compact with the state. Eli Tarbell had requested it. Brown said that present casino gambling at Akwesasne was illegal: "There is no way to make [it] legal unless the tribe receives 70 percent of gaming [bingo] revenues off the top for use in tribal projects. This is because gaming is a right of the tribe, not the individual."[46]

In an attempt to legitimize gambling at Akwesasne under the 1988 Indian Gaming Regulation Act, Jacobs and White drafted and signed a tribal council resolution permitting the issuance of gaming licenses for casino gambling. They also requested negotiations with the state of New York to meet the requirements for legalizing slot-machine gambling under federal law. Tarbell's signature was absent from the draft resolution, which was not implemented.

In a November 2 letter the Mohawk Nation Council requested a meeting with Governor Cuomo along with representatives of the Onondaga council, which acts as "firekeepers" or speakers in the Iroquois Confederacy. The letter specified that a tentative agenda for the meeting "would include taxation, gambling, jurisdiction, and how to find ways to improve communications between our respective governments."[47] Cuomo did not respond.

Snye and St. Regis Village, two of the three major Canadian settlements at Akwesasne, lie on the south shore of the Saint Lawrence River. They can be entered by road only through the United States. The 11-man Mohawk police force patrolled the Canadian side under a charter from that nation's government, but could not serve St. Regis Village, Snye, or Cornwall Island without passing through U.S. territory. When the Warriors' trucks rammed their squad cars on U.S. territory, the Canadian Mohawk officers could do little but grimace. The Warriors did not stop there, however. They sometimes pumped AK-47 fire into their station house and even fired at the homes of the officers.

The Warriors' assault on the Mohawk Police continued for several months. For example, November 2 and 3, reports filed by Mohawk police included the following incidents:

> *4:45 A.M., November 2.* While officers were at the Akwesasne Police Station, several shots from a 9-millimeter weapon were fired into a patrol

unit [squad car]. Several shots struck the unit, two in the rear window, two in the trunk, and one flattened a rear tire. Suspects sped away onto the United States side of the reservation in an unknown make or model vehicle.

11:30 A.M., November 3. While police chief and constable were en route to the station after patrolling, they were struck from behind by a Warrior vehicle. The vehicle struck the patrol car three times. An attempt by Akwesasne police to apprehend the driver failed, after which the driver struck the patrol car again.

2:30 P.M., November 3. While on patrol in Snye, Quebec, a Warrior vehicle was spotted by Mohawk police. An attempt to pull over the vehicle was unsuccessful. A chase began, for approximately two miles. The police unit drove close to the vehicle in an attempt to identify the driver, but due to tinted windows, identification was impossible. An occupant in said vehicle stuck the barrel of a rifle, believed to be an AK-47, out the back window. The police then terminated the chase.

9 P.M., November 3. At Canada customs, an arrest was attempted by the Royal Canadian Mounted Police on a female reservation resident on a warrant. Several members of the Warrior Society showed up, and during negotiations, the female disappeared.[48]

As 1989 came to a close, violence continued to escalate at Akwesasne. *The People's Voice* reported that nine shots were fired at its office on November 15. State police described the incident as an apparent drive-by shooting. On November 17, five shots were reportedly fired into an unoccupied police car.

That same day the Mohawk Council of Akwesasne asked residents to adhere to a voluntary curfew to "limit their use of the public roads after 10 P.M., [and] ensure that all minors are at home or supervised by an adult after 10 P.M." The council also limited use of firearms to "authorized personnel" warning that Akwesasne police would confiscate all "visible restricted weapons." The council's restrictions were blamed on the Warriors' "campaign of terrorism."[49]

A few hours before dawn on Monday, November 27, about 10 vehicles encircled the Akwesasne Mohawk police station, illuminating all exits with searchlights and headlights. One police cruiser was rammed. A citizen coming to the aid of police officers inside the building was assaulted and injured. Warriors and other gambling supporters then tried to blockade the village of St. Regis near the police station. However, a sizable crowd of local residents tore down the barricades. The Warriors and their supporters fled. Four hours later, just at sunrise, a man firing a semiautomatic rifle in all directions drove through St. Regis Village in a brown Blazer just as children were beginning to arrive at a nearby school. Mohawk Police gave chase until the Blazer and its armed driver crossed the international boundary. The vehicle was well known to them; it had been used to ram at least four vehicles in St. Regis owned by the Mohawk Police or Akwesasne residents opposed to casino gambling.

Despite the violence, the casinos remained open as Canadians and U.S. citizens from off the reservation apparently accepted the danger of violence as the trimming on a high-stakes gambling adventure. By December 1 the casinos along the strip reportedly were grossing $200,000 a day.

In early December, shortly before being paralyzed by the gambling crisis, the St. Regis Tribal Council voted to establish a reservation police force utilizing $150,000 appropriated for that purpose by Congress. This amount seemed very small next to the $3.3 million the state police had spent on overtime due to reservation violence during the preceding summer and fall. The council also resolved to enact gun-control laws on the reservation (a resolution that chiefs Jacobs and White never implemented) and asked the New York state police to resume routine patrols on its territory until the new tribal police force was in place. The Council also asked the state police not to notify the Warriors before entering the reservation. The Warriors had demanded that the state police seek their permission to enter, contending that any intervention without their sanction was a violation of Mohawk sovereignty.

On December 23 the Onondaga Nation Council of Chiefs condemned the casinos and the Warriors. The council said that the casino operators "follow no rules, keep all of their revenues, and hire armed guards (including the MSSF) to protect their operations."[50] According to the Onondaga Council, the casinos and Warriors were not only snubbing U.S. law but also Iroquois law. The Onondaga chiefs also denounced the Warriors for covering their activities with a patina of Indian "activist" rhetoric. "This paramilitary organization has been denounced by all Mohawk councils as well as the Onondaga Nation," according to the statement.[51]

An early winter 1989 editorial in *Akwesasne Notes* pointed to gambling and Cuomo's repeated refusal to intervene in the crisis as roots of "the deterioration of the moral values and traditional family structure of our people." Governor Cuomo "persists in negotiating a gambling contract with the St. Regis Mohawk Tribal Council despite the clear inability of the Tribal Council to deal with the violence that characterizes life at Akwesasne." The editorial recommended that Cuomo respond to the Haudenosaunee (Iroquois) Confederacy's and Mohawk Nation Council's appeals for a meeting. "[This is] the historically legitimate government of the Mohawk. ... We at Akwesasne are having our lives and security gambled away. All of this from a man [who calls himself] 'a friend of the Indian.' "[52]

As 1989 ended, the situation at Akwesasne was summarized as follows:

The tragic result of all the controversy is a community divided against itself. Brothers oppose brothers, leaving their parents caught in the middle. Plenty are willing to take the $400 a week from the casinos, while others remain on welfare because of their convictions. Ironworkers travel 800 miles each way to walk the high steel in New Jersey, and bring home $700–$800 home to their families on weekends, while teenage cigarette smugglers make that much in an evening. Fear and anger frustrate all attempts to bring the feuding parties together. With the situation unresolved, guns pile up, fires spread, tensions rise. It is a dangerous situation for the people of the Mohawk Nation, struggling to decide who they want to be, before they destroy themselves. It is also sad. Because as time passes, the possibility of violence for the Iroquois Confederacy's Keepers of the Eastern Door becomes greater, even as the prospects for a resolution grow more remote.[53]

Notes

[1] *Observer* (Massena, NY), October 9, 1986.
[2] *Daily Times* (Watertown, NY), September 15, 1987.
[3] Ibid.
[4] *Evening Telegram* (Malone, NY), September 15, 1987.
[5] Barbara Barnes. Interview with author, Akwesasne, August 4, 1991.
[6] *Akwesasne Notes* (Akwesasne), Spring, 1988.
[7] *Times* (Washington, D.C.), September 9, 1988.
[8] On April 11, 1988, owners of the Mohawk Bingo Palace called a press conference to hand over a $40,000 check to the St. Regis Tribal Council, but the chiefs (all of whom opposed gambling at the time) refused to accept it. They seemed to look at the payment as a bribe of some sort, a way to buy franchise rights by gambling promotors who were operating without tribal permission to begin with.
[9] *Press-Republican* (Plattsburgh, NY), November 18, 1988.
[10] Associated Press, *Herald-American* (Syracuse, NY), July 15, 1990.
[11] *Times-Union* (Albany, NY), September 24, 1989.
[12] Marc Clark and Brenda O'Farrell, "Gambling and Guns," *Maclean's* (September 21, 1989): 21. Some momentum to encourage reservation gambling was gathering speed in Canada at about this time, although casinos never took root there for any length of time. In December 1988 Mohawk gambling investors at the Kahnawake Reserve south of Montreal defied a popular referendum that opposed its plans to open the $2.7 million high-stakes Super Bingo Hall on September 24, 1989. It opened under the armed guard of the Warrior Society, which claimed its defense of the new bingo hall was an act of Mohawk sovereignty.
[13] Letter to the Editor, *Daily Times* (Watertown, NY), June 22, 1989.
[14] Doug George. Personal statement in letter to author, October 3, 1991.
[15] As of mid-1992, the proposed resort had not been developed and the major industries at Akwesasne remain gambling, smuggling, and tax-free sales of gasoline and cigarettes.
[16] Associated Press, July 21, 1989.
[17] Leo David Jacobs and Lincoln White to Mario Cuomo, July 20, 1989. Copy in files of St. Regis Tribal Council.

[18] Mohawk Nation Council press release, July 24, 1989. Copy in Mohawk Nation Council files.
[19] John M. Peebles to Tony Laughing, August 12, 1989. Copy in St. Regis Tribal Council files.
[20] Associated Press, July 28, 1989. In files of U.S. Senate Select Committee on Indian Affairs.
[21] Associated Press, July 27, 1989. In files of U.S. Senate Select Committee on Indian Affairs.
[22] Associated Press, July 28, 1989. In files of U.S. Senate Select Committee on Indian Affairs.
[23] Ibid.
[24] Associated Press, July 31, 1989. In files of U.S. Senate Select Committee on Indian Affairs.
[25] *Globe and Mail* (Toronto, Ont.), August 16, 1989.
[26] Ibid.
[27] Warrior Society press release, n.d. Copy in *Akwesasne Notes* files.
[28] *The People's Voice Akwesasne,* September 8, 1989.
[29] Warrior Society press release, August 28, 1989. Copy in files of *Akwesasne Notes.*
[30] Ibid.
[31] Affidavit on September 6, 1989 incident sworn by Harold Tarbell. Copy in files of St. Regis Tribal Council.
[32] *Times-Union* (Albany, NY), September 24, 1989.
[33] Ibid.
[34] Ibid.
[35] Narrative statement of incident. In North American Traveling College files.
[36] "Gambling and Guns," *Maclean's* (September 18, 1989): 21.
[37] *Times-Union* (Albany, NY), September 24, 1989.
[38] Barbara Barnes. Interview with author, Onchiota, NY, June 3, 1990.
[39] *Maclean's* (July 18, 1989): 21.
[40] *Courier-Observer* (Massena, NY), September 29, 1989.
[41] *Courier-Observer* (Massena, NY), September 15, 1989.
[42] *Daily Times* (Watertown, NY), December 13, 1989.
[43] *Courier-Observer* (Massena, NY), November 29, 1989.
[44] *Times-Union* (Albany, NY), September 24, 1989.
[45] United Press International (from wire service), September 27, 1989. In files of U.S. Senate Select Committee on Indian Affairs.
[46] Harold Tarbell. Report of October 13, 1989, meeting with Ed Brown, et. al., at Interior Department, Washington, D.C. Copy in files of St. Regis Tribal Council.
[47] Mohawk Nation Council to Governor Cuomo, November 2, 1989. Copy in files of Mohawk Nation Council.
[48] Akwesasne Mohawk police reports. St. Regis Village, Quebec, November, 1989.
[49] Mohawk Council of Akwesasne press release, November 17, 1989. Copy in MCA files.
[50] Statement of Iroquois Grand Council, December 23, 1989. Copy in files of North American Indian Traveling College.
[51] Ibid.
[52] *Akwesasne Notes* (Akwesasne), Early Winter 1989.
[53] Ned R. Hoskin, "High Stakes at Akwesasne," *Capital* (November, 1989): 76.

CHAPTER 3

▼▼▼

A Community Under Siege

As 1990 opened, violence related to gambling at Akwesasne became more frequent, more personal, and more vicious, eventually resulting in death. The Warriors and casino operatives were armed more heavily than ever before to prevent a repeat of the 1989 raids. Without outside police intervention, gambling opponents increasingly took matters into their own hands in an attempt to close the casinos.

On January 13 Jerry McDonald, a gambling opponent, entered Tony Vegas International, drew a 12-gauge pump-action shotgun, and began shooting into the ceiling, floor, and furniture of the casino after first warning people to get out of his way. For two hours McDonald pumped about 30 shotgun blasts into the casino's walls and furniture. Many of the patrons and casino workers present were slightly injured by flying glass.

McDonald was well-known at Akwesasne. He was chosen in 1980 to carry the Olympic torch for the Mohawk Nation at the Lake Placid Winter Olympics, and in 1984 he represented the Iroquois Confederacy in a 3,600-mile native run across the United States. A construction worker in "high steel," McDonald also was known as a singer, dancer, craftsman, and teacher of native culture to young people. According to Mohawk Nation Council chiefs, McDonald was not usually a violent man, but he was fed up to the point of explosion after he had been beaten for the third time by toughs hired by gaming supporters, a reprisal for his outspoken opposition to commercial gambling at Akwesasne. The Warriors also harassed McDonald's family. Nails were placed in the driveway of the family home, and their car was constantly tailed. McDonald also had disputed Warrior interpretations of the Great Law in *Indian Time,* comparing their tactics to the fascists in Europe during World War II.

McDonald turned himself in to Mohawk Nation Council chiefs who had arrived at the casino to stop the confrontation. The chiefs then turned MacDonald over the Akwesasne Mohawk police who in turn turned him over to New York state police. McDonald was later charged with first-degree reckless endangerment, third-degree assault, and criminal mischief.[1] The Warriors quickly used the incident for propaganda purposes, claiming that they had "complete control" during the incident and saying that state police were correct when they declined to intervene.

At the St. Regis Tribal Council's monthly general meeting on January 14, during a discussion of how the tribe should spend $200,000 appropriated to develop a law-enforcement plan for the U.S. side of Akwesasne, each of the elected chiefs was asked to put forward names of people who would serve on a committee to address the issue. Chief Leo David Jacobs suggested Jerry Cook, Eli Tarbell, and Tony Laughing, all of whom had been active in promoting casino gambling. Emily Tarbell, a member of the audience, then asked Jacobs whether the tribe ought to appoint people who were under indictment for criminal activity to a law-enforcement committee. Laughter rippled through the audience as she asked sardonically whether Jacobs's nominees would commute to meetings from jail if their convictions were upheld on appeal.

On January 16, more than 100 people—Mohawks, other Iroquois, and non-Indian supporters—marched in front of the New York state capitol at Albany in an attempt to convince Governor Cuomo to intervene against gambling at Akwesasne. As he would do repeatedly during the next four months until escalating violence forced his hand, Cuomo refused to send state troopers onto the reservation.

The same day, five Mohawks received jail terms in Auburn Federal District Court for gambling-related offenses stemming from raids the previous July 20. Eli Tarbell, owner of the Bear's Den, got 18 months and a fine of $5,000; he had pleaded guilty in November to one count of possessing a gambling device within Indian country, a felony with a two-year maximum term. Tarbell said he reserved his right to appeal his case to the Second Circuit Court of Appeals on grounds that state and federal jurisdiction do not apply at Akwesasne.

James Burns, former owner of the Silver Dollar Casino, also was sentenced 18 months in prison for possessing a gambling device in Indian country.[2] Roderick Cook, operator of the Night Hawk Arcade, was sentenced to five months in prison and five months in a community facility on the same charges. Paul Tatlock, also convicted of possessing a slot machine, was sentenced to 15 months and fined $5,000. Tatlock's son, Tarek, was sentenced to two years probation and fined $500 after he pleaded guilty to one charge of promoting gambling. David Mainville, owner of the defunct Club 21, also got 15 months in prison for possessing slot machines.

Six other Mohawks, including Tony Laughing, had also pleaded guilty to various gambling charges and were awaiting sentencing in

February and March. Bill Sears, whose major business was bingo, was acquitted of slot-machine possession after Jerry Cook testified that he, not Sears, had owned Wild Bill's Grocery where slot machines were seized in the summer raids. Cook himself was later indicted for slot-machine possession by a grand jury.

On January 26, at 1:55 A.M. and again at 4:45 A.M., unidentified gunmen fired several shots at a car parked in front of the family home occupied by Doug George, antigambling editor of *Akwesasne Notes* and *Indian Time,* on Route 37 near Beaver Meadow Road. New York state police later found casings from a .9 mm and a .45 caliber firearm near the targeted vehicle.

About 10:45 P.M. the same day, an unidentified person shot at the headquarters of the Warrior Society, the former Onkwe Bingo Jack, a blue prefabricated aluminum building that looks like a cross between an space-age barn and a warehouse. The George house was shot at again January 27; shortly afterward, shots also were fired near the homes of Chief Jake Swamp, Richard "Junior" Cook, and Edward Gray, all of whom had spoken out against large-scale commercial gambling. According to police, all the shots appeared to have been fired from automatic weapons.

Akwesasne Mohawk police serving the Canadian side of the reservation arrested three Warriors, confiscated an AK-47 assault rifle, other weapons, and a Warrior vehicle on February 2. Alwyn Cook, Raymond Lazore, and Dewey Lazore were charged with possession of prohibited and restricted weapons.

Following a rash of shootings at the homes of gambling opponents, the "antis" again accused state police of ignoring the increasing violence. In a letter dated January 31, 1990, Harold Tarbell, the only remaining antigambling chief on the St. Regis Tribal Council, wrote to President Bush, requesting his "personal attention and assistance ... to resolve a dangerous criminal situation that threatens our community with anarchy over the rule of law."[3] Tarbell wrote that the unresolved conflict at Akwesasne would "undermine the sovereign rights of all Indian tribes, jeopardize the integrity of the U.S. Indian Gaming Regulatory Act, and destroy economic benefits of legitimate Indian gaming activities on a national basis."[4]

Tarbell described to the president how the five full-scale illegal casino operations and two high-stakes bingo halls at Akwesasne had been established outside of the provisions of the 1988 law. The establishments operated without the state agreement mandated by the law for casino operations and without oversight by the board that was supposed to govern reservation gambling on a national scale. Tarbell contended that required payments to maintain tribal services and programs had not been made. By early 1989, according to Tarbell, the seven gaming establishments at Akwesasne were generating more than $100 million annually in unreported income, "operating totally without the sanction or supervision of the tribal government."[5]

The gaming operators and their security force heeded the law of neither the elected councils on either side of the border nor the Mohawk Nation Council, much less federal or state law. The Warriors spoke for a tradition stressing resolution of political conflict through the barrel of an AK-47. Tarbell wrote:

> The gaming palaces "are protected by a well-armed army." They have so far intimidated the FBI and the New York state police. Incredible as it may seem, these activities are all being undertaken under the guise of Indian Sovereignty. But really, they are abusing a law-enforcement vacuum by taking the law into their own hands for one reason: profit.[6]

Despite occasional raids by state police and the FBI during the previous year, Tarbell noted that "antigambling Mohawks were unable to stop this flagrant, illegal behavior and the resulting degradation of our communities, cultural, moral, and family values."[7]

In such an environment of chaos the Akwesasne Mohawks had been unable to provide for the health and safety of the people, unable to establish a tribal infrastructure—constitution, judicial code, courts, a legitimate police force—or badly needed alternative forms of economic development that could provide employment for reservation residents without reliance on gambling enterprises. Tarbell thought that unilateral U.S. intervention would be unwise. He asked, instead, that the government work through constituted authority on the reservation.

Bush did not respond to Tarbell's letter. Appeals for outside intervention again fell on deaf ears, even as many people in Montreal and at Kahnawake also urged Canadian officials to intervene.

On February 6, less than a week after Tarbell wrote to Bush, senators Daniel K. Inouye and John McCain, chairman and vice chairman of the Senate Select Committee on Indian Affairs, wrote to Bush urging speedy action on the chief's requests. The two senators were responding to copies of Tarbell's letter to Bush that the chief had sent to them.

> We are writing to ... assure you and your staff that this is indeed a serious situation which represents a grave threat to the peace and security of the Mohawk community and surrounding areas. We are also aware that notwithstanding three major law-enforcement actions or raids, the confiscation of over 700 slot machines and the federal felony convictions of thirteen of the principals involved, this activity continues in flagrant violation of the law and at great risk to the community. Based on a recent first-hand report of a representative of the Committee who was sent to visit the reservation, we are concerned that the chief's courageous action in writing directly to you significantly increases the possibility or threat of physical harm directed at him and his family.[8]

In the February 1990 issue of *National Geographic* Warrior spokesmen Francis Boots was cast as some sort of woodland philosopher musing over the cosmic insignificance of international boundaries and the rule of law. "This line—this imaginary line where the two white people couldn't get along—does not affect us. ... It goes above our heads."[9] From his home on Cornwall Island Boots said that he didn't even recognize the tribal council that governs the part of the reservation on which he lives: "For us, Michael Mitchell [head chief of the Canadian council] has no voice. He doesn't even have a face. I no longer recognize him as a human being."[10] Boots was reacting to a statement by Mitchell, an ardent opponent of gambling, who said,

> Our traditions are breaking down. Greed, money. It's hitting us like a disease. We need education, to be doctors, nurses, and lawyers. You don't need an education to pass out bingo cards. The gambling people tell me it's about time we gave it back to the white man. We got slapped; let's slap them back. They tell me you can't eat honor. And I look back at them and say, 'But you can live it.' [11]

The magazine summarized the situation,

> Now gambling complicates all—big-time gambling [in] a strip of bingo halls and slot-machine casinos crowding U.S. Route 37. ... Millions of dollars have been made, hundreds of jobs created. The customers are mainly white Canadians—busloads weekly, filled with players from Ottawa, Montreal and Toronto. Backers, it is said, include the underworld. ... [12]

On February 26 Tony Laughing was sentenced to 27 months in prison and fined $27,000 in a Syracuse U.S. district court, the longest sentence yet meted out to any of the nine Mohawks sentenced to date on federal gaming charges. George called the sentence "trivial" observing, "The guy makes $25,000 a day. What's $25,000 to him? It's nothing."[13] Laughing's sentence was deferred until after the Second Circuit Court of Appeals determined if the United States had jurisdiction over gambling offenses at Akwesasne. The next day, Peter Burns was sentenced to 21 months, fined $5,000, and ordered not to work or gamble in reservation casinos for three years.[14]

The sentencing and fines did nothing to stop the growing gambling influence nor to ameliorate the violence. The Mohawk police continued to be the target of ever-increasing violence that extended to their families.

Dorleen Mitchell, wife of Mohawk Police officer Louis Mitchell, recalled the horror of March 3, 1990.

> At 6. A.M. our house and car were shot up. ... Me and my two daughters, Rhonda, age 14, and Krissy, age 10, were asleep in the house. I was awaken[ed] by this loud noise that hit the house. ... The windows were rattling. I thought that maybe a car had hit the house. ... [where] my daughter was asleep. I ran to the front window and looked out and didn't see anything, but I heard a loud car speed off down the road. I ran back

> into the bedroom and called my husband, who works at the Mohawk police station. In the meantime, they were also getting shot at, at the same time.[15]

Mrs. Mitchell's husband took her call as he lay on the floor of the station house avoiding gunfire.

> His voice was all hyper and scared and he told me that they had just gotten shot at and he almost got his head blown off. I told him that we had just gotten shot at, too. Then I heard a knock at the door, and it was my neighbor. He asked me if I had heard the gunshot, and I said yes. He said: "They hit your car." I ran into the bedroom to get dressed, and then we looked around outside. We found bullet casings on the side of the road. We put them in sandwich bags and turned them over to the police. When my husband got home, we were outside talking about what had happened, and then we were going into the house when we noticed bullet holes all along the front of the house. All the bullet holes were in a line with [the room occupied by] my other daughter who was sleeping on the couch in the living room.[16]

Later, the daughter told Mrs. Mitchell that when she heard the gunshots she tried to curl up into a little ball until she heard the car gun its motor and speed away.

> We assume the shooting had to do with my husband's job. His name [had come] on the Warrior [scanner] channel and they said: "That was it. He's gonna get it this time." Then the incident at our home happens. The Warriors are always threatening to break all our windows, burn our house down, or shoot it up and kill all of us.[17]

> Before we even had a chance to talk to anyone about the incident, John Boots [older brother of Francis Boots] already had a line for the newspapers. He said that the Warriors didn't do it, [that] it was a fight between two families. Well, maybe he can tell us who this other family is, since he knows all about it. ... Our children will have to live with this the rest of their lives. They are always living in fear that their father will get killed one of these days while he's at work. Children should not have to live like that. I can tell you one thing. We won't give up until we can all live in peace again.[18]

At the March 3 general monthly meeting of the U.S. St. Regis Tribal Council anger at David Jacobs' complicity with gambling promotors was boiling over. Community members had prepared a list of 32 alleged official acts of misconduct they attributed to Jacobs, essentially a bill of impeachment. In effect, the list boiled down to a point-by-point listing of Jacobs' willingness to act as an official front for gambling interests, and as a beneficiary of their gifts. During the meeting, it was moved and seconded that the "Council of Chiefs and Subchiefs conduct an in-depth investigation into [Jacobs'] activities—and if he is found guilty of any improprieties or illegal acts that he be removed from office."[19] During the investigation, the motion instructed Jacobs to step down from office and forfeit his $400-a-week salary. The motion passed by 93 votes to 31, but Jacobs remained in office.

At the same meeting, Cindy Terrance, editor of the progambling *People's Voice,* was told to stop videotaping by Head Chief Tarbell. People at the meeting feared that she might give her tapes to the Warriors. Terrance denied that she gave her tapes to anyone and she maintained the right of the Mohawk press to cover tribal meetings. As the crowd grew more antagonistic, Terrance stopped recording and then agreed to surrender one hour of tape to Tribal Clerk Carol Herne. According to Terrance's account (which appeared in a complaint filed with state police), Tarbell opened her camcorder and ripped the tape from it, as the crowd chanted, "Break it! Break it!" Finally, Tarbell had to call the unruly audience to order.

The Canadian Mohawk Council of Akwesasne, using its police and community volunteers, began to evacuate people from their homes during the first two weeks of March as Warriors continued to harass the Akwesasne Mohawk Police in several shooting and ramming incidents. Elderly and handicapped residents of St. Regis village were evacuated first by barge. The Royal Canadian Mounted Police and the Quebec and Ontario police stood by, with a police helicopter. Evacuation by automobile was ruled out because St. Regis Village is isolated from the rest of the Canadian side of Akwesasne by the Saint Lawrence and St. Regis rivers. Its only land boundary is with the United States where the Canadian Mohawk Police had no jurisdiction. "It has become a very tense situation, and we can no longer guarantee the safety of our people," said Lloyd Benedict, a chief with the Canadian council.

On March 6 Grand Chief Mike Mitchell challenged the Warrior Society: "If you're going to kill someone, kill me." During a press conference, Mitchell showed reporters bullet holes in the Canadian Akwesasne Police station house, as well as an assortment of shotguns, assault rifles, and ammunition the police had confiscated from members of the Warriors during the previous 18 months. He said that the reservation police force was outgunned by the Warriors. Mitchell also played a tape recording of a telephone conversation he said was made by two Warriors.

First voice: Mike is trying to get the people to get us to lay down our arms.
Second voice: We'll lay down our arms if he cuts his head off.
First voice: Ten-four.[20]

By March 6 the Canadian governing council said it would close the reserve to outside traffic if violence did not subside. This closure would have stopped traffic between Cornwall and the reserve as well as on the bridge from Massena across the international boundary. Mitchell, who made the announcement, had just emerged from a community meeting attended by 600 to 700 people, more than the council's community building could hold. Mitchell asked, "How did we get this far, where we are willing to kill each other? We're all from the same family."[21] Warrior spokesman Art Kakwirakeron Montour retorted that Mitchell had no authority to close the reserve. As the level of violence against the tribal police force increased, the Warriors stuck by their story that it was a result of interfamily rivalries, that they had not provoked any of it.

At this time, Thomas A. Constantine, superintendent of the New York state police, said that returning state troopers to the reservation would be similar to the 1983 decision to send U.S. Marines to East Beirut to interpose a peace between warring factions. The result, he said, was more than 200 Marine dead. Constantine took a look at the size of the arsenals on the reservation and said he did not want to lead his troopers into "a slaughter."[22] Surveying the situation early in March 1990, Constantine elaborated: "All you need is one shot fired either accidentally or fired over someone's head ... and it then becomes the potential for a tremendous amount of return fire."[23]

As the level of violence at Akwesasne continued to rise, the Canadian Mohawk Council of Akwesasne closed its offices March 19. Harold Tarbell also recommended that the St. Regis Tribal Council close its offices, but they remained open. On March 21, Tarbell released to the press the text of a death threat mailed to him that included pieces of text and illustrations cut from magazines that had been arranged to say: "We triumph over MCA [Mohawk Council of Akwesasne] and cops today. Tomorrow the SRTC [St. Regis Tribal Council] ... HT [Harold Tarbell] you are [opposite a photo of a man holding a gun].[24]

On March 23, gambling opponents, determined to disrupt the gambling operations, erected two sets of roadblocks along Route 37, one at either end of the gambling strip. One set of barricades, which came to be known as the "eastern door," stopped gambling-bound traffic in Hogansburg, within sight of Wild Bill's Grocery. The other, sometimes called "the western door," was erected at a double bridge near the Mohawk Bingo Palace, blocking traffic from Canada (over the International Bridge and Cornwall Island), as well as from Massena, New York. (The eastern and western doors was a metaphor for a traditional longhouse of the Iroquois.) At the same time, the "antis" also demanded that the Warriors' MSSF disband, to be replaced by a community-wide police force. A community-wide referendum on gambling also was called for.

The roadblocks became the major focus of the confrontation during the next month. Gambling advocates made repeated attempts to dismantle them so that the customers—the economic lifeblood of the gaming industry—could again reach the casinos and bingo halls. Ernie King, chief of the Canadian Akwesasne Mohawk police, became one of the blockades' coordinating captains. He said he was taking the action as a private citizen when the Warriors charged that his action proved that the Mohawk police had taken the "antis'" side in the dispute over gambling.

Gaming supporters tried to destroy the blockades even as they were first being built. Brian Cole, who worked as an economic planner for the St. Regis Tribal Council, was helping assemble a roadblock at the eastern door March 23 when he and others were confronted by three gambling supporters, Reginald, Virgil, and Allan White. Reginald fired a revolver into the air, then struck Cole in the ankle and face with the gun. In retaliation, Virgil and Allan White were struck with a club and taken to a hospital.

The attacks did not deter the blockade builders, however. After the barricades were erected, they distributed a leaflet to motorists that explained the blockade.

> We are blockading this road because of the casino and bingo owners, who, as individuals, took over our collective rights and used them for individual gain and profit without permission from the people. ... We are blockading this road because the Warriors, who terrorize our community with their weapons, abuse our collective border rights by smuggling, and have attacked our national and community government leaders in [an] attempt to replace them as our leaders and spokespersons. We are blockading this road for our children and their children. We are defending what is left of our 'native sovereignty.' Our rights are now being dragged into state and federal U.S. courts under the banner that gambling is a sovereign right. ... We are blockading this road because there is no law and order in Akwesasne. ... We are blockading this road without guns. The people who have put up this road block are men, women, and children who are concerned with our community rights. If any of them are injured in any way, we will hold the casino owners, Warriors, smugglers, and others responsible. ... [25]

The maintenance of the barricades became a community enterprise. Women baked bread, cakes, and pies to feed the two hundred people who rotated duty around the clock. At night, a procession of elderly people moved into the shelters. Men carrying canes and smoking pipes told stories, evoking ripples of laughter. Elderly women brought cakes, pies, and coffee and often stayed to join the conversation. The subchiefs of the Mohawk Nation Council and Harold Tarbell of the St. Regis Tribal Council were continually coming and going, carrying messages and other news from the outside.

Gambling supporters attempted to dismantle the blockades again on March 25, two days after they had been constructed. At 7:30 A.M., Warrior Steven Cooper drove a blue van directly into the western roadblock. Defenders clubbed the van and threw a nail-studded board under its tires. Cooper waved a MAC-10 assault pistol at the people surrounding him before he nursed the battered van to the parking lot of the burned-out Lucky Knight Casino. Three hours later, Warriors approached the western roadblock again and smashed a bingo parlor sign that the protestors had been using to light the area at night. The sign was quickly repaired and in use by nightfall. That evening Warriors moved on the roadblocks. An appeal for help at the blockades was broadcast reservation-wide at 7 P.M. on CKON, a radio station housed in St. Regis Village in the same building with *Akwesasne Notes* and *Indian Time*. The radio station went off the air a few minutes later; the Warriors had cut its broadcasting cable.

As opponents of gambling began to assemble March 25, Cole, who had become a captain at the blockades, was speaking for roughly 300 people gathered at the roadblocks on Route 37 near the eastern side of the reservation. He told reporters that two Warrior bulldozers had emerged from inside the reservation at about 8 P.M., surrounded by between 50 and 100 people. The antigambling demonstrators met the two bulldozers and their supporting force on the bridge just outside Hogansburg.

Cole said that Indian and non-Indian casino employees armed with firearms and baseball bats began to back off from the Hogansburg blockade one by one as demonstrators formed a human chain in front of the bulldozers and sang John Lennon's "Give Peace a Chance." Barbara Barnes said that the confrontation did not end until about 50 of the "antis" imitated the gamblers' own tactic. Bruce Roundpoint, an antigambler who had been present at the blockades, fired up another bulldozer and aimed it at the Bear's Den and Tony Vegas International. By 10 P.M., antigambling demonstrators were sitting on bales of hay around campfires, bats, and large sticks laid aside, rehashing the events of the evening, maintaining the roadblock at which the bulldozers had been aimed.

Ernest Benedict, a chief on the Mohawk Council of Akwesasne, carries a sign requesting peace at the anti-gamblers' barricades, April, 1990. (Photo:* Akwesasne Notes*)

How does one fight violence without resorting to it? The fact that gaming opponents had burned out one casino, trashed another, and sometimes retaliated physically against Warrior tactics troubled people at Akwesasne who supported their cause. Representatives of the Mohawk Nation Council of Chiefs visited the barricades to encourage the application of the Great Law of Peace's principles by the protesters, who were told to operate as a defensive, nonviolent force. The people who maintained the blockades also studied the methods of Martin Luther King, Jr., Gandhi, and others. During the months to come, the people at the blockades retaliated only rarely under repeated assault by Warriors and other gambling supporters who tried, with increasing force, to break the barricades.

Sue Ellen Herne, a Mohawk who spent many hours at both blockades, recalled that one young man was visibly disappointed with himself because he had not fought back when the blockade he was attending was dismantled by Warriors.

> He felt as if he didn't act like a man, and was berating himself and the rest of us as a whole, wondering what the next generation would think of us for not defending the blockades. Others talked to him, explaining that, by his self-control, he [was showing] that he is a man.[26]

Herne said that this incident occurred on March 27. Similar incidents recurred several times after that, involving several people. During the assault on the barricades March 27, their defenders urged each other to remain nonviolent. "Men took punches to the face without a response," Herne recalled.[27]

Cole stood at the barricades for many weeks during the harsh late winter and early spring. He became a hero to many of the gambling opponents as he withstood two beatings by gambling supporters who saw him as an enemy. Cole, an ardent "anti" who had been first through the door during the trashing of Laughing's casino, recalled the rising level of interpersonal violence at Akwersasne.

> Through all this time I've been pistol-whipped. I've ... had daily and nightly phone calls saying they're going to kill me. I've identified a lot of those people who called me. They're my friends. People I grew up with. I've been beaten half to death. ... Am I full of hate? I'm full of bitterness. But the teachings of my people are strong in me. And right now, there are many of us who are going through this internal battle. Because of my teachings, we say that people who have strayed and do damage to their own people, we are supposed to pick them up and support them, and bring them back to ... reason.
>
> It's hard for me because that's what I've been taught. And I want to uphold what I've been taught. But another side of me says, I can't do that. And people try to kill me. They try to kill all the people up there behind you, or behind me. I've had a pistol—have you ever felt the cold

barrel of a pistol against your cheek? You don't know if you're going to walk away. You have your family assaulted. It's hard to cope with it. That's why I think our people resorted to violence in a sense, because our society is crumbling. ... We didn't want that. And I think that in 1990 a lot of us made up our minds that, yes, peace is the way. And, as long as I am sitting here, I will do all I can in a peaceful manner to resolve the issues at Akwesasne. Will I defend myself? First, I will use reason all I can. And, sometimes, I wonder, because I've got enough scars on me that I wonder if this peaceful thing is working.[28]

During late March, *Indian Time* provided this glimpse of daily life at the blockades.

Underneath the dark sky at the roadblocks, Leanne Jock and Margaret Peters don't demand any attention or acknowledgement. They talk quietly to their friends, stopping occasionally to take a sip of hot coffee to warm themselves against the cold night air. They could be in your kitchen sharing everyday experiences about their children or work. They could be your friends, neighbors, or sisters ... with one exception: they have put their lives on hold to build a better future for Akwesasne. They are living the danger of being part of the blockades. They have been a part of the standoffs against the pro-gambling faction's guns, bulldozers, bats, and cars. Death became a real probability when the pro-gamblers marched on the eastern door ... and when they marched on the western door prepared to fight.

Margaret Peters [said]: "I remember thinking: they [casino workers] have finished talking. They're here to fight. Andrea Swamp asked if I wanted to be in the front line when they came. I decided I could never hit

At the anti-gambling barricades, March, 1990. (Photo:* Akwesasne Notes*)

someone, so I went [to the] front line. I couldn't sing, because I was in shock that it had come to this; two bulldozers and people with bats and guns. One girl was yelling [at me]: 'Why aren't you singing? Don't you want peace?' I told her, 'I'm not the one carrying a weapon.' I kept thinking: were their jobs so important to them that they were going to kill or hurt somebody? They denied having Warrior support, but [avowed Warrior] Fabian Hart was there with a gun. Harry Square was there. They were the first to provoke. I felt sad for these people. If I had any doubts about the blockades, they stopped when I saw them coming. We want to get rid of the violence that the casinos are bringing in. I never thought I would get hurt, but I was worried about my husband, who was behind me, and my kids, who were at home."

[Leanne Jock said] "We got the call Sunday that they were coming, [so] I took what I thought was my last walk in Hogan [Hogansburg]. Salli Benedict was shaking hands with everybody and saying goodbye. I realized we could die. I remember Andrea Swamp saying 'This is not rational,' when we were standing on the bridge, waiting for them to come. Meme David and Emily Tarbell said a prayer. We didn't care if they hurt us. I didn't want anyone to fight. We saw them coming. I saw Fabian with his gun; his eyes were glossy with hate. If he was a real Indian, he wouldn't need a gun to prove it. I saw Jerry Cook behind him with a baseball bat. I said hello to him. He put his head down. If they were going to do it, do it, I thought. Once the drivers [of the bulldozers] stepped down, we knew they couldn't do it. When we saw one person leave, I felt good. We didn't have to fight to prove a point. We were singing instead of swinging. I believe that, in their hearts, they didn't want to hurt their family."

Leanne was there again the next Saturday, when the pro-gamblers tried to tear down the blockade at the western door. She was the first to step out in front to keep both sides from violence. "I knew something was going to happen," [she said]. "They [anti's] wanted something to happen. The young guys [at the blockade] were getting mad. It's worst when *your* guys get mad. You know how mad they really are. I started to walk back and forth in front of the roadblock. They [pro-gamblers] were sitting in their cars, across the road. We couldn't see who they were, because they were shining their lights on us. People across the road were yelling obscenities. 'What are we gonna do if they beat you up?' somebody asked. 'Bring me flowers and candy,' I replied. I had to keep the mood light, because it was too crazy. I thought I was crazy. The people in the cars were revving their engines. I looked right at them. I was going to see the person who ran me over. It might have been for only a second, but I was going to see it, so I could haunt them."[29]

At 8 A.M. March 27, a black Pontiac Firebird attempted to force its way through the western blockade, but the driver lost control and drove the car into a ditch. The driver and a passenger crawled out of the car. One of them raised a rifle, according to a sequence of events published in *Indian Time*. The people at the blockade disarmed him, and took two mini-14 assault rifles from the car as they smashed its windows.

That same afternoon, gambling supporters again massed at the Mohawk Bingo Palace, where some people demanded that the barricades be removed by force. Reports circulated that the casinos and bingo parlors were losing $150,000 to $200,000 a day. The Mohawk Bingo Palace announced that 180 employees would be laid off. The next afternoon, Warriors assembled an automobile and truck caravan and drove forcibly through the western blockade. Bales of hay were set on fire and logs were rolled or carried off the road, as scattered fights broke out, slightly injuring Mike Mitchell and Bruce Roundpoint, among others.

On March 28 and 29, chiefs of the three councils governing the St. Regis reservation met to seek an end to the blockades and violence. The chiefs agreed that the casinos should close, a community referendum should take place accepting or rejecting gambling, and the blockades should come down. They also agreed that AK-47 assault rifles should be banned from the reservation and that the Warrior Society should disband. Mohawk Nation Council subchief Tom Porter said that the Warriors should disband because they had never been authorized by any governmental authority.

The Warriors refused to disband or surrender their weapons. A Warrior Society spokesman, Kaheroton, rejected the chiefs' peace proposal because "The Warriors have a peaceful function in the community ... and they must defend the territory's sovereignty."[30]

The same day, a group of gambling supporters waded into anti-gamblers at the blockade on Route 37 at the western door. The gaming advocates initiated a fistfight and forcibly removed the barrier before speeding away in their automobiles and trucks. Their opponents rebuilt the barricade, allowing cars through after identity checks. At the eastern roadblock, women carried hand-painted signs with messages of peace. They waved at passing drivers as other gambling opponents roasted a side of venison for a communal supper.

At the reservation's western door, people at the roadblock posted a large red, purple, and yellow Mohawk flag bearing the traditional Iroquois Tree of Peace, an eagle flying overhead, and a war club under the tree's roots symbolizing the burial of weapons which initiated the Iroquois Confederacy's founding more than 600 years ago. The casinos remained closed as the gambling protestors turned away busloads of gamblers; school buses also refused to enter the reservation, and government offices and schools were closed on the Canadian side.

Press reports on March 29 said that native people from other Iroquois reservations and other native nations were converging at Akwesasne on both sides. The same day, more than 300 gambling supporters gathered at the Mohawk Bingo Palace to await developments and to hear St. Regis Tribal Chief David Jacobs report on negotiations with the other chiefs. The Warriors posted a large red-and-yellow flag on a vehicle in the bingo hall's parking lot to announce their presence.[31]

Political differences among Harold Tarbell, David Jacobs, and Lincoln White, the three U.S. elected chiefs, had paralyzed that tribal council. Tarbell met with the Mohawk Nation Council and Mohawk Council of Akwesasne chiefs, most of whom stood with him in opposing gambling. Jacobs and White often boycotted the tricouncil meetings. In late March Tarbell initiated an investigation of Jacobs for alleged criminal activity. Tarbell also had attempted to have Jacobs removed from office, preparing a council resolution that White refused to sign. In retaliation, Jacobs and White tried (and failed) to have Tarbell removed from office, contending that his letter to Bush was an action that required the consent of at least one other chief.

As March ended, Art Kakwirakeron Montour went on trial on a charge of forcibly impeding state troopers during a gambling raid on July 20, 1989. During opening statements, assistant U.S. Attorney John Duncan said that Montour did not block state police himself during the raid; he was called a field commander of those who did so. Seth Shapiro, one of Montour's defense attorneys, said he considered calling Governor Cuomo to testify in support of Kakwirakeron. Leigh F. Hunt, chief of police in Syracuse, appeared as a character witness for the defendant, saying that Montour had worked to peacefully mediate disputes between native people and authorities in New York state for a dozen years.[32]

On March 29 a military helicopter on an emergency medical mission was shot down as it flew over Ganienkeh, a Mohawk settlement and Warrior haven 60 miles east of Akwesasne that had grown out of Warrior activities during the 1970s. People at the settlement apparently mistook the lone National Guard helicopter for the advance guard of a military invasion. Dr. James Kirk, a second-year medical resident traveling in the Vermont Army National Guard helicopter, was struck by a bullet that entered his arm, exited at the shoulder, and grazed his neck. Another bullet hit the helicopter's oil line causing oil pressure to drop. The helicopter had been dispatched to Massena Memorial Hospital to pick up a patient but was unable to land because of heavy rain mixed with snow. It was shot at returning to Burlington, Vermont, as the patient was driven to the same city in an ambulance. Mohawk residents initially refused to allow state troopers onto the land to investigate the incident, initiating a stare-down that lasted several days until the Mohawks allowed a limited search of the 698-acre area leased to them by the state at no charge.

The Route 37 barricades, re-erected after Warriors had torn them down during the March 29 fistfight, were attacked by gambling supporters once again on March 31. About 200 people emerged from the Mohawk Bingo Palace following a public meeting to which the press had been invited to hear the Warriors' side of the story. Elected Chief Lincoln White spoke at the meeting along with Francis Boots. The meeting included videotapes of gambling opponents allegedly guarding their blockades with firearms.

Stoked to action by several speakers, the progambling crowd emerged from the Bingo Palace and marched toward the nearby barricade at the western door. The people at the blockade stood aside as the frenzied crowd ripped bales of hay apart; dismembered boards, logs, and large metal scrap; then hauled it all into a large pile with a portable toilet on the top, looking like a white cherry atop a very large, ragged ice-cream cone. The pile was set on fire as other pieces of the barricade were piled onto a large flatbed truck and hauled away. One car carrying a Warrior flag rammed bales of hay in the road as several other vehicles screeched tires, burning rubber as their straining engines tried to remove a mobile home that was being used as a field office by gambling opponents.

A van surrounded by burning bales of hay caught fire, sending people on both sides scattering, expecting its gas tank to explode. One Warrior used a tractor to smash an old bus that had been part of the barricade. Shouting matches erupted between supporters and opponents of the blockade, but there were no fistfights and no injuries.

The blockade, destroyed at about 4 P.M., was back in place by 7:30 P.M. the same day. After destroying the blockades, the gambling supporters pulled out signs they had been carrying, as they posed for photographers. At 9:25 P.M. a truck outfitted with a snowplow tried to ram the eastern blockade as defenders battered the vehicle with bats and sticks. The truck was carrying the ash-stained remains of the toilet that had been burned earlier in the day, which apparently had been saved as some sort of souvenir by a couple of Warriors with a sense of humor.

The following Wednesday, April 4, about 35 Mohawks drove to the state capitol at Albany and marched past Cuomo's offices for almost two

Anti-gambling barricades being destroyed by gambling supporters, April 1990. (Photo:* Akwesasne Notes*)

hours. The demonstration was made up mainly of people who had no particular position on the gambling issue but were simply tired of the conflict itself. Most owned businesses in surrounding towns, such as Massena, that were suffering because of the confrontation. They wanted the barricades on the reservation removed. Representatives of the marchers met with Jeff Cohen, a staff aide to Cuomo, and a representative from the office of State Senator Ronald B. Stafford, whose district includes the U.S. side of Akwesasne.

Cuomo again refused to intervene, and the blockades remained in place. Despite occasional Warrior attacks, the day-to-day routine of maintaining the roadblocks settled into six-hour shifts as one group of gambling opponents relieved another around the clock. *Indian Time* reported;

> Captains and chiefs pass in and out of the tents, checking on the crews, bringing the latest news, or simply lending moral support. Donations of food and coffee come throughout the day from people who support the barricades but could not [be present]. Throughout the night, there is constant movement between the eastern and western barricades. The casinos are closely watched to make sure they remain closed. ... The odd traveler does sometimes squeeze through. What they see is a two-mile strip of Akwesasne marked by flashing lights and empty parking lots. With the exception of the odd car racing down Route 37, the roads are generally clear."[33]

Although deliveries of food and fuel were allowed to pass, most businesses on the reservation had closed or curtailed their open hours.

During the long hours of watching and waiting, the blockades' defenders talked mainly about the weather, wondering how much worse it could get. In early April the weather was wicked: tempestuous storms of spring mixed with the remains of winter. Rain, snowstorms, and record-setting cold lashed the blockades and their defenders.

Indian Time on April 4 published a statement from the Canadian Mohawk Council. Its head chief, Mike Mitchell, had recently offered his resignation (following the Canadian and British parliamentary model), to have it declined in a show of council support for him. "The Warriors continue to issue malicious and misleading statements about every Council (elected and traditional) in every territory who disagree with them," the statement began, as it explained that chiefs on both types of councils can be removed from office by popular will. Elected chiefs can be voted out, whereas Mohawk Nation Council chiefs may be "dehorned" for errant conduct.

> What recourse do you have when the *self-appointed* Warriors or MSSF violate the community will[?] Have you, as *Akwesaseron* [the people of Akwesasne] selected any one of them to be leaders or to decide the future of all the Mohawk people? The Warriors and their 'behind the

> scenes' leaders have their own agenda and objectives and [these are] to control the communities through fear, intimidation and distortion.[34]

In the same issue of *Indian Time,* the Onondaga Council of Chiefs, keepers of the Iroquois Confederacy's central council fire, took issue with the very name by which the Warriors call themselves: "We do not have a word for warrior [in the Mohawk language]. The men are called *Hodiskengehdah*. It means 'all the men who carry the bones, the burden of their ancestors, on their backs.' " The statement was meant to remind all Mohawks, and all other Iroquois, that their confederation was born centuries ago of peaceful intentions, a unification of factions that had once wreaked bloody carnage on one another. Furthermore, the Iroquois Council's chiefs argued that the Warriors had no business invoking the rhetoric of sovereignty to protect their own interests.

> The word [sovereignty] has been invoked in the current situation at Akwesasne. ... Sovereignty lies with the people. *Guyanahgowah,* The Great Law of Peace, states: Issues affecting the Nation or Nations must come before the people and ... there must be an unanimous decision by the Council of Chiefs before an issue can be sanctioned. Every person has a right to peace and tranquility in his or her lands. The Haudenosaunee [Iroquois] lands are ... held in common, one of the few places left in Indian country exercising that aboriginal right. Therefore, consent of all the people is required before changes can occur that will affect the lives of the people.[35]

The Iroquois Council's statement posed several questions for the casino and bingo parlor operators:

> Do they have outside non-Indian business partnerships? If they do, and if they do not get the consent of the Council of Chiefs, then they themselves will have violated the sovereignty of the Mohawk people. ... Are there revenues taken off the Mohawk Nation territories without the consent of the Mohawk Nation? Then, Mohawk sovereignty is being violated again. ... There should be an accounting of these revenues to the people. ... The [gambling] businesses have created mercenaries of some of our people. ... We have been told by a young man, who at one time upheld the values of the Longhouse, that we do not understand. We understand only too well what he meant by that statement. We do not agree with their [Warriors'] attempt to usurp the legitimate Mohawk government and replace it with the free-wheeling, unregulated, ungoverned activities of wealthy individuals protected by their personal armed security forces just like the drug barons of Central and South America. Anarchy in Indian country is directed by Las Vegas and other enclaves of gambling.[36]

On April 5, Kakwirakeron told a jury in Syracuse that he didn't order his security force to forcibly resist his arrest during the previous summer's gambling raids. Instead, Kakwirakeron said that he had been frantically making telephone calls trying to arrange mediation as 200 state troopers and FBI agents swarmed into the casinos with search warrants. Kakwirakeron portrayed himself as a man of peace. "I am not a believer in using armed force to resolve a conflict," he told the jury in U.S. District Court.[37] Shapiro, one of Kakwirakeron's attorneys, had called him "the Martin Luther King of his people."[38] Kakwirakeron was convicted of impeding execution of a search warrant and conspiracy on April 10. The jury acquitted him of a more serious felony, using a deadly weapon to interfere with law-enforcement officers executing a search warrant.

As Kakwirakeron argued his case in Syracuse, Doug George was sending to press an essay that characterized the gambling operators and their supporters in a much different light.

> We are an ancient, agricultural people who have had to weather intense economic, political and cultural changes in the past 10 years that have left us disorganized, split into innumerable factions and in desperate need of time to heal our wounds and decide what type of society we are leaving for the next generation. We have, over the past four years, had to tolerate the corruption of our people by bands of organized Indian criminals involved in such reprehensible activities as gambling, gun-running, narcotics peddling and cigarette smuggling. These criminals have tried to hide behind our treaties and our Great Law of Peace. They have abused our tax-exemption rights and our border-crossing privileges. They have used every opportunity to make money, corrupt tribal officials, and deliberately prevent our people from unifying the three Mohawk councils into one national government. By anarchy they thrive.[39]

Later, George said that the Warriors had used the legitimate issue of land rights and sovereignty to gain bargaining leverage for their gambling and smuggling operations. "Gambling has failed to provide schooling for one Mohawk kid, or health care for one elder."[40]

Not all of the actions against the blockades were on a large, organized scale. During April there was a series of individual attempts by gambling supporters to break the barricades, usually rammings by drunken drivers. Numerous bomb threats were called in to the Canadian elected council as well. During the morning of April 6, a transport trailer sped through the western roadblock at about 70 miles per hour, followed closely by a brown van. A little more than an hour later, a Cornwall taxi raced through the roadblock and back again. The next day, just after midnight, a car with Quebec plates smashed through the blockade. Two and a half hours later, according to a log kept by blockade defenders, Allan Peters, Harry Thompson, Jr., and Louie Peters arrived at the Hogansburg blockade. Allan Peters tried to provoke a fight as he smashed a car windshield with a baseball bat. No one on the blockade's defense crew took the bait; Louie Peters then tried shooting at the blockade from his truck, leaving .223 rifle casings at the site. Apparently frustrated, the three men then sped off in the direction they had come, revving their truck around Hogansburg. A half hour later, a car with its lights out drove up to the same blockade and began spraying bullets at it. At 5:50 A.M., a 4-by-4 truck raced through the roadblock.

During April, the blockades were reinforced. Mohawks with long experience in the construction trades, some of them the celebrated Mohawks in "high steel," turned bales of hay and scrap building materials, sealed with plastic, into comfortable rooms where opponents of gambling waited out the stormy weather. Barrels became impromptu stoves; bales of hay became beds and chairs. The defenders of the blockades used portable telephones to communicate with each other and kept a citizens-band radio tuned to the frequency that the Warriors used to coordinate their own activities. On the radio, the people of the blockades monitored the Warriors so often that they came to know their "handles" as well as their names: "Red Cloud" (Tommy Square), "Red Deer" (Rowena General), "Sharp Knife" (Donny Smoke), "Dull Knife" (Debbie Smoke), "Moma Bear" (Harriet Boots), "Frank Wood" (Francis Boots), and "Mama Wolf" (Minnie Garrow).

At one point in April, John Boots requested a meeting with Jesse Jackson in an attempt to bring him in on the Warriors' side of the conflict. Jackson's staff had a policy of meeting only with "responsible" leaders of Indian tribes. When Jackson answered Boots's request, the invitation went to Harold Tarbell, as head chief of the tribal council recognized by New York. While Tarbell and Mohawk Nation Council subchief Tom Porter met with Jackson at his National Rainbow Coalition headquarters in Washington, D.C., on April 18. Cuomo, to whom Jackson also had offered his aid, declined to meet with him.[41]

Returning to Akwesasne after his meeting with Jackson, Chief Tarbell said that Jackson would urge Cuomo to drop his neutral stance and work more aggressively to resolve conflicts. Jackson sent a warm greeting to the people at the antigambling blockades, along with a set of glossy photographs: "Stand tall for justice and peace. God will not forsake you. Keep hope alive."[42]

By the third week in April, sides were hardening visibly at Akwesasne. Just as many people were becoming even more disaffected by the Warriors' heavy-handed "protection" of their community, gaming supporters, along with the Warriors themselves, were readying again to bring down the blockades that had brought gambling to a stop.

On April 13 the Mohawk Nation Council issued a statement that called the Warrior Society a "lawless and terrorist cult." The Mohawk Nation Council statement, in the form of an indictment, listed 22 ways in which the Warriors had damaged the community, including:

> The doctrine of said warrior cult is twisted and manipulated the principles of the Great Law to support destructive activity;

> Said warrior group has demonstrated anarchist behavior and recognizes no government leadership within Akwesasne or the [Iroquois] Confederacy;
>
> Said warrior cult takes active criminals as members of their cult [and] protects illegal and immoral activities of some of its members;
>
> Individual members of said warrior cult have engaged in acts of intimidation, threats against lives, homes, and property of Mohawk people ... seduc[ing] individuals into a doctrine of hate that had divided families, turned children against their parents, brother against brother, Mohawk against Mohawk;
>
> [The Warriors have] promoted a doctrine which has corrupted the minds of children, which has led them to believe that killing is acceptable behavior ... [and] corrupted children into accepting personnel assault weapons as essential tools for existence within this community;
>
> Individual members ... have disrupted sacred ceremonies ... [and] protected deviant, violent and unacceptable criminal behavior ... desecrated and disturbed the burial sites of Mohawk people ... disrupted Grand Council meetings ... threatened the lives of Chiefs and Clan Mothers ... [and] practiced treasonous activities aimed at the destruction of the Mohawk Nation government. ...
>
> Those who wish to return to the Circle of the Confederacy under the Great Law [should] do so immediately. Due to the severity of crimes committed by the warrior cult ... the Mohawk Nation hereby delivers this one notice only. [43]

One month after the barricades went up, gaming supporters and Warriors began to report a series of violent acts. On April 18, according to Warriors leader Minnie Garrow, Richard Adams, a gaming supporter, was dragged from his car shortly after midnight, beaten, and dragged through the muddy median strip.[44] In retaliation, the 40 Warriors dismantled that barricade the same day, using a "liberated" state department of transportation snowplow to shove cars aside as they set hay bales afire with gasoline. On April 21 a trailer near the home of Diane Lazore, who had been active among the Warriors, was set ablaze, an act of "anti" arson, according to the Warriors. On April 23 Warrior Tommy Square was said to have been beaten unconscious by "antis," who tied his hands and then carried him in a car trunk to a traffic circle on Route 37. He was said to have been dumped at the feet of state police. On April 28 Lazore said that "antis" shot through her glass picture window, missing her brother Gordon by inches as he was answering the telephone. According to the Warriors' account, one of their protests against the barricades was rammed by an antigambler whose automobile hit one person, injuring him slightly.[45]

The Warriors maintained that such violence "provoked" them to mount one final, brutal assault that would take down the "antis'" barricades during the last week in April, a trashing so complete that they would not be erected again. Violence at Akwesasne reached a new level of vehemence as the barricades came down for the last time. Violence would become so pervasive that it began to take on a life of its own, from barricade trashings, to beatings, to nightly firefights with automatic weapons, spiralling, day by tempestuous day, toward death. As the barricades came down, the land where the partridge drums was entering its most violent week in memory.

Notes

[1] On October 29 McDonald was sentenced to ten months in jail, of which he served six. He also was fined $3,000, an amount close to the $3,800 in damages he caused in the casino.

[2] After his arrest, Burns checked out of the burgeoning gambling business at Akwesasne, turning his casino into a video-rental store.

[3] Harold Tarbell. Letter to President George Bush, January 31, 1990. Copy in files of St. Regis Tribal Council.

[4] Ibid. Tarbell is referring here to the 1988 law regulating Indian gambling which is discussed in the Introduction.

[5] Ibid.

[6] Ibid.

[7] Ibid.

[8] Senators Daniel Inouye and John MacCain to Harold Tarbell, February 6, 1990. Manuscript in St. Regis Tribal Council files.

[9] Priit J. Vesilind, "Common Ground, Different Dreams: The U.S.–Canada Border," *National Geographic* (February 1990): 110–11.

[10] Ibid.

[11] Ibid.

[12] Ibid.

[13] Doug George. Interview with author, Onchiota, NY, August 3, 1991.

[14] On January 7, 1991 the Second Circuit Court of Appeals upheld the convictions of Laughing, James Burns, Sr., Eli Tarbell, and Roderick Cook on federal gaming charges by a vote of 2 to 1, ruling that United States jurisdiction applies at Akwesasne south of the 45th parallel. Attorneys for the four men prepared to appeal to the U.S. Supreme Court, as U.S. District Court Judge Neal McCurn ordered the four to surrender to federal marshals, the first step in serving their prison sentences.

[15] New York State Assembly Hearings, *Transcript of the Crisis at Akwesasne,* Ft. Covington, July 24, 1990, pp. 514–17.

[16] Ibid.

[17] Ibid. People on both sides of the dispute at Akwesasne often communicated by citizens'-band radio "scanner"; each side used a specific frequency, which was known to the other, so such listening in was common.

[18] Ibid. John Boots was quoted in the Massena *Courier-Observer* on March 6: "The incident in Snye looks like a family problem. As far as the St. Regis incident, there are always these allegations. We've stated before that we won't lift a hand against another Mohawk."

[19] Minutes of meeting. St. Regis Tribal Council, March 3, 1990. Copy in files of St. Regis Tribal Council.

[20] *Standard-Freeholder* (Cornwall, Ont.), March 7, 1990.

[21] *Daily Times* (Watertown, NY), March 6, 1990.

[22] Between March 24 and May 1, 1990, residents of Akwesasne appealed to the state police for help at least 147 times without response, according to phone logs provided by the Mohawk Council of Akwesasne. Indeed, Constantine would tell a New York state assembly investigating committee during the summer of 1990 that the Warriors owned more automatic weaponry and other military-type ordnance than his entire force.

[23] *Daily Times* (Watertown, NY), April 21, 1990.

[24] *Sun* (Fort Covington, NY), March 28, 1990.

[25] "Why We Are Taking This Action." Leaflet distributed at blockades by gambling opponents, distributed during late March and early April 1990. Copy in files of *Akwesasne Notes* and *Indian Time*.

[26] Sue Ellen Herne. Letter to author. October 12, 1991.

[27] Ibid.

[28] New York. State Assembly Hearings, Transcript, *The Crisis at Akwesasne,* Albany, August 2, 1990, pp. 443-49. Cole also said that more than 600 incidents of violence had been chronicled against "antis" by Warriors at Akwesasne during the first three months of 1990. Charlotte Debbane, one of the nonviolent observers who had been at Akwesasne during the previous March and April, said that as she heard Cole's statement during the State Assembly hearing, "I was crying. ... He was there with swatches of hair on his forehead. He was still suffering the migraines and dizzy spells" suffered during the second and most serious beating in April 1990.

[29] *Indian Time* (Akwesasne) April 6, 1990. Emphasis added.

[30] *Daily Times* (Watertown, NY), March 29, 1990.

[31] *Press-Republican* (Plattsburgh, NY), March 29, 1990.

[32] Hunt was later fired as police chief of Syracuse by the city's mayor. Several months after that, he was appointed by Cuomo to head a new state Indian relations office. At Montour's trial, Hunt was referring in part to the settlement of an armed occupation that began in 1974 at an abandoned Girl Scout camp at Moss Lake that gave birth to Ganienkeh ("Land of the Flint"), a Warrior encampment on state land near Plattsburgh, about 50 miles east of Akwesasne. The same series of events had brought Montour and Cuomo together. Working with Montour, Cuomo in 1977 convinced the Mohawks to leave the camp and settle on land owned by New York state, which has no state-recognized tribal status. Nevertheless, it hosts a high-stakes bingo hall, and engages in large-scale, tax-free cigarette sales. Most of its residents sympathize with the Warriors' notions of Mohawk sovereignty. The area, which residents claim by treaty right, is strictly off limits to non-Indians (except those arriving for bingo) and many other Mohawks as well. Montour had figured prominently in the 1974 occupation and got to know then-New York Secretary of State Mario Cuomo during three years of legal battles following the occupation, a relationship that opponents of gambling charged kept Cuomo from sending state police to Akwesasne before two men were killed on May 1, 1990. Cuomo's relationship with Montour probably accounted for the fact that when he finally decided to send state troopers to the reservation following those two deaths, the governor violated the state's own protocol when he communicated with the extra-legal Warriors (who had obtained an agreement from progambling chiefs White and Jacobs allowing them to serve as "escorts"), treating the private army as diplomatic equals of the state-recognized St. Regis Tribal Council. Cuomo totally ignored the chiefs of the Mohawk Nation Council, which is often more influential on the reservation than the elected bodies in the United States or Canada.

[33] *Indian Time* (Akwesasne), April 4, 1990.
[34] Ibid.
[35] Ibid.
[36] Ibid.
[37] *Post-Standard* (Syracuse, NY), April 6, 1990.
[38] *Post-Standard* (Syracuse, NY), March 29, 1990.
[39] Letter to the Editor, *Evening Telegram* (Malone, NY), April 7, 1990.
[40] Doug George. Interview with author. Akwesasne, August 5, 1991.
[41] Cuomo commented, in a tape played for Fort Covington *Sun* reporter Virginia Jennings over the telephone by an aide, "It is not up to me to invite him to another nation." Cuomo also commented, rather dejectedly, "There is sufficient evidence of my failure [to settle issues there]." *Sun* (Ft. Covington, NY), April 18, 1990.
[42] *Akwesasne Notes* (Akwesasne, NY), Late Spring, 1990.
[43] Statement of Mohawk Nation Council, April 13, 1990. Copy in Mohawk Nation Council files.
[44] Rick Hornung, *One Nation Under the Gun: Inside the Mohawk Civil War* (Toronto, Ont.: Stoddart, 1991), 150–54.
[45] Ibid. Curiously, nonviolent observers posted at both barricades around the clock did not confirm the Warriors' accounts. Warriors argue that the observers were in cahoots with the "antis" and covered up their acts of violence; gambling opponents say that the Warriors fabricated the accounts to justify their own violence, especially the attacks that finally brought the barricades down for good. The observers themselves said that they were duty-bound to report any violence they saw by either side. At such times, people on each side of this community under siege seemed to be operating within distinctly separate realities, so deep and violent had the split become.

CHAPTER 4
▼▼▼

Downslide to Death

By late April life at Akwesasne had unravelled completely. A community that had been under siege was now at war—brother against brother, mother against son. During the final week of April, there was a surge of violence at Akwesasne on a level so personal and pervasive that few people in the United States have seen its equal. Allegiances hardened as the bullets flew, and violence escalated until two men lost their lives May 1.

Within the St. Regis Tribal Council, David Jacobs and Lincoln White prepared to outflank Harold Tarbell by signing an agreement with Francis Boots recognizing the Warriors as partners with the New York state police to dismantle the gambling opponents' roadblocks. When the chiefs of the Iroquois Confederacy learned about this agreement, signed April 18, they exploded in fury. The chiefs of the Onondaga Nation sent a letter to Senator Daniel Inouye dated April 19, 1990, one day after the agreement was signed, which read, in part:

> The resolution signed by Jacobs, White, [Carol] Herne [tribal clerk], and Boots (using his Mohawk name), purports to recognize the Warrior Society as a legal body of men following the will of the people is a travesty. ... It is also inflammatory and provocative. ... There are now 13 Mohawk people convicted of criminal charges stemming from these casinos and Warrior activities. This last act of recognizing a Warrior Society as legitimate by two individuals who[m] the Haudenosaunee have asked to be investigated is proof that the casino owners, Jacobs, White, and the Warrior Society have been working together all along."[1]

On April 23, Curtis Berkey, representing the traditional Mohawk Council, wrote Bill Ott, director of the Bureau of Indian Affairs (BIA) eastern-area office. He asked the BIA to notify Jacobs and White that their agreement with Boots had no legal effect. "It gives encouragement and aid to a para-military organization at a time when the responsible leaders at Akwesasne are desperately searching for a way to control the lawless activities of this group," Berkey wrote.[2]

Organized confrontations at the blockades intensified again on April 22. Warriors' cars and those of other gambling proponents paraded in front of the barricades, hovering for impending action. The same evening, a few firebombs were lobbed at the barricades from passing automobiles. Linda Champagne, an observer posted at the blockade by the New York State Martin Luther King, Jr., Institute for Nonviolence, later wrote a report to the leaders of the Iroquois Confederacy and Mohawk Nation Council.

> I had just left the fire barrel next to the road, where people were keeping warm, and was inside the frame shelter when the first explosion occurred. We looked through the plastic "window" to see a wall of flame next to the handful of people standing outside. Joellene Adams, beside me, let out a yell, [because] she thought the people were on fire. Lee Ann [sic] Jock, who was standing beside the road, later described the flash of heat that [had] flared up her back. ... She was sure her hair would ignite. It didn't. Only the hay bales burst into flames at that site.[3]

Champagne wrote that the men who threw the firebombs leered from car windows in the flame-burnished shadows, wearing ghoulish Halloween masks, one a clown, the other a devil. At one point during that terrible week, Jock listened to Cuomo's denials that people were being shot at and declared, "If he will come to Akwesasne, I'll carry him through Hogansburg on my back, and he'll see how he likes being shot at!"

The antigambling blockades were firebombed with more Molotov cocktails on April 23. The North American Indian Traveling College, a stronghold of antigambling sentiment, was one of three buildings set on fire the same day. Gambling supporters raised the ante in their attempt to destroy impediments to "business as usual" along the gambling strip. The fire at the Traveling College destroyed 20 years of reservation history in printed and videotape archives. The Warriors later denied any involvement in any of these events

On April 23, Mike Francis, a New York National Guardsman and military veteran, crossed paths with the Warriors and other gambling supporters as they threw gas bombs at the blockades. At one point, Francis watched Bill Sears, who had started the first bingo hall at Akwesasne, dodge a gas bomb. "They almost burned their own boss," he said.

> We were still dodging rocks and bottles. One of our guys, Tommy Lazore, got hit in the chest with a rock, and that was it. That's all it took and we started throwing rocks back at them. A Warrior was hiding off to the right in some trees and he yelled at me, 'Mike, quit throwing those rocks and bottles at my people.' And they were throwing gas bombs and

smoke bombs at me. I went right up to him face to face and asked him what the heck was going on. ... He was there with another Warrior. They both backed up. ... They just stood there, that's how drunk they were. I could see the Budweiser bottle in his hand. That's how close I was.[4]

At the same time, three people were injured after a live hand grenade was tossed into a crowd at the Canadian Akwesasne police station. Marie Martin, who lives across the street from the Mohawk police station, described the scene.

I heard a lot of commotion ... cars screeching, voices shouting at the police station and the band [tribal council] office. I went across the street to find out what was going on. People were milling about, and I could feel the tension in the air. I asked, "What is going on?" I was told that "We are trapped!" The Warriors had set up a blockade on the four corners of Hogansburg and Magee Road that leads to the Bear's Dean. ... There was a school bus at the police station that was battered. All of the windows were smashed out, as well as the lights (head and rear) and sides, front and back. I asked if there was anyone in it. I was told yes. There were four children in the bus at the time. The driver was a woman who was sympathizing with the antigamblers. She was screaming and terrified as the Warriors attacked the bus with bats and steel rods. The children were unhurt, but the terror of the afternoon remains with them. The woman bus driver was hospitalized from the flying glass.[5]

Two of Martin's cousins were visiting from Saranac, New York, as the day-to-day level of violence at Akwesasne approached its zenith. "Fear was on their faces," Martin recalled. "They asked, 'What is going on?

Burned-out building of the North American Indian Traveling College, April 1990. (Photo:* Akwesasne Notes*)

There are a bunch of people under the traffic light at the four corners smashing cars with bats and iron rods and attacking the drivers."[6] The two cousins told the Warriors that they were visitors, and they were allowed to pass through the barricade without harm.

In the evening, Martin crossed the street again to visit the police station, and was told by officers to get back inside her house.

> The Warriors were going to attack the police station. Around 9 P.M., when it got dark, the shooting started. Warriors came in and AK-47s were firing continuously, and were so close to our house that our 10-year-old son was terrified, as was I. We were laying on the floors and my son was crying. He was saying, "Mommy, I don't want to die. I'm too little. Please, Mommy, let's get out of here." I told him that if we got out of this alive, we would go.[7]

Lying on the floor beside her son, Mrs. Martin heard the grenade explode, followed by the sound of ambulance sirens.

> One young man, 19 years old, was hit by the shrapnel ... and the firing continued until about midnight and 1 A.M. I could see men crouching and running around with rifles and guns. In my terror, I could not sleep.[8]

Warrior spokesman Boots quickly blamed the Akwesasne police for throwing a large firecracker at the crowd in front of their own office, contradicting nearly everyone else on the scene. Observers described 15 to 20 Warriors lining their cars up in front of the police station, their high beams illuminating the crowd, as one of them tossed the hand grenade.

Several private homes on the reservation were damaged by firebombs during the same night that the barricades were assaulted and the Akwesasne police station shot up. Calls for intervention by state police again went unheeded.

As the level of violence rose, the fabric of daily life at Akwesasne began to unravel, strand by strand. On April 24 the U.S. Postal Service stopped deliveries to some sections of the reservation. An elementary school operated by the Salmon River Central School District was closed. Three people were hospitalized, and six arrested amidst numerous reports of beatings, vehicle rammings, house fires, grenade explosions, power outages, and automatic-weapons fire. A school bus had all its windows smashed by men wielding baseball bats. The driver's face was cut by flying glass.

Hundreds of rounds of gunfire poured into the eastern and western blockades on the evening of April 24 and ended with their destruction around 11:30 that same night. This time, the people assaulting the blockades were not firing into the air. They were throwing barrages of automatic-weapons fire, Rambo-style, parallel to the ground. Blockade defenders, caught with no guns to defend themselves, scattered to their automobiles under a hail of gunfire. They regrouped at the Snye Fire Station under the leadership of Chief Harold Tarbell and described a mob of gambling supporters staggering, howling, apparently drunk or high on cocaine.

Mike Francis held his ground in the midst of the gunfire to videotape the April 24 assault. The videotape was aired hours later in many cities across North America. Francis described what he saw:

> We saw a vehicle driving fast and throwing gas bombs [Molotov cocktails] at the people standing around. As we got closer, they pitched them at us. ... A couple of their gas bombs didn't explode ... and so myself and my brothers decided to get the gas bombs off the road. Then they took sniper fire at us. It went right into the vehicle and over my brother's head. ... My [other] brother jumped ... back into the vehicle, and I went to the side of the road for cover. ... I could hear on the radio that people were getting shot up. ... You could hear the Warriors on the CB saying they were coming to get us. There were about 100 to 150 people on the ground with shots firing through them. I had my camera on and I took pictures. I have bullet holes in my wife's car. I tried to take pictures of them when they started firing at me, and I got the hell out of there in my [wife's] car.[9]

Charlotte Debbane, a Canadian citizen, joined the group of observers summoned by residents of Akwesasne. She had been involved with Mohawks at Kahnawake, near Montreal, after she came to Canada from Egypt in 1973. When the call came for help at Akwesasne, she accepted without hesitation. Debbane was present during much of March and April.

> On various occasions, I think they [Warriors] burnt about fifty private vehicles. And they rammed cars, including [those of] observers. They would threaten to drive straight at the barricades, and there were people standing there always, so you always had to be on your guard, and know when to jump aside, because sometimes they would just pretend. They would come up, and swerve away at the last minute. Sometimes, they would drive their cars straight into the barricades. ... It was like a scene out of a bad movie—a John Wayne show. They were screaming, waving weapons above their heads. They ripped apart hay bales and tarpaulins, and shoved everything into a ditch.[10]

The experience that shook Debbane most intensely was listening to Mohawk women tell her how the conflict had split families.

> One elderly woman at the barricades told me: "my children are on the other side." I still get goosebumps when I think about this. It was heartbreaking. They didn't want these people killed—they are their brothers, their sisters. But the others [Warriors and other gaming supporters] were so intoxicated—some literally, others with power. ... One woman could not go to a family wedding, because she was on the other side.[11]

Debbane recalled what a gambling supporter who was active in the Warrior Society told her:

> "You are not an observer. You're on the other side." I told her I won't lie for *anybody*. If people on the "right side" are doing things they shouldn't be doing, if they are being violent, we would have noted that all the same. Our log books are open. We have nothing to hide.[12]

Debbane confirmed, for example, that a group of "antis" beat a group of Warriors as the blockades were being assaulted. The majority of the violent incidents were initiated by gambling supporters, however, according to the records of Debbane and other nonviolent observers. "We offered observers [to accompany] the Warriors," she said, "But they refused." At one point, Debbane was told by gambling supporters that the "antis" were responsible for the violence, "and I just stood there, going a-huh, a-huh, a-huh. ... I was looking at what was going on, pointedly."[13]

By late April, the Warriors were trying to force the observers off the reservation. Debbane was told that the observers had half an hour to leave the reserve "or else they had no responsibility for what happened to us." Debbane watched as two Warriors escorted one observer to their leaders.

> I felt assured that the idea was to beat him up. And because we had been told that sometimes the presence of an observer could help prevent violence, I trotted after them and I heard what happened. He was being told off by two older people who seemed to be in charge of the Warriors. They were middle-aged people, a man and a woman who were insulting him and calling him an FBI spy and telling him that if he didn't leave the reserve they would get him. A car, a gray car, came down the road, and a man got out of it. I didn't know who he was, so I called him "George Bush." He had the same long, pallid face, a tight little face. He got out of the car and began jumping up and down. ... He said that all the people at the barricades were being paid ... by either the Canadian government or the American government and that they were all traitors and spies. This man suggested that [the observer] be thrown into the river. [His] response was completely peaceful and non-violent.[14]

After that, the Warrior leaders turned to Debbane, and "told me that I had no business being there...because I was white and that I should leave immediately. And I said to them: 'No, I don't think so'. And they asked me who had brought me in, who had invited me, so I said [that] friends invited me. And they said: '*We* didn't invite you.' " One of the Warriors began to shout at Debbane that no one could go near the people on the barricades without being beaten up. Debbane, however, said that she had seen where the violence came from.

> I was looking at it. ... [It was an] ordinary every-day occurrence for the people of Akwesasne; that is to say, broken bottles thrown at them, random insults, cars swerving as they reached the barricade[s], attempts

to ram cars. ... I couldn't believe that the police were not responding. I took the telephone at two o'clock in the morning and I told them [Quebec police] in French. And their answer was: "It is too dangerous for us to come in during the night. Let them hold on." Besides, both on the American side and the Canadian side, both Ontario and Quebec, the answer was the same: "We know what is happening. We are ready. Our superiors have given us no instructions. We can not move in without instructions from our superiors."[15]

Margaret Weitzman, a resident of Potsdam, New York, also fled the barricade at the eastern door the night the Warriors and other gambling supporters attacked it. Weitzman captured the mood of people awaiting assault.

Some 70 or 80 men and women at East Gate wait out the fairly mild night. Mosquitoes gather. Inside the 300 square-foot shelter people eat, sleep, talk. The phone rings—a call for Jake Swamp. Chief Harold Tarbell is back from Albany and on his way over to report. Paul Warloski, a reporter for the *Malone Evening Telegram,* who has spent many nights here on his own time, heaves a sigh of relief. He will be able to get Tarbell's news into the next edition. "Anti," a six-month-old yellow and white puppy sprouting an adolescent's big feet, noses among tables and people's legs for scraps.

Abruptly, both CB and telephone jolt us. "All right, we're going in," the flat voice on channel 4 says. "Well, whaddaya know! They set fire to their own roadblock!" Andrea Swamp, on the phone, says "They're quitting the west gate now. ... " A pause. The Warriors are digesting the west gate. A voice, on channel 4, gloating, "I'm going to get you, Mike Mitchell. ... I'm gonna make you squeal like a pig!"

It's our turn. Nobody says it. "Half an hour?" someone asks. "get the light up," someone shouts. These are searchlights mounted on the back of a truck. The lights go on. We are flooded with light. Suddenly, we are flooded with noise—shooting. ... The gun crackles become business-like. Nobody is returning fire; nobody is armed with anything heavier than a stick of firewood.[16]

Gaming supporters had decided that no cost was too great in their effort to open the roads to gambling traffic. The Warriors and other advocates of reservation gambling continued to pummel the two blockades through the night. According to Weitzman's narrative:

The shooting started from the left, behind us. ... Most of us hit the ground by the sandbags surrounding the tent. My back was against one [sandbag]. I could feel the impacts. The fire began like rifle fire, then came in bursts—semi-automatics. From the direction and volume of fire, there were between three and five [armed] attackers. That no one or nothing came to our aid is still hard to believe. State police a half hour later were not interested in our story.[17]

The observers debated among themselves what sort of nonviolent action could help quell the gunfire. They decided that any show of bodies was too risky. Finally, they began singing a song: "We are gentle angry people, and we are singing for our lives." Some of them embraced and began to sob. Linda Champagne described tracer bullets illuminating the sky above her head as she lay flat on the pavement, face up.

Vivian Smoke also was caught in the assault on the barricades. She was at the eastern door.

> We heard that the western door had been completely demolished. They had shot up the cars first, then they set the cars on fire. They set the whole roadblock on fire. I worried because I hadn't heard from my son or anybody that was at the western door. Apparently they had all been able to get away. You could see all the [Warriors'] cars coming toward the eastern door. We got out and started cleaning out our hut where we had kept our food and everything. And then, all of a sudden, the bullets started flying. I was behind a truck and slowly made it by going down on the ground behind other cars. I met up with other women and our crowd just kept getting bigger and we kept behind the cars. There was really no place to run because shots were coming from all over. You could see the bullets ... flying right over our heads.[18]

Smoke said it was a miracle that no one was killed by the spray of semiautomatic rifle fire. The bullets raced overhead like flaming sleet driven by a furious wind. "We were on the ground and you look up and see them. They were tracers ... they had flames on them."[19]

The next day, the people who had been through that night regrouped and, in Smoke's words, "Gave thanks to the creator for seeing us through that night."[20] She and others called off-reservation police agencies for help.

> I called the New York State Police, I called the OPP [Ontario Provincial Police] and nobody ever responded to our calls. [The Quebec police] said that their plan was for us to be evacuated tomorrow morning. I said that tomorrow morning was too late. We need help now. He said they were meeting. They were forever meeting, but nothing ever got done.[21]

Amazingly, no one was seriously injured during the night of April 24. Indicative of the state of anarchy on the reservation, no one was arrested, either. By morning, the burned-out shells of more than 20 cars lined Route 37. The Warriors set up blockades that they said were not being used to stop traffic but to make sure their opponents would not re-erect blockades of their own.

Akwesasne now resembled a war zone, its roads littered with broken glass, spiked planks, and the shells of burned-out vehicles, their windows cracked and grills smashed. The cars had been damaged by the men attacking the blockades. Observers described roads laced with roadblocks within roadblocks. "A normal night here is like going through Belfast," one person said. At one point, local non-Indians who live near the reservation had set up their own roadblock as a publicity stunt to demonstrate the problems caused by the other barricades. In Hogansburg, gambling supporters refused to let reporters through their roadblock to talk with gambling opponents, waving them off with baseball bats and angry words.[22]

The Warriors claimed that blockade defenders were torching their own vehicles on WPTZ-TV during the evening of April 25. Mrs. Paul Herne, a resident of Akwesasne, called the station to say that the gambling opponents were not burning their own vehicles and blockades. A reporter on the news staff told her that they had to report the assertion as part of the news. The reporter then asked Mrs. Herne, "What would you do if they [the Warriors] threatened to shoot you?" Mrs. Herne replied, "What do you think the Warriors are doing to us?" Having observed the newspaper and television press coverage of the crisis at Akwesasne carefully, Mrs. Herne found much of it fragmented, contradictory, and confusing, often because assertions by the Warriors were reported as if they were facts. She also objected to being called an "anti" because she spoke out against the Warriors. "I am a responsible resident ... of Akwesasne," she said. "I believe in law and order. I take offense at people who left the reservation, and then came back to upset our way of life."[23]

Damage to a Mohawk Council of Akwesasne police cruiser. (Photo:* Akwesasne Notes*)

By April 25, after the barricades had been destroyed, some of the antigambling Mohawk Nation chiefs moved to safe houses at undisclosed locations outside of Akwesasne as other residents also began to flee. The U.S. side of the reservation was becoming a no-man's land, rent by bursts of automatic-weapons fire day and night. On one of the most violent nights of that week, Debbane recalled watching one Hare Krishna devotee decide, against the expressed desires of the nonviolent observers, to take his quest for peace directly to the streets of Akwesasne. She watched him set out in his flowing saffron robes, armed only with a small drum, walking slowly into the night as automatic rifle fire crackled in the distance. He descended in measured paces over a low hill, his body disappearing inch by inch behind it, chanting, over and over, to his solitary drumbeat.

The lone man wandered the roads of Akwesasne until early the next morning as the firefight roared around him. When he could drum and chant no more, Father Egan, a Catholic priest at Akwesasne, took him in for the night.[24]

On April 26, the Mohawk Council of Akwesasne asked people on the Canadian side of Akwesasne to evacuate en masse. Lloyd Benedict, a chief with the Canadian Mohawk Council, ordered evacuation of all women, children, and elderly people under that council's jurisdiction. Some already had moved away. One hundred fifty residents were evacuated by boat from the village of St. Regis. Residents of the U.S. side also were beginning to leave their homes without an evacuation order.

Vivian Smoke stayed on the reservation at the request of Mohawk Police Chief Ernie King, whose force of 10 men had been overwhelmed by the violence. She took two days' change of clothing and went to the Mohawk police station on the Canadian side to help answer the telephones. One call urgently requested help evacuating people from an old-age home on Cornwall Island. Smoke left the police station to aid in that evacuation.

> I got on the barge with them and I never felt so helpless in all my life. We fled our land and our homes on the barge. And there I was with these 25 people, and this was all they had left in their lives. I sat on that barge and I was so angry. The anger I felt in me, I was ready to go back home and pick up a gun and shoot anybody that was in my way, that's how angry I was. I am still angry for what they did to us. But we survived it. We still have some spirit left. I worked for many years to build my home, my husband and I. But for those few days, I was able to give it up. We gave each other comfort when we were at the transport center in Cornwall [used as a refugee center]. We just had one another, that's all we had left in this world. We gave up everything [else] for the terror that was going on in our lives.[25]

During the last week of April, as violence at Akwesasne assumed an intensity so personal and vindictive, one incident stood out in the memories of many people. On April 26, Brian Cole, a former principal of the Akwesasne Freedom School, was jumped while he was searching a wooded area at Akwesasne for a missing observer, Horace Joseph Cook, who had been sent to the antigamblers' barricades by the Iroquois Confederacy. Cook, a diabetic, had fled the attack on the blockade at the eastern door. Cook emerged from the woods 24 hours later, tired and dirty, but uninjured. He had survived on a diet of edible plants and cedar needles.

Cole was hospitalized in critical condition after he was beaten with baseball bats. His attackers knocked Cole out, after which they continued to pummel him. Cole's skull was partially crushed, one of his cheek bones broken, and his jaw dislocated. (Two sons of traditional subchief Jake Swamp and a son of traditional chief Ross David, also an opponent of gambling, were assaulted, hospitalized briefly, and released the same day.) The Warriors asserted that Cole had tried to rebuild the eastern door barricade at Hogansburg, close to Billy's Bingo, and was beaten by "angry citizens" who wanted to keep the road open. "I hate to say this, but not too many people feel sorry for him," said Cindy Terrance, editor of *The People's Voice.*[26]

The same day that Cole was beaten, the home of Barry and Barbara Montour, on Route 37, near the Akwesasne reservation's eastern border, was riddled with gunfire. Barry, 28, a son of Art Kakwirakeron Montour, had stood alone among his brothers in opposing casino gambling at Akwesasne.

Barry and Barbara were not at home when it was riddled with bullets. They had been studying for spring exams at the State University of New York at Plattsburgh, 70 miles from home. Family ties aside, the Montours found themselves a target of Warrior harassment. At 10 P.M., April 26, Barry took a phone call from one of his sisters, who warned him of impending danger to the family home. The nature of the danger was not made clear, but the caller said, "If anything happens to your house, I want you to know that I'm not responsible."[27] Around midnight, a light green automobile cruised slowly down the road in front of the house, its lights out. As the car rolled to a stop, semiautomatic rifle fire rattled the evening stillness, startling Barbara's uncle in a nearby house. Everyone in that house hit the floor instantly until the gunfire stopped and the light green car roared quickly down State Road, its lights still extinguished.

Early the next morning, the Montours, still in Plattsburgh, learned from Barbara's brother that their house had been shot up. Gathering up their son, Barry and Barbara drove home as quickly as they could to inspect the damage—the home's siding was splintered, and two 4-by-4-inch pieces of lumber supporting the swimming pool had been pierced by bullets, entering on one side, passing through the water, and exiting. Some of the bullets had sliced through the house into Taylor's bedroom.

Having surveyed the damage and gathered spent shells, the Montours then called the New York state police, who arrived eight hours later after an insurance adjuster had already visited the scene. When they did arrive, the state troopers, accompanied by a Warrior escort, spent only 10 minutes at the scene. Barry and Barbara shouted at the Warriors to get off their property. The Warriors backed away to the property line but continued to leer at the nervous troopers, who recorded their impressions on a single 3-by-5-inch index card. As she and her husband picked up more than 40 AK-47 and rifle shell casings near their home on April 26, Barbara said, "We thought no one would get hurt because of family. But the Warriors won't stop at family. Money is more important."[28]

Following a week of terror on the reservation, Senator Daniel Inouye sent a letter to Governor Cuomo urging him to intervene with state police, as requested by the Mohawk Nation Council under the 1794 Canandaigua treaty. Cuomo communicated most often with Montour, a frequent spokesman for the Warriors, while one of Inouye's most frequent sources of information was Harold Tarbell, head chief of the U.S. elected council and a gambling opponent. Inouye was also in frequent communication with officials of the Canadian government who had long advised Cuomo to intervene in a situation they regarded as anarchistic. Inouye reminded Cuomo that the casinos were operating illegally. Inouye wrote:

> It is only a matter of time until members of the community are injured and perhaps killed by gunfire attacks. ... Waiting until the Warrior Society members 'settle down' continues to expose the rest of the community to clear threats of deadly violence and is a situation that would not be tolerated by the state or Federal government in any other community or under any other circumstances.[29]

The day after Inouye's letter to Cuomo, the Canadian government asked the U.S. Department of State to pressure the governor to send police to the reservation. Cuomo once again refused and reiterated his support for legalized gambling on the reservation. Cuomo said that people were not being shot at. He said that the dispute was "internal to the Indians at this moment."[30]

Major Robert Leu, a New York state police commander with jurisdiction over the area, said "It's almost like a family fight. ... The Mohawks are all friends. They are all relatives."[31] In another interview, Leu gave a more practical reason for the state troopers' reluctance to enter the reservation: "Right now, we're out-gunned."[32] As the state police demurred, Chief Tarbell urged that the National Guard be called in. Without intervention, Tarbell said, "It's like he has an Indian death penalty because that is what it seems it will take before he acts—a death."[33]

By April 28 the number of persons evacuated on both sides of the international border had risen to at least 2,000, almost one-quarter of the reservation's population. Estimates of the number of people who left their homes ranged from 1,000 to 4,000—no one knew the exact number. On the same day, Akwesasne Police Chief Ernie King reported that roughly 200 rounds were fired at the police station by unidentified men carrying AK-47 assault rifles and other firearms.

As refugees streamed out of Akwesasne, New York State Police Superintendent Thomas Constantine defended his and Cuomo's refusal to intervene. "It's easy for somebody to sit back there, sucking on a martini someplace, to say some trooper should get his butt shot off." Constantine accused gambling opponents of playing up the violence for political purposes and of calling politicians in Washington, D.C., instead of the state police to complain about violence at Akwesasne. "If they have an immediate complaint like that, and their first call is to a politician in Washington. ... Well, I didn't fall out of a Christmas tree." Constantine also disputed the Akwesasne Mohawk police's account of the assault on their station house. "If the number of rounds reported had actually been fired, that building would look like the Alamo." He disputed reports that Warriors had tossed a hand grenade at the station house the previous week. "We established a listening point where we could hear generally all over St. Regis from two o'clock in the morning until dawn [the previous Thursday, April 26]. There were a total of five shots fired ... all of those shots were fired on the Canadian side."[34]

Constantine's "listening post" may have been Chief Jacobs, who said much the same thing, the same day, in another newspaper. "Despite reports from antigambling partisans, gunfire on the reservation has only been sporadic since the blockades were removed. Alleged reports of hand grenades are unconfirmed, and no evidence of grenade explosions has been verified ... at present, relative calm prevails on the reservation."[35] Montour, who by his own account, spoke to Cuomo, Constantine's boss, by telephone on April 29, went so far as to say that the level of violence had actually decreased since what he characterized as a small number of gambling opponents had left the reservation. He said the evacuations were a sympathy ploy. "The Warrior Society does not promote violence or the use of arms to achieve a political end," he said.[36]

On April 28, Chief Tarbell again urged Cuomo to send in the National Guard. Cuomo replied in the press that he had "no intention of ordering in the National Guard. He said he believed that reports of violence may have been overblown."[37] The governor said this as the reservation came, day by day, to resemble a free-fire zone. Cuomo himself told the Associated Press that reports of violence on the reservation could be overblown by "individuals who are seeking to advance their own political cause." Cuomo also repeated Major Leu's earlier assertion that the state police would not move onto the reservation because they couldn't match the Warriors' firepower.

As residents of Akwesasne appealed for help during the last week of April, Cuomo pitched his plan to legalize gambling on the reservation. Cuomo said he would appoint a mediator, State Operations Director Dr.

Henrik Dullea, to help negotiate a settlement but only when violence ceased. Receiving reports of the latest violence, Cuomo finally directed the state Division of Military and Naval Affairs to take steps to be prepared for military action as a last resort. Chief Jacobs applauded Cuomo's initiative, while Chief Tarbell said it contained no provision for a reservation-wide referendum on the gambling issue and no way to disarm the Warriors.

Traditional Mohawk subchief Jake Swamp had moved off the reservation with his family. He released a press statement from an undisclosed location.

> This is Jake Swamp. I'm calling in regard to a shooting that happened this morning at Akwesasne. We need to get [New York] Governor [Mario] Cuomo off his "bum" and start doing something. ... Right now I am ... with my wife Judy and three of my children. They are not able to go to school right now. We are like refugees from our land of Akwesasne.[38]

Swamp and his family had moved off the reservation after automatic weapons fire was aimed at his house. He described one in a series of incidents of this type.

> The last time, during the month of April, there were three people in a car driving by and one of them shot at our home and hit the house this time. My wife and my daughter were at the kitchen sink washing dishes; my daughter was wiping. If that bullet would have penetrated [the wall], in the direction it was [heading], it would have gotten one of them in the head ... Then they parked in front of the house in direct view of my wife and daughter. ... They opened the door and then got ready to shoot again. But for some reason this person changed his mind and instead got back in and closed the door and then they drove off.[39]

Swamp then chased the car from which the shots had been fired for half an hour. After Swamp filed a complaint with police, they visited the house to investigate.

As fighting intensified at Akwesasne, Doug George and his brother Dave decided to make a stand at Dave's house in Snye. The firefight around the George house culminated with the deaths of Mathew Pyke and Harold Edwards, Jr., during the early morning hours of May 1. The only part of the reserve not under Warrior control was Cornwall Island, on the Canadian side where travelers from the United States must pass through customs. This kept some weapons from crossing the border.

> It was a very hot day, Friday, April 27. It was the day after we were looking for Horace Cook, and Brian Cole was beaten up. There was a lot of gunfire on the reservation, and people began to evacuate. Mike Mitchell passed the word, through various sources, that the Canadian militia was coming in ... I wasn't sure if I should leave, but because of my stance against the Warriors, who now controlled most of Akwesasne, I decided I should go. I was told I should leave. I started loading papers

> and clothes, and someone came over and said that my brother Davey had shot someone, a Warrior, in the chest.[40]

Instead of driving to Cornwall, Doug went to his brother's house, to discover that the rumored shooting hadn't happened. Instead:

> Davey had put stones in the road [to impede Warrior vehicles]. He said he wouldn't leave until the militia came in. We expected them that evening. If a Warrior vehicle came by to see if he had left the house, he would tell them they couldn't pass. He gave them three warnings. After the third, he shot out their tires. He did that to two vehicles. Very quickly the Warriors retreated from that area, and the word over the scanner was "Don't go near that area. Dave George is crazy. Don't provoke a fight with him."[41]

Many families around them decided to evacuate; the Georges had decided to remain on the reservation. The George brothers secluded themselves along with four other Mohawks in David George's house in Snye, built of stone and brown-stained wood, overlooking the Saint Lawrence River. When the firing began, they found themselves "boxed in," according to Doug. "They kept firing and firing, but they couldn't hit anything." The men inside the house returned fire with shotguns and .223 caliber firearms. A citizens-band scanner in the house that had been fixed on the Warriors' frequency constantly crackled with threats aimed at the people in the house.

> On-and-off gunfire went on for two days after that, until Sunday morning [April 29]. We were really tired. We were under a lot of stress. We didn't fire at anything specific. Our aim was to make a lot of noise, so we fired over the tops of trees. There was no place for us to go, because my brother's house is surrounded on three sides by water, and by a hill on the other side. Our intent was never to hurt any one, but just to maintain our position until the bloody Canadian militia got there. ... People would come over in the middle of the day, and give us supplies, thinking it was safe.
>
> Sunday morning, I asked Darren [one of the people in the house] to relay a message to the Warrior Society, whom we assumed were the ones shooting at us. Sure enough, he contacted Tommy Square, meeting him a quarter of a mile down the road where Davey had felled a tree to keep them from using their vehicles to attack us. The message was that the people in the George house didn't want to hurt anyone. They just wanted to maintain their position until we could get help.[42]

The terms seemed agreeable, and Doug gave Square some clips from an AK-47 that had been confiscated as a gesture of good will. "I asked him if he would go to the Warrior base, ask them to leave us alone. He said he would agree to that." Later, Darren went to the Warrior base and got the word that the people in the George house "could go fuck themselves."

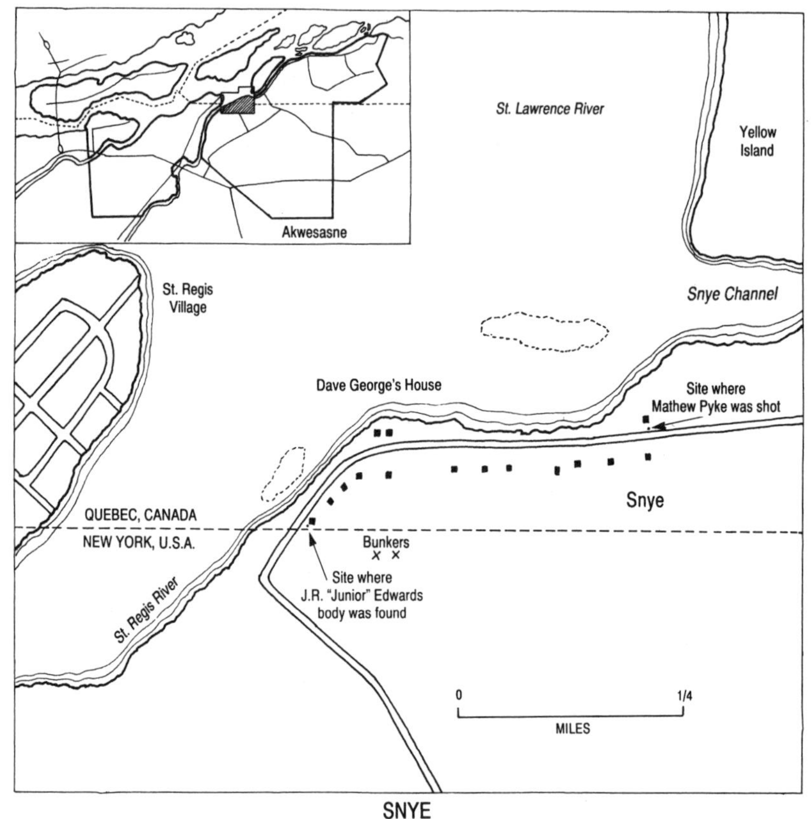

SNYE
Site of Gun Battle Late April–May 1, 1990

> That night was when we got the really intense gunfire, on and off, for quite a few hours. The next evening [April 30], we finally got a break at my brother's house, and I went over to the Traveling College [on Cornwall Island]. We had to go by a very roundabout way, miles and miles out of our way ... Several people there agreed to come back with us, but we couldn't take any weapons across the border. There were a number of extra firearms at my brother's house, mainly hunting rifles. People had brought them over.[43]

Two Canadian journalists joined them a little later. Doug warned them of the risk, but they agreed to take the risk.

> Those of us who had been there for four days previous were desperate to find any corner to get some rest. ... We now had several people. I was given a rifle, I'm not sure where it came from, an AR-15. I was shown how to use it. We were assigned positions. The leaders at this time were Ron Lazore, a police officer and a former Marine, and Cartoon, my brother-in-law, also a Marine. We made it plain that this was a defensive position. Shortly after nine o'clock, I was down by the river, behind a wood pile. Ronnie was showing me the characteristics of this rifle. ...

> Gunfire then came at us from the hill [south of the house]. We realized that we were three-quarters surrounded, and that we had only one avenue of escape, down the River Road. There was an intense amount of gunfire. It really shook us up, but we held our positions.[44]

The house got a phone call from the Traveling College, which was serving as the center of communications, with news that Cuomo was being interviewed on a television talk show as the firefight raged outside. Returning to the house from his position outside, Doug was told "that I could talk with him, toward the end of the show." Following an hour-long television talk show, "Inside Albany," at WMHT-TV in Schenectady, Cuomo was walking out of the television studio when he decided to say hello to operators who had fielded calls for the show. After the show ended, Cuomo, as he sometimes does, reached over and picked up a line at random. Doug was at the other end.

> The conversation lasted about 10 minutes. I told him, in a very calm way, that we had just taken a lot of gunfire, and that we were afraid that someone could be killed. He was very clever in his words. ... He asked me if I was exaggerating, and I said, "No, I'm not exaggerating." He said it was an internal matter, and I knew that the governor was going to wait until somebody died.[45]

Less than half an hour after the conversation ended, the rain of fire began all over again, shattering the short-lived peace among the river-front stands of beech trees. Moments before George's conversation with him, Cuomo had told the television audience that shots being fired on the reservation "were not ... at people." During ensuing hours, some of the nonviolent observers tried to call Cuomo at his personal residence, to be told first that he would call back, then that he was asleep. They also repeatedly called all various police agencies in the United States.

Meanwhile, after talking with Cuomo, George had become even more convinced that

> the person who had the governor's ear was Art Montour, and, in the governor's eyes, we were expendable. We weren't getting any relief. The day before, the RCMP, in all its glory, had sped by in a number of speedboats—they went right by us! They had this huge flotilla, and they turned and ran! Meantime, thousands of rounds were being fired ... I don't know how you count rounds from automatic weapons, but it was a lot of rounds. Cartoon kept us going, because he was a combat veteran. When we were on the verge of losing control, under the stress of constant violence, he could stand outside and smoke a cigarette. But we weren't scared now; we were mad. We weren't breaking. And, besides, they were afraid of the woods. Cartoon had set a lot of booby traps in the woods.[46]

Doug, Davey, and the others continued rotating in and out of the house all night long.

> About daylight, about 4:45 A.M., I was inside, listening to the bullets whistle overhead. The men outside heard a woman's voice, screaming, "You can't do that." And then I heard gunshots—pow! pow! pow! A few minutes later, it was daylight, and I went over to the residence of Louie Mitchell, just east of my brother's house. Along comes this photographer, walking along the riverbank. Bullets were going over his head. "Don't do that," I shouted. "You'll get killed. I'll show you how to crawl." So I crawled, with the rifle, and then he snapped that picture.[47]

George would later joke about how he hardly knew how the weapon worked, but the photo of him was transmitted worldwide by the Associated Press/Wide World Photos becoming an instant visual metaphor for the armed agony of Akwesasne.

Cecilia King, an employee of the St. Regis Mohawk School and a neighbor of David George, described the days before the fatal shootout. "I was beginning to dread the thought of going away to school every day and not knowing if my family would be safe and if they would still be there when I came home. I began to wonder each day when I left my house if I would be coming back alive." She had arranged in late April to move her 90-year-old grand uncle from the house to a hospital in Cornwall. Still King worried about her disabled husband who would not leave. King was afraid the house would be vandalized by Warriors while she was away, because she had been an outspoken opponent of them, as well as commercial gambling.

Doug George, Editor of the* Indian Times *newspaper, hits the dirt under a volley of gunfire near the end of an overnight gun battle between pro and antigambling factions on the Akwesasne Mohawk reserve in Snye, Quebec. The battle, which saw over 3,000 rounds of ammunition fired, lasted nine hours. (Photo: Associated Press/Wide World Photos)

> During these few days, David George erected a blockade in front of his home. The reason for his doing this was to protect himself, his family, and their property, and to keep a watch over the homes of the friends of the anti's who had evacuated. There began to be much talk on the scanner from the voices of the Warriors. I could tell from their voices that they were up to something because they kept talking about Dave. The language that was coming out of their mouths was very dirty. This went on for about two days. At various times, they were threatening the Akwesasne (Mohawk) Police. I realized that the types of threats that they were sending were quite serious, so I got my recorder ready and began to record some of their voices.[48]

Shooting began about 9 P.M. the evening of April 30.

> The gunfire was coming from a westerly direction behind our house, and the shots were loud. After the shots, the voices [on the scanner] would say remarks to Dave and ask if he was ready to give up. Around about 11 P.M., the shooting began again, with more harassing words aimed at the antis. During this time, there was even a false alarm called in. Firemen responded, but couldn't find the fire. ... The continual shooting began again around 1:10 A.M. and the sound of it was much closer now. I was terrified by now, and all I wanted to do was get my family and get out. Now there seemed to be a retaliation from the direction of [George's] blockade. The sound of [that] gunfire was hardly anything compared to the sound that was coming from behind our house.[49]

At about 5:30 A.M. on May 1, King told her husband that she was leaving.

> I could tell that he was very afraid, also, as he walked around crouched low, trying to throw some clothes in a bag. He still wasn't going to go with me, but he told us to be careful and to drive fast. Our nephew was with us, and he also heard the guns throughout the night. We got to my car, and the shooting [seemed] very close to us. I drove until we got to my cousin's house, which is one mile down the road ... she encouraged me to try to get my husband out. I called him, and he said he was going to stay.[50]

After King had been at her cousin's house about an hour, her daughter-in-law came running.

> I ran out to meet her, and the news was not good. The voice they heard on the scanner said: "King's [house] is history." His house was shot up with five bullet holes. Three had gone into the area of their bedroom, and one went into the kitchen. I was furious and so afraid for everyone, and [I] wondered what would happen next.[51]

Several people stopped by King's cousin's house during that early morning; many of them left to check the home of King's son and the George's residence to offer help. One of them was Mathew Pyke. Cecilia King was one of the last people to see him alive.

> One of the men came running and told us to call the Fort Covington rescue squad and [to] have them meet then at the end of the road, that there was a man who was shot in the back, and his name was Mat Pyke. ... These men, along with Mathew, went down to help our son and his family to evacuate.[52]

During the early morning of May 1, along the road that runs along the Saint Lawrence River in front of the King and George houses along the north end of Snye, the blizzard of bullets fatally injured two Mohawk men. Mathew John Wenhisseriio Pyke, 22, was shot in the back by a sniper using an M-16 as Pyke approached the David George house. He was taken immediately to the hospital in Malone, New York. J. R. "Junior" Edwards' body was found at 3:30 P.M., some nine hours after Mathew was shot.

Pyke was cut down about 300 yards east of his destination. George said that Pyke had parked about a quarter mile from the house and was killed by gunfire as he walked toward it. The occupants of the car in which Pyke was riding were forced to stop short of the George house and scatter for cover because rifle fire began to hit their car. Some of them returned fire as they ran.

Late the previous evening, Pyke had left his girlfriend Linda Lazore at the Transit International Training Centre in Cornwall, where she and more than 1,200 other Mohawks had taken refuge from the gun battles raging on the reservation. They had known each other for six years and had joined other gambling opponents at the blockades during March and April, every day except Easter Sunday. One day, the two of them had talked about death. Mathew had told Linda that when he died, he wanted to be buried in a cardboard box, "So I can get back to the earth, quickly." By the end of April, with many of the reserve's residents away from their homes, Pyke and others were returning from time to time to look after their homes, some of which had been burglarized over the weekend. "We all knew something was going to happen," Lazore said after Pyke was killed. "But we never knew how far they'd go. We never thought they'd do this to their own people."[53]

Mathew Pyke was shot at about 6:30 A.M., not far from the location of several Akwesasne Police officers who were pinned down by gunfire. "He was shot in the back ... and was bleeding profusely. Bruce Roundpoint tried to get him to the hospital, but he was stopped at a Warrior roadblock," Doug George said. (Hospital officials confirmed that Pyke had been shot in the back.) He believes that the time that Roundpoint had to stop may have cost Pyke his life. "He was fully conscious. He was even talking up until he went into emergency, into the operating room."[54] (The Warriors later denied this and said that Pyke had been shot from the George house after which "antis" impeded attempts to transport him.) Pyke died in the operating room of Alice Hyde Memorial Hospital at 10:50 A.M.

Harry Pyke, Mat's father, said later that his son's life could have been saved if Cuomo had heeded the Mohawks' appeals for help before two men died. The senior Pyke said the delay was just more evidence that the Mohawks were regarded as second-class citizens. He had served in the U.S. armed forces, but when he appealed for help, he was ignored until his son was killed.

By 7 A.M., the gun battle that had killed the two men was winding down. Many of the Warriors got into their vehicles and rumbled away. "We had them in our sights, and we could have gone after them, but we didn't," George said.

Roughly nine hours later, the body of "Junior" Edwards, 32, was found roughly 500 yards from where Pyke had been shot, 200 yards west-southwest of the George house along the road. Edwards had been killed by a blast to the stomach. On the NBC Evening News Tom Brokaw reported, "Police sealed off a Mohawk Indian reservation today after a tribal war claimed two lives. The issue is gambling. Traditional Mohawks believe it corrupts their culture. Mohawks who favor it see economic advantage."

The place where Edwards' body was found may not have been where he died. According to Doug George, the defenders of Davey George's house had "secured" the area near where Edwards' body was later found at 9 A.M. May 1.

> We sent four men, including myself, west on River Road to accept the surrender of Arthur Yopps. Three of our men approached Yopps directly, while I provided cover in case of an ambush. Our men were exactly where the body of Harold "J. R." Edwards was found later that day, (lending credence to the belief that the body was moved after Edwards was shot). It would have been impossible for them not to have seen Edwards, absolutely impossible if he had been at that location.

Pathology conducted on Edwards's body indicated that he had remained alive for an undetermined amount of time after he was shot. The same evidence indicated that he fell forward on impact, not on his back, as the body was later found, and photographed by the press.

Joseph Gray, regional editor for the Massena *Courier-Observer,* had strayed from the press pack to investigate the death of Pyke when he discovered the lifeless body of Edwards. Driving toward George's house, Gray was forced to stop because a tree had been felled across the road near a sign reading Warrior-free Zone erected by Dave George. The afternoon was warm and sticky, Gray recalled, but a fresh breeze off the Saint Lawrence River kept the early spring heat from becoming oppressive.

> Because I was forced to walk on the edge of a ditch to get around the tree, my line of vision was taken from the road to the side yard of a small

> white house just beyond the concrete post which marks the U.S.–Canada border. I noticed a man's body lying near the house. It was about 3:30 P.M. At first I was unsure if he was injured, dead, or simply asleep.[55]

Gray described the body as being clothed in boots, blue jeans, work gloves, and a Carhart work jacket. A hat was laying at one side of the body, near the foundation of the house. His gloves were coated in dirt. It looked as if he had been burying a water pipe just a few feet from where he fell. Blood was spattered on the house wall behind him, and there was blood on the ground near him. The soles of his shoes were also covered in blood as if he had walked around after being shot. "When I walked along the road past the house, the man did not stir. It was then that I first thought he was dead. He was sprawled on his back with his arms at his side and his legs spread," Gray wrote.

Gray sought assistance from a man doing carpentry work outside a nearby house.

> I told him about the body lying in the yard, and he immediately jumped in a car with a woman and headed toward the house. I followed in my own vehicle. When I arrived again at the house, the man who accompanied me was walking onto the lawn. When he approached the body, he immediately took a few steps back and waved the woman and [me] off. He told the woman to get in the car and drive to the Warrior base for assistance and an ambulance.[56]

While they waited a half hour for the ambulance, Gray talked with the man, who identified himself as Thomas Square, a Warrior who had been injured several days earlier in a skirmish. Square described the dead man as Edwards, a high school classmate and friend. Edwards had been at Square's house the day before he was killed.

Harold Edwards, Sr., the father of "Junior" Edwards, said after his son was killed that the young man had been an innocent victim most of his life. The younger Edwards lived alone in a house owned by his father near Snye, drew welfare, and "at times, drank too much."[57] While the younger Edwards did not overtly support gambling interests (the senior Edwards said his four remaining sons were gambling supporters), he was impressionable and sometimes hung out with gaming sympathizers. Edwards said that the blame for his son's death lay with the people who had brought the guns to Akwesasne to begin with. "Whoever killed my son, I don't blame them as much as the people bringing in the weapons in the first place. It's some other people who are bringing them in, and giving them to the Warriors, and then they go crazy. I want the police to get the people who are bringing in the guns and the dope, even if they have to search every house to do it."[58]

The Warriors rejected blame in both deaths. They said Pyke had been killed in cross fire between his friends.

The two shooting deaths created an ironic coincidence. May 1 had been declared a national Mohawk holiday in 1985 by the Canadian Mohawk Council of Akwesasne in memory of Jake Fire. He was shot and killed at 4 A.M., May 1, 1899, by a contingent of the Royal Canadian Mounted Police as he was protesting the imposition by Canada of the band system mandated by the Indian Advancement Act of 1884.

On the ninety-first anniversary of Jake Fire's murder, the police on both sides of the border finally got their orders. After hundreds of appeals for help, including requests to church officials, police converged on the reservation from both sides of the border. Debbane recalled that "at the Traveling College [which had been gutted by fire] all these young policemen [who] had arrived were white as sheets. They had spent the night there and just couldn't believe that they were still alive." To Debbane:

> The night of the firefight was the most horrible thing I have ever seen. ... At my age, I saw the bombings that happened during World War II, so this wasn't something new to me. But never have I seen people so desperate. Never have I seen people so absolutely helpless asking for help with nobody answering. Never have I felt so useless and so helpless.[59]

Later during the morning of May 1, Doug George and the other people occupying Davey George's house were ordered to leave by

A house burns on the Akwesasne reservation at the height of violence, May 1, 1990. (Photo: Nancy Ackerman,* Montreal Gazette*)

police. By then the surrounding area had been secured, as the Warriors withdrew after the night of terror. Entering Diane Lazore's house (from which they had taken intense fire for four days) in search of snipers, they found the house vacant and strewn with beer bottles and other trash. At about 2:30 P.M., the house burned to the ground. Although Doug told a television crew that the burning of the house was "a small price to pay for his [Mathew Pyke's] death," he and the other defenders of Davey's residence said they did not start the fire.

During the days following the killings, about 500 police and troops converged on Akwesasne from north and south. New York state police occupied the U.S. side under a declaration of martial law. Royal Canadian Mounted Police, Ontario Provincial Police and the Sureté du Québec occupied the Canadian side. Gunfire subsided, and a tense calm descended.

On May 3, a list was released containing the names of about 200 Mohawk leaders and other gambling opponents. Gambling opponents who released the document contended that persons whose names were marked with a D, double D, or triple D were regarded by the Warriors as "dead meat." Mathew Pyke's name appeared on the list annotated with a D. Canadian head chief Mike Mitchell's name was preceded by a double D, as was U.S. council head chief Harold Tarbell. The list also included the names of many Mohawk Nation Council chiefs who had opposed gambling as well as members of their immediate families. Doug and David George also were listed.

Asked about the list, Francis Boots said, "Unequivocally, the Warrior Society does not know about any such list that could be considered a hit list." Instead, Boots said the list was drawn up by "community people" to

***(Courtesy of the Ottawa* Citizen)**

list those people who had maintained the antigambling blockades between March 23 and April 24. These unnamed community people, according to Boots, were going to turn the list over to Canadian and U.S. officials to show "that these paid servants of outside governments were actively blockading our people in our territory, causing an economic siege."[60] This Warrior response fit a pattern. It accused gambling opponents of razing their own blockades and maintained that the same people killed two Mohawk men by shooting at each other. Following the two deaths on May 1, John Boots said "as far as we know, the antigamblers are fighting among themselves. Our policy is not to lift a hand against another Mohawk." Boots then slipped in an uncharacteristically candid aside. "Maybe we don't have 100 percent control over our own men, so things happen."[61]

The scenic area where the two men were killed was enveloped in an eerie quiet the day after the shootings, as police sealed off the reservation. Hundreds of spent rifle shells littered the wooded landscape. Empty ammunition boxes stood on end near the roadside, and the frame of a burned-out house smoldered nearby. Several vehicles lined the side of the road, their windshields smashed. Mohawk artist and teacher John Kahionhes Fadden, who grew up at Akwesasne, visited the area May 2, driving from his home in Onchiota, New York. "From Dan's (my brother-in-law's) house, I looked across the river to the 'Raquette' section of the reserve and down the river toward the St. Regis village. It was beautiful ... quiet, with gulls and other feathered life flying about. It was hard to believe that anything was going on. However, it took 500 police officers from two countries to achieve that misleading peaceful look."[62]

In Akwesasne people looked at their surroundings with a new set of eyes, the kind of eyes that death installs. At this traumatic time the Mohawk Nation and the Iroquois Confederacy were now in a crisis so deep that the Great Law of Peace had been soiled with blood. For many Mohawks, early May 1990 also marked the beginning of a new road back, a search for ways to heal a community so severely divided against itself.

Notes

[1] Iroquois Confederacy chiefs to Senator Inouye, April 19, 1990. Copy in files of North American Indian Traveling College, Akwesasne.

[2] Curtis Berkey, Mohawk Nation Council, to Bill Ott, Bureau of Indian Affairs, April 23, 1990. Copy in files of Mohawk Nation Council, Akwesasne.

[3] Linda Champagne, "Under Fire at Akwesasne." Report of Martin Luther King, Jr., Institute for Nonviolence to Iroquois Confederacy and Mohawk Nation Council, May 9, 1990, p. 2. Copy in files of Mohawk Nation Council.

[4] Mike Francis, testimony submitted to New York State Assembly Hearings, *Transcript of the Crisis at Akwesasne,* Fort Covington, July 24, 1990, pp. 461–64.

[5] New York State Assembly Hearings, Transcript, *The Crisis at Akwesasne,* Albany, August 2, 1990, pp. 569–72.
[6] Ibid.
[7] Ibid.
[8] Ibid.
[9] New York State Assembly Hearings, Transcript, *The Crisis at Akwesasne,* pp. 461–63.
[10] Charlotte Debbane. Interview with author. Akwesasne Freedom School, August 4, 1991.
[11] Ibid.
[12] Ibid.
[13] Ibid.
[14] Ibid.
[15] Ibid.
[16] Weitzman's account, originally a report to the Iroquois Confederacy, was published in the late spring 1990 edition of *Akwesasne Notes.*
[17] Ibid.
[18] New York State Assembly Hearings, Transcript, *The Crisis at Akwesasne,* Ft. Covington, July 24, 1990, pp. 440–43.
[19] Ibid.
[20] Ibid.
[21] Ibid.
[22] *Press-Republican* (Plattsburgh, NY) April 25, 1990.
[23] Mrs. Paul Herne. Personal communication to author, October 1991.
[24] Stories emerged from that final week at Akwesasne that would be told for years afterward. Tom Porter, one of the Mohawks' traditional subchiefs, stood on a river bank, as semiautomatic rifle fire sprayed at him from all sides. The people who saw this, or heard of it, credited the Creator with shielding him from death. During one of the intensely violent firefights that eventually took the lives of two Mohawks, Mark Narsisian, whose appetite for a good joke and a good meal is legendary, rolled under an ambulance, only to find himself wedged between the ground and its chassis. He asked the Creator not to send the vehicle on an emergency run until he could get someone to roll it off him.
[25] New York State Assembly Hearings, Transcipt, *The Crisis of Akwesasne,* pp. 441–42.
[26] Rick Hornung, *One Nation Under the Gun: Inside the Mohawk Civil War* (Toronto, Ont: Stoddart, 1991), 160.
[27] John Kahionhes Fadden, "Barry, Barbara, and Taylor Montour: A Vignette of a Young Family at Akwesasne," typescript, n.d., p. 4. Copy in author's files.
[28] *Evening Telegram* (Malone, NY), April 27, 1990.
[29] Senator Daniel Inouye to Governor Mario Cuomo, April 27, 1990. Copy in files of North American Traveling College.
[30] *Daily Times* (Watertown, NY), April 27, 1990.
[31] *Inquirer* (Philadelphia, PA), April 29, 1990.
[32] *Post-Standard* (Syracuse, NY), April 25, 1990.
[33] *Standard-Freeholder* (Cornwall, NY), April 30, 1990.
[34] *Daily Times* (Watertown, NY), April 29, 1990.
[35] *Courier-Observer* (Massena, NY), April 29, 1990.
[36] *Standard-Freeholder* (Cornwall, NY), April 30, 1990.
[37] *Times* (New York, NY), April 30, 1990.
[38] Jake Swamp in a press statement, n.d. Copy in files of *Akwesasne Notes.*
[39] New York State Assembly Hearings, Transcripts, *The Crisis at Akwesasne,* Fort Covington, July 24, 1990, p. 233.

[40] Doug George. Interview with author. Onchiota, NY, August 3, 1991.
[41] Ibid.
[42] Ibid.
[43] Ibid.
[44] Ibid.
[45] Ibid.
[46] Ibid.
[47] Ibid.
[48] New York State Assembly Hearings, Transcript, *The Crisis at Akwesasne,* Fort Covington, July 24, 1990, pp. 429–38.
[49] Ibid.
[50] Ibid.
[51] Ibid.
[52] Ibid.
[53] *Native Beat,* June 4, 1990.
[54] Doug George. Interview with author. Onchiota, NY, August 3, 1991.
[55] *Courier-Observer* (Massena, NY), May 2, 1990.
[56] Ibid.
[57] *Standard-Freeholder* (Cornwall, NY), May 2, 1990.
[58] Ibid.
[59] New York. State Assembly Hearings, Transcript, *The Crisis at Akwesasne,* Fort Covington, July 24, 1990, pp. 401–10. After Debbane made a statement to the New York State Assembly hearings into the crisis at Akwesasne during the summer of 1990, Assemblyman Steven Sanders said he appreciated Debbane's courage. She replied: "I have no courage. The courage was with the people who were inside. For us to be observers, we were there sometimes a few days a week; sometimes two or three weeks at a stretch. But ultimately we had our homes and we went back ... to the peace and back to our families. The people of Akwesasne had nothing else but what was happening, and it was happening all the time. They were in the middle of it, and they had nowhere else to go."
[60] *Standard-Freeholder* (Cornwall, NY), May 4, 1990.
[61] *Gazette* (Montreal, Ont.), May 2, 1990. Joellene Adams's experience with her Warrior sympathizer son Richard cast a new light on the two Boots brothers' frequent statements that the violence was the fault of "antis" feuding among themselves and their pledges that the Warriors would never "lift a hand" against other Mohawks. One night late in April, the night that the "antis" roadblocks were forcibly dismantled for the last time, Joellene fled the attack, heading for her home in the Quebec sector of Akwesasne. There she met her husband, and both of them headed for Richard's house where she planned to check on the safety of her six grandchildren. According to an account published in the Ottawa *Citizen* May 4, as the couple drew into Richard's driveway, Joellene's husband shouted, "Watch it. He's on the porch, and he's got a gun." Then Joellene rolled down her window and said, "Go ahead and shoot your mother." Richard then fired three shots in the air as Joellene and her husband gunned their automobile out of the driveway and down the road.
[62] John Kahionhes Fadden. Personal correspondence with author, May 5, 1990. Copy in author's files.

CHAPTER 5

▼▼▼

Law of Peace, or Law of Power?

In early May 1990 the people of Akwesasne buried their dead and went about their lives slightly more peacefully but no less tensely. Police barricades replaced those of the Warriors and gambling opponents. Cuomo no longer downplayed the potential for violence. Life on the reservation very slowly returned to what might have seemed normal to a visitor who had not survived the agonies of previous weeks. People walked alongside roads, in and out of homes and shops; children played in the woods or fished on the riverbanks. People ventured outside their homes very cautiously, however, amid several hundred police who cruised the back roads in a menagerie of vehicles and uniforms representing almost a half-dozen jurisdictions, carrying shotguns and wearing flack vests. While the shooting had stopped, the world of Akwesasne was suffused by tension that filled the newly stilled air like an electrical current.

The St. Regis Tribal Council's office opened for the first time in two weeks as a single receptionist struggled to keep up with a barrage of telephone calls from residents and the press. The Warriors' headquarters at the Onkwe Bingo Jack was open for business as reporters and television correspondents interviewed Francis Boots and others outside its bullet-shattered front door. Alison Caulkins, a reporter for the Plattsburgh *Press-Republican*, who had covered the crisis for some time, watched with some degree of awe as the reservation filled up with media people from around the world drawn by the killings, lending "a twilight-zone atmosphere of police presence and the fast-talking reporters who want to interview everybody and photograph everything."[1]

Hilda Smoke, a subchief on the U.S. elected council, said,

> We have an uneasy calm at Akwesasne right now, people are expecting something drastic to happen. The whole community is suffering from lack of sleep. [People] have trouble socializing, are paranoid, and families are having difficulty trusting one another. It is an uneasy trust. A great number of families are still at odds. Father against son, mother against daughter, sisters against brothers, *et cetera*. Our children and grandchildren are having the same problems. They are quiet, not really playing, not smiling. [They are] fighting, very unhappy, and clinging to whoever can protect them. The children have lost their faith in Akwesasne. [2]

On May 5 Lee Ann Jock stood shivering in a cold drizzle outside the refugee center in Cornwall. "I want to get back to my house, my kitchen," she said. Jock had been living with her three children in a small room at the transport center, clothing them with items she had managed to stuff into a large green trash bag before she fled her home at Akwesasne. "I'm not afraid to die," she said, "But it's my kids. I don't want them to see any more violence." Jock said that during their last days at Akwesasne, when the firefights reached their peak, her 4-year-old daughter would scream whenever she heard bullets. Her 10-year-old son asked her for the *Bible*. During that horrible week, her younger brother, a Warrior, had faced off with guns against her husband and father. "My brother, who I still love, was pointing a gun at his family," Jock said, falteringly. "This is what it has come to."[3]

One of the faces in the press pack during the week after the shootings was Rick Hornung, who was preparing a long piece for the May 15 issue of the *Village Voice*.[4] The piece was virtually a Warrior manifesto. Hornung managed to take back to Manhattan whole episodes that do not appear in other eyewitness accounts or in the daily newspaper coverage. The night of the firefight when Pyke and Edwards were killed, for example, Hornung wrote that the George brothers and others accompanying them helped initiate the whole thing by firing on a Warrior speedboat on the river north of David George's house.

Hornung also mixed up the complex geography of the area. For example, he said that Snye (the area where the two men were shot to death) was also the site of blockades meant to block charter buses full of Canadians from reaching the casinos. Snye is on the Canadian side of the reservation, isolated from Route 37 on the U.S. side, which is the site of the casinos. Had he studied a detailed map of Akwesasne, Hornung would have quickly realized that there was nothing to blockade in Snye.

Hornung portrayed Art Kakwirakeron Montour as ". . . a strapping, six-foot-four Warrior with black braids who has been a leader of Indian struggles for 20 years. 'Our whole way of life is on the line' [Montour said]."[5] Similarly, Warrior Mark Maracle, who had earlier been forced to run a gauntlet of angry gambling opponents, was presented as "an imposing, six-foot-six man who speaks in rapid-fire cadence."[6] Hornung painted gambling opponents as "Tontos," or toadies to the white man. Hornung quoted Maracle: "You can say that we have our Tontos, who you would call the good, patient Indian, who says 'O.K., Kimosabi, it's a pleasure to work with the white man.' " Jake Swamp didn't know quite what to make of Hornung's description of him as a "roly-poly" apologist for gambling opponents' purported "sellout" of Mohawk sovereignty.[7] The *Village Voice* piece presented the casinos as the Mohawks' modern economic salvation; the gaming establishments were said to employ 700 people, generating ancillary jobs in gas stations, restaurants, and gas stations along the "strip." Hornung did not tell *Village Voice* readers that many of the casino employees were nonnatives hired from small towns around the reservation.

In his *Village Voice* piece, Hornung elevated Francis Boots (whom he called a "spindly chain smoker") to "elected war chief" of the Mohawks (the Warriors maintained that their own clan mothers had authority to do such things), and a man of peace. He quoted Boots, "We [the 'Warriors'] would never attack a fellow Mohawk."[8] Hornung came away from Mohawk Country with a conception of Iroquois governance that appears nowhere else in historical or later anthropological accounts, not to mention Iroquois oral history. He called the Grand Council the "Fire Council," stated that the Mohawk Nation Council was created by European colonization, and presented the Warrior Society as a "resurrection" of some unnamed ancient Mohawk tradition.

The Mohawk language does not even contain a word that can be translated as *warrior*, although it *does* contain 26 terms related to basket making. Mohawk history contains nothing comparable to the role the Warriors were asserting at Akwesasne in the late twentieth century. The Iroquois governmental system that predates European contact *does* employ the term *war chiefs* who mobilize people in time of conflict with outside aggressors. In peacetime these individuals revert to advocates for the benefit of the people at large, engaging in such tasks as bringing people's concerns before the Grand Council. There is no precedent in Iroquois history or tradition for a para-military Warrior force maintained to defend economic interests of some Iroquois against others within the confederacy.

Two days after the deaths of Pyke and Edwards, 25 officials representing five different governments in the United States and Canada met in suburban Montreal to search for a long-term solution to the gambling crisis. The Canadian government had long insisted on such a meeting. The most important proposal to emerge from the one-day meeting favored a single, unified council to replace the three that governed the reservation. While the meeting sounded like a powerful initiative, it had some flaws. The biggest problem with the meeting was that no Mohawks were invited. In typical paternalistic style, the officials told the Mohawks they would be briefed.

Harold Tarbell liked the idea of a single council. Most of the Mohawk Nation Council chiefs and Canadian-council members also endorsed the proposal. Francis Boots summed up the Warriors' feelings:

> We didn't know about the meeting, nor were we participants in it. That's the problem. The people are never consulted about decisions made for their benefit. How can it benefit Akwesasne if we are not part of the solution?[9]

At the same time the officials met near Montreal, some of the Canadian Army that had been rushed to Cornwall pulled out. Hundreds of police from the United States and Canada remained. New York State Police Superintendent Thomas Constantine, who had been so reluctant to send his troopers onto the reservation, said, "We don't want any further violence to occur. There has been no firing at night and no assaults. It's stable now, but that's because there's a tremendous police presence."[10]

Fletcher Graves, a conciliator in the community-relations office of the U.S. Justice Department, said that no easy long-term solution to the crisis was in sight. Graves had observed the situation at Akwesasne for 15 years and had not expected the two murders. "If the casinos would close down tomorrow, there would still be a good deal of strife. ... It is about gambling, but not just about gambling. Gambling is a major issue, but ultimately who governs the reservation is the overriding issue."[11]

During the spring of 1990 gambling advocates continued their strategy to fill the elective council on the U.S. side with their supporters. Two of the three chiefs, Leo David Jacobs and Lincoln White, openly sided with them. In a month, gambling supporters would have a shot at the third and final seat on the council occupied by gambling opponent Harold Tarbell.

The gamblers' growing dominance of the U.S. council was no accident. All the gambling enterprises and most of their Mohawk workers lived in areas under U.S. jurisdiction. Many Mohawks often refused to vote for the elected council as well, so the election results overstated support for gambling.

Despite widespread opposition to gambling on the Canadian side of Akwesasne, gaming proponents tried to fashion a crude coup during the first week in May. By their account, they "impeached" the 12 chiefs of the Mohawk Council of Akwesasne along with Grand Chief Mitchell. The gambling supporters claimed they had assembled 500 names on a petition to support the impeachment. The elected chiefs said that only 200 people had signed the petition. Canadian government officials continued to recognize the elected council.

Funeral services for Mathew Pyke began at 2 P.M. May 4 at the St. Regis Catholic Church. Several hundred mourners had marched, arm in arm, one mile from the home of Mathew's parents to the church's limestone sanctuary along a river bank. During the hour-long walk, mourners sang "Give Peace a Chance," the John Lennon song that had been a favorite at the blockades.

Mourners carried the body to the church in a mahogany coffin along with a picture of Mathew. "We are stunned ... paralyzed with the realization. Does it really have to be this way?" asked the Rev. Thomas F. Egan. More than 400 people packed the church, standing shoulder to shoulder along about 20 rows of wooden pews. Despite police blockades at a dozen places around the reservation and official pledges that only friends and relatives of the Pyke family would be allowed through them, at least 100 reporters and camera operators swarmed around the funeral procession. They even invaded the graveyard as Mathew was buried. Only in the church did the mourners achieve some relief from the intrusive reporters.

Funeral services for "Junior" Edwards were held the following Monday in St. Patrick's church at Hogansburg. About 500 people attended, both supporters and opponents of gambling. "Junior" was buried in St. Joseph's Cemetery in Hogansburg. Police had been asked to bar all nonresidents of the reservation, including the press, from the brief service. Several hundred people, many of whom had known "Junior" as an ironworker, also had paid their respects at a wake, held in a local parish hall, the previous weekend.

"I never heard him say anything about closing the casinos, or keeping them open," said Clayton Jackson, a cousin of "Junior." "He was friendly with both sides—he had relatives on both sides. He loved playing bingo, but other than that, he minded his own cup of tea."[12] "There's no hard feelings. Everybody was at the wake," said an unidentified Warrior. "He was just at the wrong place at the wrong time," said Rev. Thomas F. Egan, the priest who conducted "Junior's" funeral service.[13]

As the number of days of police-enforced peace on the reservation stretched to a week, some of the people who had fled the reservation began to return to their homes. Others were reluctant. "I'd like to go home, yet I don't want to," Sharon Wheeler said. "People shooting at you. It's a horrible experience to go through."[14]

Estimates of the number of people who fled Akwesasne at the height of the violence vary from a few hundred (according to gambling supporters) to more than half the population. According to the Mohawk Council of Akwesasne, 2,667 of 3,920 people living on the Canadian side of the reserve left their homes, while roughly 1,000 of 4,239 people on the U.S. side moved out. A number stayed in Canadian motels and hotels or moved to similar temporary accommodations on the U.S. side. Approximately a thousand people stayed with relatives off the reservation and another 1,000 people were listed as "displaced but not evacuated from [the] community." The Mohawk Council of Akwesasne estimated that about 2,000 people were sheltered in public facilities at the Transport Canada Training Institute in

Cornwall, where they crowded into a space meant to accommodate 600. Many lived eight to a small room. Some were even taken in by residents of Cornwall, Ontario, who did not even know them. They knew only that the Mohawks were fleeing in danger of their lives.[15]

On May 7, almost a week after the two deaths caused Cuomo to reverse his opposition to a police presence on the reservation, the governor said that his conditions for negotiations had been met. Violence had stopped, the extra-legal barricades had come down, and the casinos had remained closed. Cuomo refused to include Mohawk Nation Council chiefs in his proposed negotiations, however. Elected chief Tarbell took issue with this display of historical ignorance during a meeting with the governor on May 8. "If you want a solution that's going to be effective, and you want peace at Akwesasne, that's the way it will have to be done," Tarbell told Cuomo. "That's a practical reality and a political reality."[16]

While he fought Tarbell on the inclusion of Mohawk Nation Council chiefs in the negotiations, Cuomo also began to pick up an idea that had been advanced long before by Harold Tarbell and other gambling opponents: the bill would have created a legitimate police force on the U.S. side of the reservation. The area had gone without a police force since 1981. The existing one was disbanded by a tribal vote of 325 to 307 after complaints from Mohawks that it had become a "goon squad," a private instrument of the elected chiefs, whom many Mohawks had long maintained were corrupt.

In the face of allegations that the Mohawk Sovereignty Security Force were progambling "goons" themselves, John Boots said that the Warriors were the traditional people on the reservation. He asserted that leaders of a unified tribal council should be selected by clan mothers from lineages maintained by the Akwesasne Mohawks' three clans—Turtle, Wolf, and Bear. As for the chiefs *already* so installed, Boots said they all ought to be replaced, presumably because they did not see things the Warriors' way.

On May 9, after six hours of negotiations with Henrik N. Dullea, a state operations officer who was acting as a mediator for New York State, St. Regis Council chiefs Tarbell, Jacobs, and White signed an agreement seeking a U.S. reservation police force. The action itself was hardly newsworthy. The council had long been on record advocating such a force. The real news was that the three elected chiefs met as a group. They had not spent more than a few minutes in the same room together for more than a month. Jacobs and White said they thought the new force should operate only on the U.S. side of the border, but Tarbell agreed with Cuomo's assertion that both sides of the reservation should have a unified force. Such a force would have been much harder for the Warriors to influence because it would be under partial jurisdiction of the antigambling chiefs of the Canadian council. Gambling supporters, including chiefs Jacobs and White, seemed to be looking for ways to deputize the Warriors along the lines of the previous April 18 agreement that had so infuriated the chiefs of the Mohawk Nation Council and Iroquois Confederacy. Tarbell said that such a move would repeat the degeneration of the reservation police into a "goon squad," the same problem that had led to its dissolution a decade earlier. Tarbell said that a "law-enforcement vacuum" on the U.S. side of the reservation had made possible the inroads of "illegal casinos, drug-running, cigarette smuggling ... all done in the name of Mohawk sovereignty, but done for personal advantage."[17]

Meanwhile, the 26 members of the Black and Puerto Rican Caucus in the New York State Assembly endorsed Tarbell's demand that Cuomo include Mohawk Nation Council chiefs in negotiations. At the same time, the caucus' members expressed "drastic concern" regarding Cuomo's relationship with Art Kakwirakeron Montour, Warrior spokesman and self-proclaimed voice of Mohawk sovereignty. "No one is condemning [Cuomo] for having a relationship with Mr. Montour," said Paul C. Webster, secretary of the caucus. They have questions about him dealing with a convicted criminal and not the leaders of the Akwesasne nation." Mr. Webster compared Cuomo's dealings with Montour to official sanction of drug-running gangs in New York City. Would Cuomo ignore constituted authority and do official business with the drug lords?[18]

On May 12 and 13 the Iroquois Confederacy's Grand Council drew more than one hundred chiefs, subchiefs, and other delegates to Onondaga to discuss the crisis at Akwesasne. After talking for eight hours each day, the Grand Council decided, by consensus, to ask Cuomo to postpone the scheduled June 2 U.S. tribal election. The council also requested a state investigation into the conduct of elected chiefs Jacobs and White. Acting with his usual ignorance of Iroquois politics, Cuomo did not acknowledge the Grand Council's requests, much less act on them.

However, by mid-May Cuomo laid aside his objection to meeting with the Mohawk Nation Council's leaders. Tom Porter, one of several Mohawk Nation Council chiefs who met with Cuomo in Albany May 17, also had attended the Grand Council meeting four days earlier. Porter emerged from the meeting with the governor skeptical of what he had heard. Perhaps Porter felt a little manipulated by a master politician adept at sounding capable of being all things to all people.

> When you get up in the morning and the sun is shining and the wind is warm, you feel good. After this meeting, my feeling is comparable. But even though the morning is bright, what happens the rest of the day remains to be seen. The good words, the friendliness from the governor. We'll be able to measure it in the days to come if there's any substance to it other than friendliness.[19]

Porter elaborated on his characterization of Cuomo saying, "He mesmerizes people. You think he's the most wonderful uncle. You feel like, gosh, I can trust [him]."[20]

Porter said that Mohawk Nation Council chiefs had been requesting a meeting with Cuomo regarding the gambling crisis at Akwesasne for more than a year. It had taken a year of violence, including two deaths, followed by a crash course in Iroquois governance for Cuomo to acknowledge the role of the Mohawk Nation Council.

Nancy J. Johnson, an Onondaga, had resigned her position on the New York State Humanities Council to protest Cuomo's refusal to negotiate with traditional Mohawk chiefs. Cuomo had appointed her in 1986. Johnson, a doctoral student in American studies and law at the State University of New York at Buffalo, said, "The traditional people are the stabilizing force on the reservation."[21] Johnson had mailed her resignation letter the day after Pyke and Edwards were shot to death.

As she resigned her position on the state Humanities Council, Johnson underscored the powerful role of the confederacy among the Iroquois. She told the press that she had never voted for the governor. As an Iroquois, Johnson said that she does not vote in U.S. elections but reserves her political participation for the Iroquois government that was formed before European contact. While no accurate count exists of the number of Mohawks at Akwesasne who do not participate in elections off the reservation, New York Assemblyman Chris Ortloff said in hearings into the crisis during the summer of 1990 that "only maybe a few hundred residents of the U.S. side are registered to vote in New York elections."[22]

Even after their meeting with Cuomo, the Mohawk Nation Council chiefs still felt that the governor wasn't listening to them. The Mohawk Nation Council chiefs advocated a territorywide police force under Mohawk control. Cuomo's two bills would have created a police force for the reservation and given the governor authority to negotiate compacts with Indians that would allow legalized gambling on native land, subject to certain restrictions and taxes. The gambling bill proposed to ban slot machines, lottery games, sports betting, keno, jai alai, poker, video gambling, and six other games of chance. The proposal would permit blackjack, craps, roulette, and twelve other games of chance. The bill also would have prohibited operation of casinos on the reservation by anyone previously convicted of gaming charges. Cuomo's proposal also would have taxed winnings in the reservation casinos. The Mohawk Nation Council called on the state assembly to reject two proposals that the governor was sponsoring as part of his effort to bring peace to the reservation. "If these two bills are passed, [they] will effectively promote a continuing war within the territory of Akwesasne."[23]

Many gambling opponents saw Cuomo's proposals as a back-door attempt to legalize gambling while creating a police force that would be impotent in the face of the Warriors' sophisticated weaponry. Doug George called the proposals "politically naive." How could a small, local police force stand up to a paramilitary group that had outgunned the New York state police, George asked.[24]

Micha Menczer, an attorney speaking for the Mohawk Council of Akwesasne, said that the situation of its police officers was "almost like running into a glass wall. They [his officers] are pursuing a criminal and all of a sudden it is like a Star Trek movie where a force field comes up and they have to stop [at the border]."[25] The situation was compounded by the fact that two of Akwesasne's three main communities in Canada may be approached on land only from the United States. The village of St. Regis (where the Mohawk police station house is located) is isolated from Snye and Cornwall Island, the other two Canadian communities, by water. Creation of a separate police force for the U.S. side of the reservation seemed to be no solution. The reservation needed a single police force that could enforce law over all its territory. Additionally, the Warriors needed to be disarmed. Thus, the governor's proposals seemed too narrow, too little, too late, a doomed attempt to tinker with but not replace what Harold Tarbell called a jurisdictional jungle.

On May 9, about 100 gambling supporters met at the Mohawk Bingo Palace. Their major objective was to field a candidate to oppose Tarbell in tribal elections June 2. Melvin White, an organizer of the May 9 meeting, openly blamed Tarbell for the two deaths May 1. "It will be the voice of the people whether they want the terrorist antics of Tarbell to continue," White told the sympathetic crowd.[26]

On May 10 more than 100 police on the Canadian side arrested 21 people, 15 of them Mohawks, on weapons and drug charges. They confiscated drugs, mostly cocaine, worth at least $800,000 in an attempt to break the smuggling pipeline into Canada from Akwesasne. Police also announced warrants for 16 other people. The early-morning raid, nicknamed "Trident," netted almost 4 pounds of cocaine, one-half pound of marijuana, $39,500 in cash, and 12 weapons, including three assault rifles.

According to a 14-month investigation by Ontario Provincial Police and the Royal Canadian Mounted Police that preceded the bust, cocaine was being smuggled from the New York City area to Akwesasne, then into Canada for distribution in Montreal, Toronto, Quebec City, and other population centers. It provided yet another lucrative source of smuggling income along the route followed by cigarettes, liquor, and weapons. The drug-related arrests and confiscations came at a time when unconfirmed reports indicated that up to 50 percent of the young people at Akwesasne also were using cocaine, a percentage that exceeded usage in any North American inner city. Doug George said that the 21 men arrested were not "the big guys." The big traffickers, the ones bringing it across the border for outside groups, they're still there. ... [The arrests] confirm what is common knowledge here. This fight isn't about Mohawk rights. This is about drugs and money."[27]

The scope of smuggling (much of it not by Indians) through the area was indicated by the sophistication developed by customs agents in the area. During March and April, the height of the violence at Akwesasne, U.S. customs agents in northern New York and Vermont seized more than $1.9 million in cash and 19 pounds of cocaine worth $600,000 in street value. During April, roughly $750,000 was seized in an automobile at Champlain, near the New York and Vermont border with Canada. About $302,000 was found in another car at the same crossing March 8. Agents found so much money that they had to import a high-speed computerized cash-counting machine from the Boston customs office to keep track of their haul. The machine was brought in after two inspectors spent two working days counting the $750,000 haul. John O'Hara, customs special agent in charge at Rouses Point, said that agents were tracking one drug ring in Montreal that was grossing $40 million a month. Agents had found $190,000 sealed at the bottom of a gas tank, and $37,000 stuffed into an air filter.[28]

Quebec police took four men into custody at 6 A.M., Mother's Day Sunday, May 13, for questioning in the death of Edwards. David George and Ken Lazore, a friend of George, had opposed gambling from the beginning. The other two, Steve Lazore and Roger Mitchell, were employed by the Canadian Mohawk police force, which the Warriors had long claimed was an instrument of their opponents. John Boots quickly jumped on the arrests, saying that they supported the Warriors' belief that the Canadian Mohawk police force had been responsible for much of the reservation violence. Ernest King pointed out that the four were taken in as witnesses, not suspects. No one had been charged for the murder at the time. However, the four men were intensively interrogated for about 12 hours. They also were denied access to counsel despite repeated requests.

Ernest King volunteered to accompany the four men flown to Montreal by police helicopter. All four had been in or near the George house the night of the firefight that killed Pyke and Edwards. Quebec police prefer to arrest people on Sunday because Canadian law says that a person taken into custody must be charged or released within 24 hours, Sundays excepted. The law was meant to protect civil rights, but it gave the police until Tuesday to question the four men before deciding to charge or release them.

Shortly after Quebec police detained two of its officers, the entire Mohawk police force resigned its commission with the Sureté du Québec in protest. Chief Lloyd Benedict, co-chairman of the Akwesasne police commission, said that the Mohawk police had repeatedly asked for Quebec police backup to deal with the Warriors and been refused. He also said that the resignation of commission from the Quebec police would not interfere with the reservation police's legal duties to patrol the Canadian side of the reserve because they retained their commission with the Ontario police.

On the afternoon of May 13 Doug George surrendered and was arrested and charged with second-degree murder in the Edwards case.

Many who knew George well expressed astonishment at his arrest for murder. His uncle Angus George, who had filled a father's role for George, his brothers, and sisters after their mother died, said the bookish newspaper editor was the only one of the 12 George children who did not like to hunt. "He was a little cross-eyed," Angus recalled. "He had a patch over one eye, and he was always pulling it up. He never could shoot a rabbit." Angus said, "He always sat in a corner reading. If he got an idea in his head, he would never let go of it."[29] At Mathew Pyke's funeral, George had stood nearest the coffin, softly singing "Give Peace a Chance." To his friends, the Quebec police's primary suspect was not the murdering type. Edwards's father did not think Doug George had murdered his son. "You've got to blame someone, but he's not the murderer. ... The whole thing is the gambling dispute. Who brought the easy money, the guns, and the smuggling in? That's who is guilty."[30]

After 10 days in jail, George was released on $10,000 bail raised by friends within three hours. Supporters of George were not allowed to put their homes up for bail because of a Canadian law that prohibits the seizure of native-owned property. As he walked out of the courthouse in Valleyfield, Quebec, George was met by more than 50 supporters who embraced him and offered him rides home to Akwesasne. "Come on, we've got a deadline to meet," said Konwawihon Fox, who worked with George at *Akwesasne Notes* and *Indian Time*.

The problems with the prosecution's case against George became manifest almost immediately, but the legal system ground on for three and a half months until the Quebec police's main witness, Ken Lazore, recanted a statement implicating George, which the Surete du Quebec had forced him to sign. George was exonerated but left with more than $55,000 in legal bills. Lazore testified that Quebec police had told him he was being charged with the first-degree murder of "Junior" Edwards and that he would go to jail for 25 years if he did not put the gun in someone else's hand. On that basis, the Sureté du Québec suggested that Lazore incriminate George.

Lazore said that Quebec police even presented him with a scenario in which Edwards jumped out onto a road where Lazore was walking. The police "script" called for Lazore to say that he shot Edwards because Edwards' sudden appearance had frightened him. Lazore also testified that Quebec police denied his request for legal representation at least eight times, and that he was threatened and called a liar during a 12-hour interrogation May 13. "They kept telling me I'd never see [my kids] again," Lazore said. The piece of creative writing that the police had composed and forced Lazore to sign during that interrogation was the only evidence that the prosecution produced implicating George in the murder. Once Lazore repudiated it, the prosecution case fell apart.

The prosecution case collapsed during the third day of a preliminary hearing in Valleyfield, Quebec, which was held to determine whether enough evidence existed to hold George for trial, a procedure similar to that performed by a U.S. grand jury. By the end of the day, it was clear that George was innocent. Thus, the slaying of Edwards remained unsolved as evidence at the hearing indicated that he was not directly involved in the gunfight that had killed him. Apparently, Edwards was walking to his uncle's house during the May 1 firefight.

Even before Lazore's testimony cleared George, Quebec police investigators seemed less than convinced that they had a case. They did scant investigative work on the scene, spending a trivial amount of time and money for a charge of murder. On two occasions, police investigators even skipped court dates during which they were supposed to lay out their evidence. After the second day that the prosecutors "skipped school" George's attorney Philip Schneider said, "It seems to me to show a lack of desire to communicate a lack of evidence. ... They are in no hurry to rush and tell us that they have no evidence on Doug George." Scheider had stuck by that reasoning since George was arrested in May, when he said, "I'm not convinced that the crown has a case against him. He is presumed innocent. We're saying that not only is he not guilty, but that Doug is innocent."[31]

Lazore had been present in David George's house the night of the firefight, with about 13 other men, who were returning gunfire from outside the house. Arriving about 9:15 P.M. the evening of April 30 with his brother and two nephews, Lazore was carrying a 30.06 rifle that he later lent to Doug George. Quebec's prosecutors had planned to enter the 30.06 into evidence as the murder weapon and to have Lazore testify that he had heard George say, "I got one" as he returned the rifle. That was the version on the police report. Later in the preliminary hearing, a ballistics expert said that the bullet that had killed Edwards could not be positively linked to Lazore's 30.06 rifle anyway, virtually vaporizing the prosecution's case against him and George.

According to Lazore, the police got excited when he told them that George had mumbled something that Lazore couldn't understand. The police, not Lazore, reconstructed the comment as "I got one," according to testimony at the evidence hearing. To build their case against George, the police put words in Lazore's mouth that they hoped would help prove that George had committed the murder. Lazore's own recollection of George's comment was "He said something like he couldn't spot any."

Such bald contradiction might seem absurd until one understands that a language barrier existed with some people speaking English, others French; apparently the Mohawks understood French better than the police thought. The police sometimes became angry, combining their misunderstanding of English with a desire to close the case on their terms, according to their own story, as they attempted to address the Mohawks in a pidgin French.

Defense attorney Schneider theorized that Edwards may have been shot by accident on a night when thousands of rounds of gunfire were being exchanged. This contention was supported by statements from some of Edwards' friends that while he may have sympathized with the Warriors, he was not active among them. "We don't even have any proof that Doug George, or anyone else for that matter, intentionally shot and killed Mr. Edwards," Schneider said. He maintained that the case was complicated by the fact that Quebec police did not arrive to pick up Edwards's body until 24 hours after his death. There were also no witnesses to the death. Testimony also indicated that George had used Lazore's gun for less than a minute, too little time for him to run to a house about 200 yards away, kill a man, and return.

George was formally acquitted of the second-degree murder charge November 1. Quebec Judge Pierre LaBerge described how he had pored over the file the previous evening before deciding that the evidence against George simply wouldn't stand up in court.

The judge said that under ordinary circumstances, he would have had to weigh evidence for several weeks, but that this case was so without merit that George should go free immediately. Sitting in the courtroom, George looked up from a legal pad on which he had been writing, took two very deep breaths, and then walked out of the courtroom as a small group of supporters cheered him outside. After his acquittal, George said, "They [Quebec police] were looking for someone to charge, and I guess I was the one with the biggest mouth."[32] He said the Associated Press photograph showing him crawling with a rifle the night of the firefight had been a major reason Quebec police had tried to pin Edwards's murder on him.

Even after police roadblocks that had been in place on the reservation for six weeks were reduced to checkpoints in early June, occasional incidents reminded police that they were in a war zone. On June 16 Quebec police officers were forced to take cover after about 20 shots were fired at one of their roadblocks in St. Regis Village. Two days earlier, two New York state troopers had narrowly escaped injury when a speeding van rammed two of their roadblocks on Route 37.

Over the Memorial Day weekend, Warriors and other gambling advocates staged what they described as a "peaceful protest." They drove back and forth in front of the Akwesasne house occupied by Mathew Pyke's parents, screaming profanities at them. The harassment of the Pyke family was part of an organized campaign by gambling supporters, many of them not Mohawks, to "buzz" the homes of their opponents during that weekend. The homes of Jake Swamp and Doug George also became targets of random gunshots that the gambling supporters used to accentuate their verbal insults and profanities.

The May 30 issue of *Indian Time* carried the first in a series of articles dissecting Louis Karoniaktajeh Hall's Warrior manifesto, "Rebuilding the Iroquois Confederacy," a 50-page, mimeographed booklet. Hall is regarded as the ideological founder of the Warrior movement in Mohawk country. He was a member of the Kahnawake reserve's traditional council in 1971 when it decided to sanction a group of young men who said they wanted to "revive" a warrior society there. As "keeper of the well," Hall took the young men's request for sanction under advisement and placed it on the council's agenda.

During 1990 the events in Mohawk Country were accompanied by a rising, often emotional, debate over the future of the Iroquois Confederacy as a whole. At the heart of this debate were two interpretations of history. One belonged to the Onondaga elders, the Mohawk Nation Council, and many of the other national councils that comprise the Iroquois' original political structure. These people reject violence and look at the Warriors as illegitimate usurpers of a 1,000-year-old history. The other interpretation, espoused by the Warriors and synthesized by Hall, rejects the governing structure as a creation of white-influenced religion and advocates a revolution from within to overthrow it.

According to John Mohawk, a professor of American Indian Studies at the State University of New York at Buffalo, the seeds of frustration among Mohawks and other Iroquois that gave rise to the Warrior Societies were sown during the 1950s, when the governments of the United States and Canada ignored native protests against construction of the Saint Lawrence Seaway. Mohawk, a Seneca, also traces frustrations running from the first contact with Europeans intent on imposing their languages, cultures, and religions as they usurped native lands. Ignoring native complaints about the Seaway fit well during the 1950s with the official federal policy of "termination," by which native reservations were to be broken down and Indians absorbed into the mainstream in both the United States and Canada.

Since the 1950s, a larger number of native people have asserted their rights to a lifestyle and land base of their own choosing, sparking the well-known confrontation at Alcatraz Island in 1969, the occupation of Wounded Knee in 1973, and many other less-publicized incidents, as well as court battles over land claims and treaty rights. After so much effort, native people, including the Mohawks of Akwesasne, Kahnawake, and Kanesatake, continue to be pushed and poisoned off their lands. According to Mohawk:

> The Warriors arise from a culture of hopelessness. That's why they can be so adventurous. They strongly believe that everything they are doing is for their own people. That makes them very dedicated. What gives birth to Warrior rage is government intransigence. Canada [and the United States] has to act right and give up real things and not fake things, so [that] there is hope. [At times, Warrior rage runs so deep that its ideology seems, to them, to justify violence against fellow Iroquois.] The Iroquois Confederacy has to do some internal house mending. Cigarettes and gambling don't bother me. Violence against fellow Indians is what's so hard to mend.[33]

In 1990, the 72-years-old Hall was living in a mobile home at Kahnawake surrounded by beech and maple trees. Hall's trailer was crammed with books surrounding the old Olympia typewriter on which he pounds out Warrior wisdom. He is a painter of stark images—many Warriors hang his works in their homes—and designer of the Warrior flag as well as a Warrior recruiting poster modelled after the famous World War I image of Uncle Sam. While some Iroquois have compared him to Adolph Hitler, Hall admires Jewish people, saying that they have suffered persecution much like American Indians, and that they make "damn good lawyers."[34] However, his manifesto was inspired by a former Nazi.

Like Hitler, Hall is manifestly homophobic, but he is an Indian supremacist who believes that white men have hairy chests because they were born in biological union with monkeys. He is also fond of pointing out that jackasses, like white men, have hair on their chests.[35]

While Hall is hardly a cardboard cutout of Hitler, many of his adversaries in Mohawk Country believe that his ideology is fundamentally fascist. An *Indian Time*'s series dissecting Hall's ideology carried a small drawing of Hitler with one difference: One has to look closely to see two native-style braids dangling from the back of his head.

Hall's manifesto, "Rebuilding the Iroquois Confederacy," claims that the Warriors hold the true heritage of the Iroquois and that today's traditional council and chiefs at Akwesasne have sold out to elitism, the Quakers, Handsome Lake, and white interests in general. Hall regards the religion of Handsome Lake, which began as a series of visions in 1799, as a bastardized form of Christianity grafted onto native traditions. He regards its followers, including many gambling opponents, as traitors or "Tontos."

Handsome Lake, who lived from about 1735 to 1815, rallied the Iroquois at a time when some of them were selling their entire winter harvest of furs for hard liquor, turning traditional ceremonies into drunken brawls, often dying of exposure in drunken stupors during winter.

Handsome Lake stopped his own heavy drinking after an illness-induced trance brought him a vision of the Iroquois' future. He later committed to writing the Code of Handsome Lake, a code of nonviolence. He quit drinking and persuaded many other Iroquois to do the same. Many also accepted his concepts of social relationships and concepts of good and evil that closely resemble Quakerism, which he had studied. Handsome Lake borrowed heavily from the Iroquois Great Law of Peace, popularizing such concepts as looking into the future for seven generations and regard for the earth as mother. These ideas became part of pan-Indian thought across North America and were incorporated into late twentieth-century popular environmental symbolism.

Louis Hall calls Handsome Lake's visions the hallucinations of a drunk. Opposition to these teachings is one plank in an intellectual platform that allows the Warriors to claim that the Mohawk Nation Council at Akwesasne and the Iroquois Confederacy Council are enemies of the people and that the Warriors are the true protectors of Mohawk sovereignty.

To protect this vision of sovereignty all adherents, even women and children, are taught to use firearms. Despite an emphasis on arms and fighting, Hall said in 1989 that the most important things in the world are peace and happiness. "I'm glad you don't think I'm a killing person, because others think I'm good for a few hundred dead white people."[36] The reporter saw no twinkle in Hall's eyes. In another Hall-style joke, in front of rolling television cameras, he declared that soon herds of buffalo would be bearing down on whites' homes all over upstate New York.[37]

Hall is quite direct on the subject of fear, stating that it is a major engine of human action and reaction. His preferred way of instilling fear is by force of arms and intimidation, the threat that such force will be used. "What can warrior societies do? Dump bridges into rivers—which are now sewers—and into the [Saint Lawrence] Seaway, canceling all traffic, knock out powerhouses, high-tension power lines, punch holes in the reactors of nuclear power houses."[38]

By such measures, Hall measures the ascendancy of native national liberation. "Legal extermination of the Indians as a distinct people is an act of aggression. Oppression is an act of war against the people. Legislating Indians into extinction by way of assimilation is an act of war."[39]

Any Iroquois who does not subscribe to Hall's ideology is a racial traitor in his eyes, a sell-out to Handsome Lake and the Quakers. In 1984 Hall said that many of the Iroquois chiefs (including the entire Onondaga council) should be executed for following the peace-oriented path.

The *Indian Time* analysis of Hall's ideology found frightening parallels to Nazism, especially the "big lie" techniques of Rudolph Hess and Joseph Goebbels. Like many *Indian Time* articles during 1990, this analysis was unsigned, to protect the identity of authors.

> Promotion of 'nationalism' among an oppressed people enables them to rise above their oppression with a sense of invincibility to a willingness to kill and die 'for the cause. ... Hall appeals to the young in the same fashion Hitler appealed and won over young Germans to enlist as cadets and soldiers.
>
> Those in society who have been labelled as "rejects" are actively recruited ... and are made to sense oneness with others, and a sense of "false love." As Diane Lazore, a founding mother of the Warriors, [has] said: "We take the rejects in and make them feel good about themselves. ... Hall bases his army on the insecurities, social isolation and low self-worth of its recruits. It's this false sense of nationalism which, in the mind of Hall and his followers, justifies their actions. Violent acts on the "betrayers of the nation" with murder the ultimate violent act is justified as protecting the nation. Terrorism is advocated in the name of nationalism. [40]

Hall does not impress all Mohawks with his rhetoric or psychological manipulations. Mohawk Nation Council subchief Ron LaFrance, an Akwesasne Mohawk who also was acting director of Cornell University's American Indian Program during the most acute days of the crisis in his homeland, said, "They [the Warriors] make these guys feel good about themselves, then they give them a gun. It's a cult."[41] Richard Powless, a Turtle Clan subchief who stood with the Warriors early in the 1980s, but turned against them, said, "They have assimilated more than anyone else into the non-Indian type of lifestyle .... They have picked up this feeling that you can do anything to anybody for any reason, as long as you get money for it."

On June 2 a distant cousin of Harold Tarbell, Norman "Nummie" Tarbell won the open seat on the St. Regis Tribal Council. "Nummie" was best known around the reservation as a stock-car driver and a gambling supporter. The election was close (637 to 538). Many Mohawks who sympathized with Harold Tarbell's politics refused to vote because they were boycotting the state-sanctioned system, even though the last antigambling seat on the council was at stake and Harold Tarbell was a long-time ally of the Mohawk Nation Council's chiefs. Only about one-third of the eligible voters turned out despite the charged nature of the election.

The two Tarbells were vying for a leadership position on a tribal council that was still reeling from the violence. On May 30, insurance companies had canceled the reservation's municipal liability coverage. Not even Lloyd's of London would insure the St. Regis Tribal Council's offices. Individuals were also being denied loans. Banks refused to extend credit for car purchases, or economic development.[42]

White and Jacobs had decided prior to the election to allow only U.S. residents to vote, a rule that previously had not been strictly enforced. Following a challenge by supporters of Harold Tarbell, the elected chiefs took the matter to the state supreme court, which upheld the letter of the law. The result created some patent absurdities. For example, Rosemary Bonaparte, a former St. Regis elected chief (she served between 1985 and 1988), was stripped of her voting rights because her home was in St. Regis village, across the Canadian border. Neither Doug George, whose house is on the U.S. side, nor his brother Davey, who lives just across the border in Canadian Snye, was allowed to vote. Many other Mohawks who retained their status on the tribal roll but lived in Canada also were turned away. Generally, Mohawks living off the reservation were allowed to vote if their addresses were in the United States. If they lived off reservation in Canada, they were denied.

When it served their purposes, gaming advocates ignored their generic position that Mohawk sovereignty rendered the international border an invisible-line. The invisible-line argument worked well to justify illegal gambling and smuggling. In the 1990 tribal council elections on the U.S. side, however, such an exercise in situational ethics came in handy; it denied the franchise to several gambling opponents who were residents of the Canadian side, but enrolled on the U.S. side. Had they been allowed to vote, this group might have reelected Harold Tarbell.

Following the election, Tarbell supporters asserted that Carol Herne, tribal clerk and a gambling advocate, had accepted or rejected requests for ballots by people living on the Canadian side with reference to their political inclinations. Tarbell supporters charged that Herne could "find" records for people in the tribe's computer and permit voting if she chose. Conversely, she could also "lose" them. In this way, up to 500 potential voters disappeared, allegedly through mistakes by an errant computer. About 100 people who showed up to vote were not allowed to do so.

Harold Tarbell asked Herne for the list of people who had actually voted, but was told it was confidential. Tarbell said that at one point his own name was even taken off the voting roll. Franklin County Attorney Brian Stewart, one of the officials asked to oversee the election, said he had counted 62 people who asked to vote but were not allowed ballots. Harold Tarbell said the actual number was twice Stewart's figure. "The results of the election came as no surprise to either political camp. Pro-gamblers hailed the advent of 'a new age of prosperity,' while anti-gamblers predicted the beginning of a new dictatorship."[43]

Elected Chief David Jacobs hailed Norman Tarbell's election as an event that would allow the St. Regis Council to make "tremendous strides" toward the Cuomo agenda of installing a tribal police force and legalizing gambling on the reservation. Norman Tarbell himself said his main priority would be to "get our people back to work" by reopening the casinos and bingo halls that had been closed since antigambling blockades went up March 23.

For several days after their electoral victory, gambling proponents went on something of a celebratory spree despite the police presence on the reservation. Men in speeding cars fired volleys of bullets at the family homes of Brian Cole, subchief Jake Swamp, and Doug George just after election day. Mohawks on the reservation who opposed gambling began to talk openly of abandoning Akwesasne, of banding together and starting over on a new plot of land in the Mohawk Valley. One of the subchiefs who talked most avidly about that plan was Tom Porter, who had been roughed up and physically expelled from the Kahnawake Mohawk reserve May 28 by Warrior sympathizers there. At the time Porter had been visiting the Kahnawake reserve with his family to scout a location for a film on substance abuse being produced by Bear Traks Productions of Ottawa. Like many Mohawks, the Porter family was beginning to feel like strangers in their own land.

By the middle of June, the police presence at Akwesasne was provoking nicotine fits in and near Kahnawake, where Warriors and other

Mohawks had used their reserve's proximity to the Montreal metropolitan area to build a large, lucrative trade in "buttlegged" cigarettes. While the police occupied the Akwesasne, the "buttlegged" smokes were going into Canadian police evidence files (sometimes thousands of cartons at a time) instead of onto the shelves of roughly 70 Kahnawake smoke shops.

Taxes and duties accounted for $21.66 of the $30.00 usually charged for a carton of cigarettes in Canada in 1990. The Kahnawake smoke shops were able to undercut off-reservation prices and still reap a very handsome profit because they paid no taxes. Non-Indian smugglers, who used to take advantage of Canadian customs looking only for Indians, withdrew from the supply line that stocked Kahnawake's shelves. Newspaper reports described Montreal smokers driving from shop to shop on the Kahnawake reserve, looking for smokes but finding only empty shelves.

Police blockades remained at Akwesasne through June and most of the gaming establishments stayed closed. Billy's Bingo did reopen during the second weekend of the month after reaching an agreement with the St. Regis elected council that stipulated sharing profits with the tribe. The parking lot at Billy's filled quickly on a Friday afternoon. Customers' cars flanked a display of bulldozers carrying signs announcing that the property was privately owned and policed.

During the early summer of 1990, John Mohawk tried to bring all sides together for a referendum on commercial gambling at Akwesasne. Fairness had been a crucial issue after past referenda on this question were promoted by each side. Mohawk suggested a nonpartisan referendum that would decide whether the people of Akwesasne wanted commercial gambling on their land and, if so, whether it ought to be operated privately as a tribal enterprise.[44] Should casino gambling be allowed or just high-stakes bingo? Mohawk proposed the referendum as an exercise in Mohawk sovereignty and sought the support of all parties in abiding by it. If private gambling won at the polls, it would be allowed. If not, it would cease. The idea was eminently sensible but impractical in a community in which the basis of trust necessary to carry out (much less enforce) a truly valid popular referendum simply did not exist.

As the intellectual struggle over the future of the confederacy continued, tensions heated up again at Akwesasne between police agencies and the Warriors. The police agencies represented troops of foreign occupying armies to the Warriors. In early July unknown persons burned the initials NYSP (New York state police) into the pavement in front of *The People's Voice,* Akwesasne's progambling newspaper. Cindy Terrance, editor of the newspaper, said that the half-inch-deep set of ruts in the asphalt appeared sometime during the night of July 5 in full view of a 24-hour state police checkpoint. She called the act "harassment," retaliation for the newspaper's publication of photos showing state police snoozing at their checkpoints. The newspaper also had published photographs of similar defacings at other places around the reservation. Capt. Richard J. Garrant, commander of the state police's Troop B while Major Robert Leu was on vacation, denied knowledge of the graffiti.

On July 10, almost a year after the gambling raid that had prompted his arrest, Art Kakwirakeron Montour was sentenced to 10 months in prison for conspiracy and obstruction of a federal search warrant. Kakwirakeron made an emotional 15-minute final statement to U.S. District Judge Neal McCurn.

> It's not criminal to stand up and defend our people. You can't arrest the spirit that is in me, and all Native American peoples . ... People in our community tried to find an economy to help us survive. You condemned it. You criminalized it.
>
> You may be able to arrest my physical body. You may be able to injure my body. You may be able to incarcerate me. You may even be able to terminate me. But the spirit that lives in me and all Mohawk people who sincerely believe we have a right to exist here as equals, you cannot extinguish that spirit. The spirit of sovereignty will not be quashed by this court.[45]

Kakwirakeron's appeal for freedom on bond pending appeal was denied. He was led away by federal marshalls, as his supporters shouted curses at the judge. Lorraine Montour shouted at Judge McCurn that *he* was the criminal. She yelled at FBI agent Jack McEligot, "Don't let me see your face on the reservation again."[46]

Mohawk Nation Council subchief Jake Swamp put the criminal shoe on the Warrior foot.

> [This trial] represents part of what we'll be seeing in the future for people who are acting in a criminal manner . ... [Montour] got drawn into the fast-buck scheme of the community. We don't need to base our sovereignty on illegal activity.[47]

Although Judge McCurn had recommended that the Federal Bureau of Prisons send Montour to a minimum-security "Club Fed" type prison in the Northeast, the Warrior spokesman was transferred on July 15 to a medium-security lockup in Petersburg, Virginia, where a majority of the 900 other inmates were serving an average of 10 years each for convictions on drug offenses or for violent crimes. Eugene Ray, executive assistant to the warden at the Petersburg facility said, "We have some security concerns at this point which we believe require Mr. Montour to be under more security than is available at a minimum-security camp." Seth Shapiro, one of Montour's attorneys, said "That's obvious discrimination. There's no reason whatsoever for him to be there." Kakwirakeron's wife Verna speculated that he might be murdered in the prison system and that officials would try to pass her husband's death off as a suicide. If such a thing were to happen, she warned, "There will be hell to pay all over Indian country."[48]

In a 90-minute interview at Petersburg Federal Correctional Institution, Kakwirakeron described opponents of gambling and the Warriors as traitors who mouthed words that the tides of history would swamp with Kakwirakeron's own "patriotic statements ... in support of true sovereignty for Mohawk and other Indian people. Gambling and 'buttlegging' or profits from them are not the real issues at hand."[49]

Late in July Brian Cole, whose skull had been fractured in a beating two months earlier, visited the Onchiota home of John Kahionhes Fadden, Mohawk artist and teacher. Fadden observed:

> He is tough and is recovering quite well. I guess he still gets headaches, but to me he seemed the same. He told me that the [Franklin County] Grand Jury hasn't even considered his case because of the backlog caused by so many arrests at Akwesasne ... Brian's assaulters haven't even been arrested! They wave at him triumphantly when they pass. I don't know how he can stand that.
>
> Some of Brian's stories weren't particularly encouraging. Little Warrior kids are playing in the streets wearing camouflage clothing and they have bandanas over their faces. They also carry plastic automatic guns as they ride their bicycles. A group of them beat another kid seriously with sticks—the next generation in training. These stories really sickened and saddened me.[50]

At roughly the same time, children at Akwesasne were playing a game called "Pros versus Antis," often fighting in school and on buses. According to Carol Francis, a youth counselor on Cornwall Island, "Children are learning that if they have a big gun, they win. If they have a lot of money, they're happy. Our culture isn't like that. We believe in family, and community, and peace." She said that the night that Mathew Pyke and "Junior" Edwards were killed at Akwesasne the Warriors had their kids out. "They were smashing cars and hammering the walls of the community center with baseball bats."[51] Francis's own daughter was "petrified at night" by the violence. "She's woken up at night, screaming 'The Warriors are going to kill me!' "[52]

One observer of the children's activities at Akwesasne wrote, "Stories of young children from antigambling and progambling families fighting with each other are common. Sometimes they fight because of the messages on the anti- or progambling T-shirts they wear, the children said."[53] A 17-year old Mohawk said, "Sometimes, it's like being in a movie, and I don't like it. A lot of the time I just feel sorry and sad."[54]

The superintendent of the Salmon River Central School said that the violence had created post-traumatic stress syndrome in many of its Native American students, a psychological affliction usually associated with war veterans. Native Americans comprise half of the 1,700 students enrolled in the Salmon River Central School District, the largest concentration of Native American students in New York state. By April 1990, according to Superintendent Robert Jaeger, absenteeism in the district's three schools reached 18 to 25 percent; at the St. Regis Mohawk School on the reservation, between 33 and 66 percent of pupils were unable to attend classes. The school had to be closed several days. Usually, attendance averages 94 to 97 percent.[55]

The New York State Assembly convened two days of hearings on the crisis at Akwesasne at Fort Covington's Salmon River High School, near the Akwesasne reservation on July 24 and in Albany on August 2. The hearings were cosponsored by assembly bodies dealing with governmental operations and environmental conservation as well as the Black and Puerto Rican caucus. Mohawk Nation Council Subchief Jake Swamp offered a traditional thanksgiving prayer to open the hearings, which dealt with environmental problems as well as the governance and gambling issues.

The roll call of witnesses was heavily weighted in favor of gambling opponents as the result of a Warrior boycott of the hearings. Most of the Warriors and other gaming proponents declined to testify because of the bias in favor of opponents to reservation gambling. Several of them sounded off to reporters assembled outside the meeting hall, however. Minnie Garrow, Loren Oakes, and others agreed that the hearings were a kangaroo court and not a true representation of the community, Most of the "antis" testifying inside were regarded as traitors and sell-outs to the Mohawk Nation. Oaks said, "You people are having a field day in there. You don't see the Warriors there. You don't see a true representation of the community."[56] According to Francis Boots, "We were not invited, and we did not participate. As I understand it, they were just going around collecting gossip and rumor from the antis. I guess it was pretty much of a Warrior-bashing party, a Warrior-bashing extravaganza."[57]

While gambling-related violence was the main reason for calling the hearings, the future of the St. Regis Tribal Council became the main subject of discussion. Assembly members were given a detailed description of the council's history. Much of the testimony came from Mohawk Council of Akwesasne staff people as well as the subchiefs of the Mohawk Nation Council. Speaker after speaker told assembly members that the St. Regis Tribal Council had been imposed on the Mohawks from the outside and, a century after it was created, that the council had still not won the respect of people there nor brought democracy to portions of the reserve under U.S. jurisdiction.

During the hearings, Mohawk Nation Council subchief Tom Porter traced the evolution of the three governing bodies on the reservation. Porter said, "We can never say that the Akwesasne Mohawk people are not one. ... We were there long before the borders were put there." Akwesasne was started as a permanent settlement before 1755, near a

Jesuit mission that the French called St. Regis. Mohawks and other native peoples had occupied the area on a continuous basis for at least 3,000 years before that, although individual settlements were temporary. The Mohawks owned the land by right of original occupancy, and they didn't need the sanction of the Jesuits.

Salli Benedict, a Mohawk historian who works with the Canadian Mohawk Council of Akwesasne, said that New York first recognized trustees but not elected chiefs. In the early nineteenth century, their main job was to act as translators for the Mohawk Nation Council chiefs and not as legislators. In the early nineteenth century, the trustees dealt with the whole community at Akwesasne and not only with the Mohawks on the U.S. side. The present U.S.–Canada border was not drawn until after the War of 1812.

Over the last century, the people of Akwesasne voted several times to do away with the elective system, but New York state insisted they keep it. In the mid-1940s, an unnamed Bureau of Indian Affairs agent filed a then-classified report in which he wrote that the traditional system of governance "has persisted continuously from prehistoric times ... and is still recognized by overwhelmingly preponderant number of tribespeople."[58]

Chief Vince Johnson of the Onondaga Nation spoke out against the divisive system of government that split Akwesasne nearly in half, in a fashion he likened to Germany before 1989.

> The world is applauding the destruction of the wall between East and West Germany and the reunification of the German people. This act has been promoted and supported by both Canada and the United States. Are the Mohawks any less important? We demand an answer from the State of New York, the provinces of Quebec and Ontario, the Canadian government and the United States government.[59]

The hearings called on representatives from all state and national agencies involved at Akwesasne. Thomas Constantine, head of the eighth largest U.S. police force, testified that his 4,100 New York state troopers were outgunned by the Warriors. He explained that as a civilian, not military agency, state troopers carried only shotguns or rifles that were no match for such automatic weapons as the AK-47.

> There has been on this reservation the introduction of wide-scale armament probably unparalleled in this state. The number of assault weapons purchased and being held on this reservation are more than held by the entire New York state police. Hundreds of thousands of rounds of high-caliber very powerful ammunition, which would go through our bullet-proof vests like a knife through butter, have been purchased by people on the reservation.[60]

Many of the weapons had been illegally smuggled into the reservation, in vast numbers, as the tangle of overlapping jurisdictions and general atmosphere of anarchy kept police from doing anything. An underlying problem, according to Constantine, was the legality of assault weapons in New York: "If you want to go down to the gun store in Watertown tonight and buy a Ruger Mini-14 and a 90-round tubular magazine and 100,000 rounds of .223 ammunition, you have committed no violation of law. Not even a license is required."[61] During the days before the two Mohawk men were killed at Akwesasne, New York military officials estimated it would take a force of 2,000 men, half the New York state police's entire force, to restore order. Yet, after the two deaths, the state police occupied the reservation with a fraction of that number. "People had shocked themselves so much [by the deaths] that everybody was in hiding for the most part and in a state of trauma," Constantine said.[62]

Constantine estimated that 1,000 officers had rotated on and off the U.S. reservation during the weeks following the shooting deaths of Mathew Pyke and "Junior" Edwards, creating at Akwesasne the greatest ratio of police to civilians anywhere in the United States. The police presence at Akwesasne had put the state police budget in the red, costing the agency more than $6 million in overtime, lodging, and food allowances by the end of 1990. The cost continued to mount, although at a slower rate, after that. During 1990 the state spent more on overtime for police at Akwesasne than it did for agricultural research, consumer protection, or investigation of hazardous-waste disposal sites. At the same time, Quebec's minister of public security reported that policing the Canadian side of the reservation was costing that province $75,000 (Canadian) a day.

The violence also was stretching the budgets of area business owners who testified that their livelihoods had been endangered by the blockades and violence. Tourism in the area was said to have declined 30 to 40 percent. In addition, the Franklin and Saint Lawrence county judicial systems were reported to be woefully overloaded by the additional caseload generated by the police presence on the reservation. Roads in the area had suffered so much damage from vandalism and extra traffic that local governing bodies had to request special appropriations from the state for repairs.

The hearing reconvened August 2 in Albany. St. Regis Tribal Council Chief David Jacobs told the panel that intervention by state and federal police at Akwesasne following the deaths of Pyke and Edwards heralded a return to Great White Father paternalism.[63] "The police harass and intimidate residents and violate Mohawk sovereignty." He laid the blame for the violence on Canadian Mohawks who wanted to gain control of the entire reservation. However, Jacobs ignored the role of gambling and the Warriors in bringing about a state of anarchy.

Jacobs claimed to have no knowledge of how the Warrior Society had started. He, White, and newly elected chief Norman Tarbell also denied knowing that semiautomatic weapons had been smuggled through Akwesasne to Warriors in Canada. If that were true, gambling supporters had somehow managed to build an arms cache described as the most powerful in the state without any of the elected chiefs knowing anything about it. However, some of them, Lincoln White in particular, had operated openly as progambling spokesmen at rallies.

During this day of hearings in Albany, Jacobs and White were grilled for more than four hours by the members of the assembly's panel. Jacobs repeatedly said "I don't know" and "That's not what I said" to pointed questions about gambling, arms smuggling, and other problems afflicting Akwesasne. At one point, Arthur O. Eve, deputy speaker of the New York Assembly, reread testimony by Constantine at the first day of hearings in Fort Covington describing the size of the arsenals at Akwesasne.

> Eve: The state police have knowledge of all of this armament, and you have literally none whatsoever, and you're their leadership?
> Jacobs: That's correct.
> Eve: That's absolutely amazing![64]

At one point during Jacobs' testimony, Maurice Hinchey, chairman of the Assembly's Environmental Conservation Committee, asked Jacobs to identify the Warrior Society "war chief" who had cosigned a St. Regis Tribal Council resolution also signed by Jacobs and fellow progambling chief Lincoln White on April 18. The resolution requested state police to intervene on the reservation with the Warriors acting as escorts to dismantle the blockades. The agreement said that the Tribal Council and the Warriors had a "working relationship on behalf of the safety of the community." Jacobs replied that he could not read the signature. Despite the fact that Jacobs, White, tribal clerk Carol Herne, and the Warrior representative had signed the agreement at the same time and place, Jacobs said at least a dozen times that he could not remember the name of the Warrior signatory. The line of questioning returned to this signature at least five times within two hours.

> Hinchey: Do you know a man by the name of Francis Boots?
> Jacobs: Yes, I do.
> Hinchey: How do you know Mr. Boots?
> Jacobs: From being from the reservation.
> Hinchey: What position does he hold?
> Jacobs: I think he has a store on the reservation.
> Hinchey: Does he hold any official position, to your knowledge, with any particular group?
> Jacobs: No—wait. I think he is a subchief or something. I believe he has a position in the Longhouse.[65]

Thus ended the assembly members' final, unsuccessful, attempt to get Jacobs' acknowledgement that Boots had signed the April 18 agreement for the Warriors. The mercurial Jacobs said that Hinchey was insulting him. He threatened to walk out of the hearing. Representatives of the Warriors walked out of the hearings in Albany following Hinchey's exchange with Jacobs. They accused the assemblyman of "baiting" Jacobs into admitting a relationship with the Warriors. Minnie Garrow, who lead the Warrior exodus, complained that the forum had become a circus.

Michael Gus Pyke, brother of Mathew Pyke, showed photographs of Warriors and other gaming supporters attacking and beating him in his truck April 26. "There is a conspiracy to commit murder by the Warriors, the pro-gamblers, and possibly the tribal chiefs," Pyke said.[66]

> Chairman Sanders: Now, in the second picture that I'm holding, the baseball bat is very clear to the eye. The door, the passenger side of the door is open. What is it that happened here? Were you forced out of the—
>
> Pyke: I got out of the vehicle of my own choice. I tried to reason with the people. There's no way.
>
> Sanders: And what happened? What was the result of this?
>
> Pyke: Well, they were going to tie me up to a tree. Take my clothes off and leave me there. But there was a witness there that started yelling at them. Told them to get off her property. And when everybody, all the Warriors and progamblers looked at her, I was outside, I was driving. I got around. I jumped back in the vehicle ... just before they hit me.[67]

Pyke also testified that his brother Mathew was assaulted one year before he was shot to death.

> He got hit with a steel pipe because he didn't like it when the Warriors had their roadblock up last summer. Nothing ever happened with that incident. And I told him—he wanted to go and shoot the guy ... and he put his gun down. He wouldn't go and shoot the guy. My father told me, brought us up not to hate people, [but] to love and respect them. It's hard, but there's hope for these people [Warriors]. They can be cured, I hope.[68]

Cuomo did not testify at the hearing, but some witnesses criticized him for appearing to share in the epidemic of collective amnesia that afflicted Jacobs. Pressed by reporters later in August, Cuomo, who was fond, at other times, of bragging about how close he was to the Mohawks, said he didn't know that slot machines were being used in Akwesasne casinos before the July 1989 state police raids there. Mohawks at the hearings asked if the governor listened to his staff. Beverly Jackson, a resident of Akwesasne, expressed astonishment at Cuomo's attitude.

> How could the Governor not know what was going on? We wrote letters addressed to the Governor. No one reads his mail? The Governor does not read his mail? We made over 200 phone calls for help between March

> 24th and May 1 [1990]. ... I would like the people here [in the hearing audience] who were shot at in your homes, in your cars, in the Traveling College, on the road blocks at the [Canadian Mohawk] police station to please stand.[69]

The hearing transcript indicated that a large number of the audience members stood.

While the assembly hearings were being conducted, the three progambling chiefs on the St. Regis Tribal Council undertook a purge of their opposition. They fired or suspended four council staff members who had publicly opposed gaming. Sakakohe Pembleton, tribal administrator for five years, was fired for what Jacobs called "at least two counts of insubordination within a week's time." Jim Ransom, head of the Mohawk Environmental Health Department for 10 years, also was fired. Jacobs also suspended Brian Cole, an economic planner for the tribe and his boss Wesley Laughing for undefined "prohibitive conduct." Jacobs denied that the dismissals and suspensions had anything to do with anyone's views on reservation gambling.

Ransom had no doubt he was fired because of his position on gambling. Ransom's expertise as an environmentalist was not at issue. As a civil engineer, he was widely recognized as the staff person on the St. Regis council who knew most about the area's environmental problems.

> On July 26th, to be exact, I was confronted by Chief Jacobs. ... [and] accused of creating trouble for the tribe. He used vulgar language with me and said that any time I wanted to resign he would gladly accept my resignation. And a week later I was suspended.[70]

The assembly issued its report on the hearings in the fall of 1990. It recommended repeal of the 1802 state law that had established the St. Regis Tribal Council on the U.S. side of Akwesasne. "The current structure is part of the problem," said Assemblyman Steven Sanders, a Manhattan Democrat who chaired the government operations committee. He believed that the state-imposed system was part of the problem. According to Sanders, repealing this enabling act would allow the Mohawks to choose their own form of government without state interference.

The assembly report also recommended adoption of a new statewide special prosecutor to handle investigations of gambling and smuggling as well as the creation of a state division on Native American affairs to develop economic development projects for Indian reservations, among other initiatives. Mohawk Nation Council subchief Tom Porter said he thought the Assembly's proposals could be realized, although such a process would take a long time. Elected chief L. David Jacobs blasted the proposals, calling them presumptuous at best, and paternalistic at worst.

Jacobs' comments illustrated the clash between consistency and convenience that now faced gambling supporters. On one hand, their nationalistic ideology would seem to indicate their unwillingness to support a tribal structure imposed on the Mohawks by the state of New York. On the other hand, they now controlled that council and did not want to give it up. Jacobs also criticized the state's proposals to help Indians find economic development projects other than gambling. "The state legislature should not labor under the illusion that the Mohawk people are interested in making beads and weaving blankets," Jacobs said.

As the assembly panel issued its report, the Mohawk Bingo Palace reopened following an agreement with the tribal council similar to that signed by Billy's Bingo, which had reopened in June. Bingo operations had been cleared for operation by the state, unlike casinos. The casinos at Akwesasne remained closed pending an agreement with the state that would allow them to reopen under the terms of the 1988 Indian Gaming Regulatory Act. The progambling chiefs of the St. Regis Tribal Council were becoming anxious enough to conclude a gambling pact with the state and filed suit in late August claiming that the state was not negotiating in good faith.

By early fall of 1990 the FBI was documenting links between the Mafia and Akwesasne gaming establishments, something that the Iroquois Confederacy had suspected all along. The FBI tracked shipments of slot machines to the reservation for two years and linked them indirectly with Paul Tatlock (a non-Indian married to an Akwesasne Mohawk). Tatlock had been sentenced to 15 months in prison the preceding January for operating a casino. John Ernest "Johnny Mash" Mascia of Hartsdale in Westchester County, New York, had been charged with interstate transportation in aid of racketeering, specifically supplying slots to Tatlock's operation at Akwesasne. Mascia's partner, Pepper Hailey of Las Vegas, Nevada, was charged with the same felonies. The FBI alleged that Hailey built bootlegged slot machines at Casino Graphics in Las Vegas that were sold by Mascia to a casino at Akwesasne. Burk Smith, an FBI agent in Las Vegas, Nevada, called Mascia a "New York talent" with alleged ties to reputed mob boss John Gotti, the former "Teflon don,"[71] who was convicted on 45 federal counts, including five murders, in New York City on April 2, 1992. The FBI was unclear regarding whether the relationship entailed business or was purely social. "What we are looking into is where machines were going to, and who controlled them. Yes, we're looking into La Cosa Nostra involvement in illegal gambling operations back there," said James P. Weller, special agent in charge of the FBI's Las Vegas, Nevada, office.[72]

In early fall of 1990, a Franklin county grand jury charged 20 Mohawks with riot, arson, and criminal mischief in connection with the April 24 attack in which Warriors sprayed semi-automatic weapons fire at 200 defenders of the antigambling blockades. Six were arrested October 10 after they turned themselves in to state police. Thirteen more Mohawks turned themselves in shortly after that, as the list of indictments continued to grow, including for the first time, cases against the men alleged to have beaten Brian Cole with baseball bats almost six months earlier. Police kept the names secret until arrests were made to keep suspects from fleeing.

By late October Anthony Hope, chairman of the federal Indian Gaming Commission, visited the Mohawk Bingo Palace and found blackjack and roulette being played "in direct contravention of federal law." Hope visited the bingo palace without telling anyone that he was a federal gaming official. The New York State Wagering Board had already ordered the Crystal Room of the bingo palace closed because table games, such as blackjack and roulette, were being played there. The St. Regis Tribal Council took the wagering board to court to prevent the state from raiding the room, and won an injunction. The federal court did not rule on the merits of the case, however, because the owners of the bingo palace said they would close the room after October 22. Jacobs complained that the Mohawks were being singled out for prosecution; the two games of chance, Kwik Bingo and Three-way Bingo, only resembled blackjack and roulette. The next day, federal officials ordered an end to such forms of "modified" bingo. Hope was powerless to act, however. Twenty-six months after the federal board had been created under Reagan's signature, Hope was its only member.

Late in July 1990, as the situation at Akwesasne simmered and new violence broke out in Oka, Quebec, the Iroquois Confederacy's Grand Council had gathered at Onondaga to hear a complete recitation of the Great Law of Peace. The Great Law of Peace is available in English but only in a vastly condensed version that leads many to forget that a complete, oral recitation can take as long as a week. Such a recitation is repeated only once every five years in a simple log building that today functions as the heart of the traditional confederacy on the Onondaga Nation, near Nedrow, New York, a few miles south of Syracuse.

Chief Jake Thomas, a Cayuga, perhaps the only person alive who knows the complete ceremonial recitation in the native language, pointed to wampum belts in glass cases, returned to the Iroquois the previous October after a century of possession by the state of New York. Thomas deciphered the symbols on the ancient beaded belts in the Onondaga language, reciting the law, tenet by tenet, until his feet ached and his voiced cracked, recalling the ancient story of the Iroquois League's founding as a union of native nations that previously had waged vicious war against each other.

Chief Thomas told a story similar to the one subchief Tom Porter recited before the assembly hearings into the crisis at Akwesasne.

> I am going to uproot the tree which is a symbol of life and peace. And when I uproot the tree there is a cavity that goes deep into the earth. And at the bottom of that tree there is a swift river. All the generations that

> you have cried because of the war clubs, the spears and the weapons that killed and injured your fellow men left you in grief. So, therefore, it has been proven that that is not the answer to peace. ... Now I call upon all the men. All the war leaders come forth and bring your spears and your clubs and all your weapons of war. ... And I ask you now to throw them in that hole. ... And they all put their weapons of war [into] that swift water that took the weapons to the unknown regions. ... There can be no peace unless there is logic and there is reason. Peace cannot be attained through intimidation. Peace cannot be attained with fear and threats.[73]

During this summer of discontent, as Iroquois again battled Iroquois, Porter recalled when such things had happened two centuries earlier.

> [As Joseph Brant] began to seek mercenaries and he ... pulled out the weapons of war ... under false pretenses—he was not a chief—[Brant] signed a treaty that was fraudulent, and he sold, with no permission from any of the chiefs or any of the people ... ten million acres in the state of New York.[74]

During this melancholy summer of 1990, the Law of Peace was said to bark out of the barrel of an AK-47, or ride on a poker chip or a bingo card. With contradictions so enormous, with the toll in blood and anguish so high, the retelling of the Great Law seemed to evoke a special sense of sadness and historical reflection. In the future, people asked, would this native political heritage that did so much to shape the societies that grew up later in America be remembered as a law of peace, or a law of power?

Notes

1. *Press-Republican* (Plattsburgh, NY), May 10, 1990.
2. New York State Assembly Hearings, Transcript, *The Crisis at Akwesasne,* Albany, August 2, 1990, p. 237.
3. *Star* (Toronto, Ont.), May 6, 1990.
4. Rick Hornung, "One Nation under the Gun," *Village Voice,* (May 15, 1990), pp.22–33.
5. Ibid., 23.
6. Ibid., 28.
7. Ibid.
8. Ibid., 29.
9. *Standard-Freeholder* (Cornwall, NY), May 4, 1990.
10. *Post-Standard* (Syracuse, NY), May 4, 1990.
11. Ibid.
12. *Times* (New York, NY), May 7, 1990.
13. *Sun* (Ottawa, Ont.), May 7, 1990.
14. Associated Press, *Press-Republican* (Plattsburgh, NY), May 6, 1990.
15. Handwritten notes in MCA files. Copy provided to author.

[16] Associated Press, *Courier-Observer* (Massena, NY), May 9, 1990.
[17] *Press-Republican* (Plattsburgh, NY), May 12, 1990.
[18] *Daily Times* (Watertown, NY), May 18, 1990.
[19] *Times-Union* (Albany, NY), May 18, 1990.
[20] Ibid.
[21] *Daily Times* (Watertown, NY), May 10, 1990.
[22] New York State Assembly Hearings, Transcript, *The Crisis at Akwesasne,* Albany, August 2, 1990, p. 115.
[23] Press releases, Mohawk Nation Council, May 7, 1990, May 29, 1990, June 29, 1990. Copies in Mohawk Nation Council files.
[24] Doug George. Interview with author. Onchiota, NY, August 3, 1991.
[25] New York State Assembly Hearings, Transcript, *The Crisis at Akwesasne,* Fort Covington, July 24, 1990, p. 280.
[26] *Press-Republican* (Plattsburgh, NY), May 10, 1990.
[27] Doug George. Interview with author. Akwesasne, August 6, 1991.
[28] *Herald-American,* (Syracuse, NY), May 20, 1990.
[29] *Daily Times* (Watertown, NY), May 18, 1990.
[30] *Daily Times* (Watertown, NY), May 15, 1990.
[31] *Courier-Observer* (Massena, NY), May 24, 1990.
[32] Doug George. Interview with author, Onchiota, NY, August 3, 1991.
[33] Bill Weinburg, "Civil War and Armed Uprising Shake Mohawk Country," *The Guardian,* December 18, 1990: 12-A.
[34] Associated Press, *Evening Telegram* (Malone, NY), July 11, 1990.
[35] Hall also reportedly has a long-held love of big band music as well as the songs of Judy Garland.
[36] Ed Hale, *Daily Times* (Watertown, NY), December 3, 1989.
[37] Ibid.
[38] *Evening Telegram* (Malone, NY), July 11, 1990.
[39] *Star* (Toronto, Ont), November 25, 1990.
[40] *Indian Time* (Akwesasne), May 30, 1990.
[41] Ron LaFrance, et. al. interview with author. Akwesasne, August 4, 1991.
[42] In early August insurance coverage was restored for municipal functions at Akwesasne through state intervention.
[43] *Akwesasne Notes* (Akwesasne. Early Summer 1990.
[44] Ibid.
[45] *Post-Standard* (Syracuse, NY), July 11, 1990.
[46] Ibid.
[47] Ibid.
[48] *Post-Standard* (Syracuse, NY), July 19, 1990.
[49] Jonathan Salant, *Post-Standard* (Syracuse, NY), August 13, 1990.
[50] John Kahionhes Fadden. Personal communication to author, August 1, 1990.
[51] *Citizen* (Ottawa, Que), August 3, 1990.
[52] Ibid.
[53] *Press-Republican* (Plattsburgh, NY), July 6, 1990.
[54] Ibid.
[55] New York. State Assembly Hearings, Transcript, *The Crisis at Akwesasne,* Fort Covington, July 24, 1990, pp. 379–385.
[56] *Post-Standard* (Syracuse, NY), July 25, 1990.
[57] *Courier-Observer,* (Massena, NY), July 25, 1990.
[58] "Report to area office," n.d. Typescript in MCA files.
[59] New York State Assembly Hearings, Transcript, *The Crisis at Akwesasne,* Fort Covington, July 24, 1990, p. 74.
[60] New York State Assembly Hearings, Transcript, *The Crisis at Akwesasne,* Fort Covington, July 24, 1990, pp. 89–91.

[61] Ibid.
[62] Ibid.
[63] Ibid., 13.
[64] Ibid., 144–47.
[65] Ibid., 116–24.
[66] Ibid., 229–35. The photos were taken by occupants of a house near the scene of the beating, unknown to the participants, and later given to the Pyke family.
[67] Ibid., 231–33.
[68] Ibid.
[69] Ibid., 350–52.
[70] Ibid., 253–54.
[71] *USA Today,* April 3, 1992. Gotti was nicknamed the "Teflon don" by the press after two earlier innocent verdicts on similar charges. After the April 1992 convictions, James Fox, FBI special agent in charge of the bureau's New York City office, said, "The Teflon is gone. The don is covered with Velcro, and all the charges stuck."
[72] *Review-Journal* (Las Vegas, NV), n.d. Reprinted in *Akwesasne Notes,* Winter 1991.
[73] New York State Assembly Hearings, Transcript, *The Crisis at Akwesasne,* Fort Covington, July 24, 1990, pp. 164–66.
[74] Ibid.

CHAPTER 6

▼▼▼

The Cultural Anatomy of a Golf Course

The resort town of Oka, Quebec, population 3,000, lies amid rolling, forested hills about 25 miles west of Montreal, at the confluence of the Ottawa and Saint Lawrence rivers. Oka is usually a quiet place, engineered that way to calm the nerves of vacationing urban dwellers. During the summer of 1990, however, this village of solid bungalows and manicured lawns suddenly became a symbol of native land rights, a clash of cultural symbols that rather effectively summed up five centuries of American history since Columbus hit a beach in the Bahamas and called it India.

The issue that sparked a clash of cultural and historical symbols that set off a political crisis across Canada during the summer and fall of 1990 was very mundane on its face. The town proposed to expand its nine-hole golf course to eighteen holes. By proposing to expand its golf course, Oka residents enmeshed themselves in native grievances across North America, including ignored land claims and respect for native burial remains. By the summer of 1990, native people across Canada would be using the land under the proposed golf-course expansion as proxy for their own long-denied land claims.

After more than four centuries, some of the original immigrants' sons and daughters in Oka were still discovering America, belatedly realizing that Mohawks had occupied this land before them. When the armed confrontation that killed Quebec police officer Marcel Lemay erupted around them on July 11, 1990, most citizens of Oka did not know that the proposed extra nine holes of golf (to be flanked by a new condominium development) were to be built on an ancient Mohawk burial ground. To the Warriors of Kahnawake and Akwesasne, the historic arrogance of Oka's city fathers was a godsend. At a time when they were accused of being frontmen for gambling and smuggling at Akwesasne, Oka handed them an issue

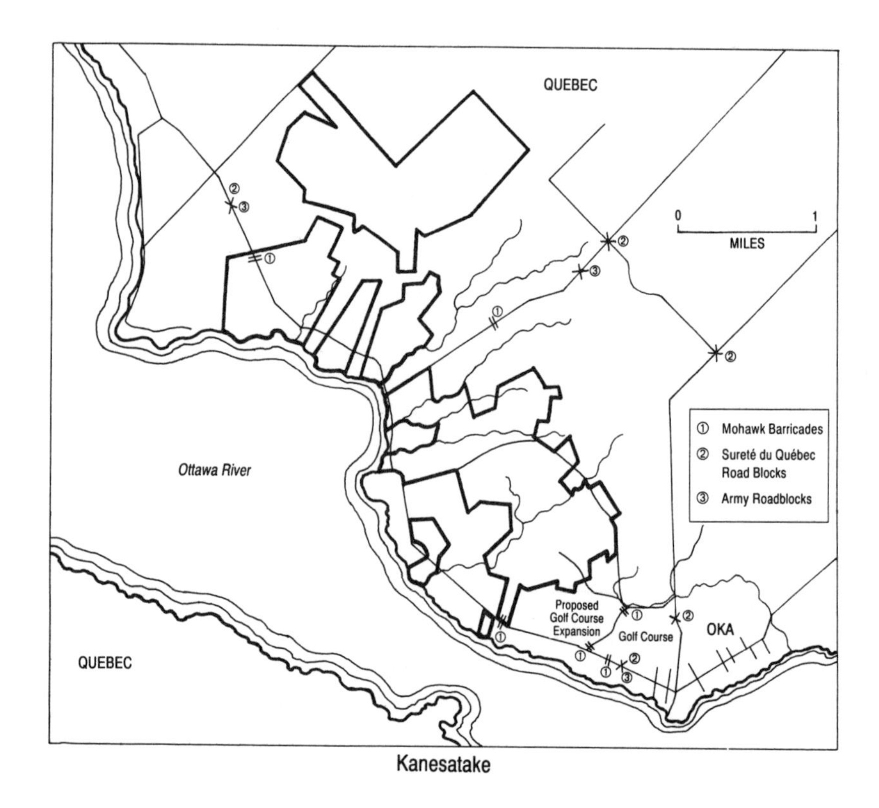

Kanesatake

grounded in land rights, along with the whites' disrespect for native remains that touches a nerve in almost every American Indian.

As tension rose at Oka during late June and early July 1990, Warriors from Akwesasne and Kahnawake streamed into Kanesatake, the small native community at Oka. When the Kahnawake Mohawks were to blockade the Mercier Bridge between Montreal and its southern suburbs, French Canadians in those towns would retaliate with some of the largest anti-Indian marches and riots ever seen in Canada. The Mohawks' actions were to spark dozens of native peoples to seek resolution of their own land-claim cases and throw up blockades across Canada during the long, hot summer of 1990. The standoff at Oka (which lasted longer than the 1973 confrontation at Wounded Knee, South Dakota) raised the long-standing land-rights issue and prodded Canada's laborious land-claims bureaucracy, which had been more a hindrance than a help to dispossessed native peoples.

The native land base around Oka had been shrinking for almost four centuries when violence flared there in 1990. In 1609 and 1610 Samuel de Champlain and a band of Algonquins attacked the Mohawks. In 1717, France's King Louis XV exercised rights to land he didn't own and granted ownership of the 2,400 hectares to a mission at Oka, meant to introduce the Indians to the soul-saving wonders of European-style farming. The

French Catholics planned to convert the Indians to their faith, and assimilate them into the developing French-Canadian society until England took control of the area in 1763.

In 1945, Canada's federal government purchased a small piece of land for a Mohawk reserve, leaving the native people with a small fraction of their former territory. Two years later, the federal government expropriated land from nine private owners to create facilities for public recreation. Much of that land, including Oka's proposed golf course expansion, remained under Mohawk claim.

Oka's original nine-hole golf course was built in 1959, adjacent to the community of Kanesatake. In 1961, Emile Colas, an attorney representing the Mohawks, told the Parliamentary Standing Committee:

> [Oka represents] the sad story of Indian reserves everywhere in Canada: the continuous encroachment of the white man, armed with legal documents, upon the pitifully small portions of the country ... [that remained] after the white men, both French and English, had taken all the rest.[1]

The same thing could have and had been said about native lands in the United States.

During the 1970s, the 1,600 enrolled Mohawks at Kanesatake (about 900 of whom lived on the reserve) pressed their claims to 675 square kilometers in and near Oka's rolling hills, farms, and single-family frame houses. They used legal channels set up by the Canadian government,

***(Courtesy Syracuse* Herald American.)**

sometimes combining efforts with other native peoples in southeastern Canada. They got nothing; Canadian officials told them they could not prove possession of the land from "time immemorial" because other native bands had also occupied the area before colonization by the French and their religious missionaries. The federal office of native claims in the Canadian Department of Indian Affairs also said that the Mohawks' aboriginal claim had been eroded by the French grant to the Catholic Church as well as later actions by the British after 1763.

Even with four centuries of struggle behind the confrontation at Oka, most Canadians, as well as citizens of the United States, knew very little about the grievances of the Mohawks living there. It took a headline-grabbing, gun-toting crisis to do that. According to the archbishops' report:

> It is a tragic commentary on Canadian society that it took some Mohawk Warriors willing to defend their land and people with guns ... to press home the urgent need for governments and society to deal justly with the land rights of aboriginal peoples. ... The frustrations of the Mohawks have been experienced by many aboriginal peoples across Canada. ... Government policy and action has only aggravated the situation. ... [U]ntil recently, [the churches] were willing participants in it.[2]

The report said that the shrinkage of the native land base in Canada had been compounded since 1970 by the Canadian government's cooperation with multinational corporations to exploit the natural resources of the Canadian North, the country's "last frontier." Ironically, governmental and corporate collaboration tended to bring the churches in on the natives' side of land-claim issues.

When the municipality of Oka voted to expand its golf course by 22 hectares (just under 10 acres) of forest early in 1990, the action set off a spark that had long been smoldering. On and off for two years, the Mohawks had confronted surveyors on the land. Sometimes, borrowing a tactic from environmental activists, they combed the woods, plucking surveyors' marking stakes out of the ground.

On March 9, 1990, about 100 Mohawks marched through the forest, past their burial ground, to the parking lot of the golf clubhouse. Allen Gabriel, who had long researched the land-claim issues, read a letter to the crowd, and a few chants went up before the shivering participants dispersed. No one with power to decide anything came out of the clubhouse to watch.

Two days later, frustrated that no one was listening, the Mohawks erected a blockade across the Chemin du Mille, a seasonal, unpaved road between two other more heavily traveled ones. The blockade was placed at a point where the road nears the Kanesatake settlement and on land long claimed by the Mohawks living there. At the time, it was blocked by snow, and for the first two of four months, the blockade attracted very little attention.

Many residents of Oka also opposed the housing development. The previous summer almost 1,300 people had signed a petition organized by environmentalists that opposed the golf course expansion and the condo development. Several residents pointed out that membership in the club that controlled the golf course cost $10,000 a year, a sum that most people could not afford even in relatively affluent Oka. Jean Remaud, a resident of Oka, said, "The mayor should have told the boys to be happy with their nine holes. The Indians are protecting us, also. We don't want to lose the forest. We in Oka have always lived in harmony with the Indians."[3]

The Warriors began to filter into the 2,300-acre Kanesatake reserve about a month before the fatal shootout. While they debated the Warriors' importation of arms onto the reserve, many Kanestake Mohawks were happy to have support in their struggle as the Warriors brought in communications equipment, vehicles, and supplies. Many Warriors appeared to have come from Ganienkeh, the Mohawk settlement negotiated with New York state in 1977, as well as Kahnawake and Akwesasne. By July Desilets said, "I realized the Kanesatake population was no longer controlling the situation."[4]

On July 2 Oka got an injunction from the Quebec Superior Court requiring that the blockade be dismantled. The Mohawks refused, and on July 10 Jean Ouelette, mayor of Oka, stepped into the Warriors' strategy by asking Quebec police to remove the barricade.

The Sureté du Quebec (SQ) massed roughly 100 officers around the Mohawk barricade before sunrise on July 11. Wearing olive-green fatigues and gas masks, the Surete officers apparently hoped they could bring the barricade down with a show of force without actually moving against the people behind it.

When the sun rose on Oka that day, few of its residents realized that the previous day's sun had set on the last normal day of their lives for many months to come. Few figured that their town and their lives were about to become a worldwide stage for a confrontation between cultures. The muffled roar of automobiles pulling out of well-kept driveways melted into the sounds of Indian drumming from the nearby woods.

At 8:45 A.M., about 100 police attacked the barricade protected by approximately 300 Indian men, women, and children. The police unleashed tear gas that a sudden switch in wind direction blew back into their faces. The Mohawks fired in self-defense. Apparently surprised by the Mohawks' fire, the police retreated in such pell-mell fashion that they left behind an assortment of vehicles, including two vans, four patrol cars, and a large front-loader vehicle brought in to dismantle the blockade. The Mohawks and their supporters confiscated the front loader and used it to dump the abandoned vehicles onto a new barricade across Highway 344, built as an obstacle course with vehicles tilted on their sides across the road.

The police said later that they had been ordered not to shoot because women and children were present. Many of the Warriors asserted that some of the police fired anyway, perhaps in panic, as most of the SQ officers and Warriors ran for cover. During the gunfight, which lasted less than a minute, SQ Corporal Marcel Lemay was fatally injured under conditions so chaotic that, after a year of forensic testing, Canadian officials were still not sure from which side of the conflict the bullet had come.

Lemay, 31, left behind his wife Lorraine, who was pregnant, and a three-year-old daughter. Doctors at St. Eustache Hospital said that Lemay suffered massive injuries to his mouth and chest. Although he was alive on arrival at the hospital, Lemay was "in very serious condition. ... He was in cardiac arrest," according to a St. Eustache physician.[5] Lemay was well-liked by fellow officers of the Quebec City SWAT team. He had played on the Quebec police ice-hockey team after joining the force in 1979. "He was the kind of guy who everyone liked. You could talk to him. He was

A Warrior raises his weapon as he stands on an overturned police vehicle blocking a highway along side the Kanesatake reserve near Oka, Quebec after a police assault to remove Mohawk barriers failed. One policeman was killed in the assault. (Photo: Associated Press/Wide World Photos)

funny," said fellow officer Real Ouillet.[6] Lemay's funeral was held in the Quebec city suburb of Ancienne-Lorette on July 16.

After the bloodshed on July 11, both sides dug in at Oka, settling into a protracted standoff. The early days were occasionally punctuated with emotional outbursts. The SQ officers constructed checkpoints made of sandbags and concrete blocks throughout the area. Wearing flak jackets, carrying shotguns, the police searched all vehicles entering the reserve, requiring people to prove they lived there. While the police said that food and water were being allowed past their checkpoints, one Mohawk family from the reserve said it had to go through four police roadblocks, repeating the search each time, to pick up mail and groceries in Oka. Sheila Jacobson, a Mohawk who lives on the reservation said that she had been unable to deliver food to her 12-year-old daughter and handicapped 69-year-old mother because she was stopped outside an Oka grocery store and forced to surrender her food to police who suspected she might use it to feed the defenders of the blockades.[7] All together, the police erected 10 roadblocks, and used two boats to patrol the Ottawa River, which borders Oka's south and west side.

In the meantime, the Mohawks opened talks with John Ciaccia, Quebec's native affairs minister, who arrived at the Mohawks' barricade in a chauffeur-driven limousine on July 13, two days after the shootout. The talks went nowhere because the Indians asserted that the police must withdraw before they would agree to anything. The Mohawks also demanded immunity from prosecution. Despite the lack of progress, Ciaccia told the press that his first day of talks had ended on a positive note. Like Ciaccia, Prime Minister Brian Mulroney seemed to be all smiles as he told the press that the situation was being handled correctly by the police. He added that native issues were now at the top of his political agenda.

On July 17, police gave William Kunstler, the activist attorney from New York City, abundant reason to resent their heavy-handed control of the Oka area. Police kept him waiting in a bus for 10 hours while they checked his identity. Kunstler had arrived at police barricades with Stanley Cohen, a civil rights attorney also from New York City, to join the Mohawks' legal team. On another occasion, an ambulance carrying a woman with severe chest pains was held up at a police barricade for 35 minutes. On July 20, a delegation from the Quebec Human Rights Commission (Ligue des Droits et des Libertés) was refused access to the Mohawk reserve by police who continued to tighten their grip on Oka. Two days earlier, the same delegation had been allowed through. The delegation was looking into allegations that the police blockades had deprived the Mohawks of essential goods and services, including food and medical care.

On July 13, as Ciaccia was opening negotiations at Oka, a ballistics expert said that the shot that had killed Corporal Lemay could not have come from a police gun as some of the Warriors had alleged. Jianfranco Cazallo, chief of ballistics for the Parthenais Laboratory of Scientific Crime, did not say what type of gun had been used. Montreal police also did a ballistics analysis that was inconclusive; their report, which was not made public, indicated that both Mohawks and police were firing the same type of semiautomatic rifle. "We can't say for sure from which side the bullet was fired," a police spokeswomen said.[8]

The report of coroner Paul Dionne, released in May 1991, concluded that the bullet that killed Lemay was fired by one of the Mohawks. Dionne rejected two other theories: that Lemay had been accidentally killed by police fire, or that he committed suicide. Dionne said that investigation of Lemay's death was hindered by the fact that the scene of the death could not be examined until after the 78-day standoff ended. Another problem that hindered investigation was the lack of a murder weapon.

Just before the July 11 police raid at Oka, Quebec police faced a second confrontation developing closer to Montreal. Mohawks at Kahnawake used concrete barriers to block two highways that cross their reserve leading to the Mercier Bridge. The Mercier Bridge connects Montreal with its southern suburbs and carries about 60,000 vehicles a day.

A blockade of the Mercier bridge was a symbol to many Mohawks. Shortly before the turn of the last century, many of Kahnawake's Mohawks first worked in high steel on those same spans before they helped build many of New York's bridges and the Manhattan skyline. Some of the people who blockaded the Mercier span worked the high steel themselves; some of their ancestors had died on it.

By using either a construction platform on the bridge or by lowering a railroad bridge that crosses Kahnawake, the Warriors could also have blocked shipping traffic through the Saint Lawrence Seaway. Instead, they lounged at their blockade, training their binoculars on people passing under them on pleasure boats. Some of the Warriors leaned against pick-up trucks carrying AK-47s, banana clips of ammunition, food, and toilet paper among other supplies.

Others listened to a portable radio during a talk show as callers speculated that the Warriors had tied dynamite to the bridge. An explosives expert, France Goupil, president of Geophysique GPR International, Inc., a demolition firm, even told the Warriors how to destroy the bridge on the front page of the *Gazette*. "Five or six little charges can easily bring down a bridge, just like in the war movies. The Indians know that—they're experts in metal structures."[9] The Warriors listening to the radio chuckled loudly at the suggestion that they might blow up the bridge and considered finding some wire that they could use to taunt the police into believing that they were about to plant a bomb.

At a community meeting three days after the blockades were erected, many Mohawks voiced objections, which the Warriors ignored. Some reservation residents said afterwards in a broadcast over Canadian

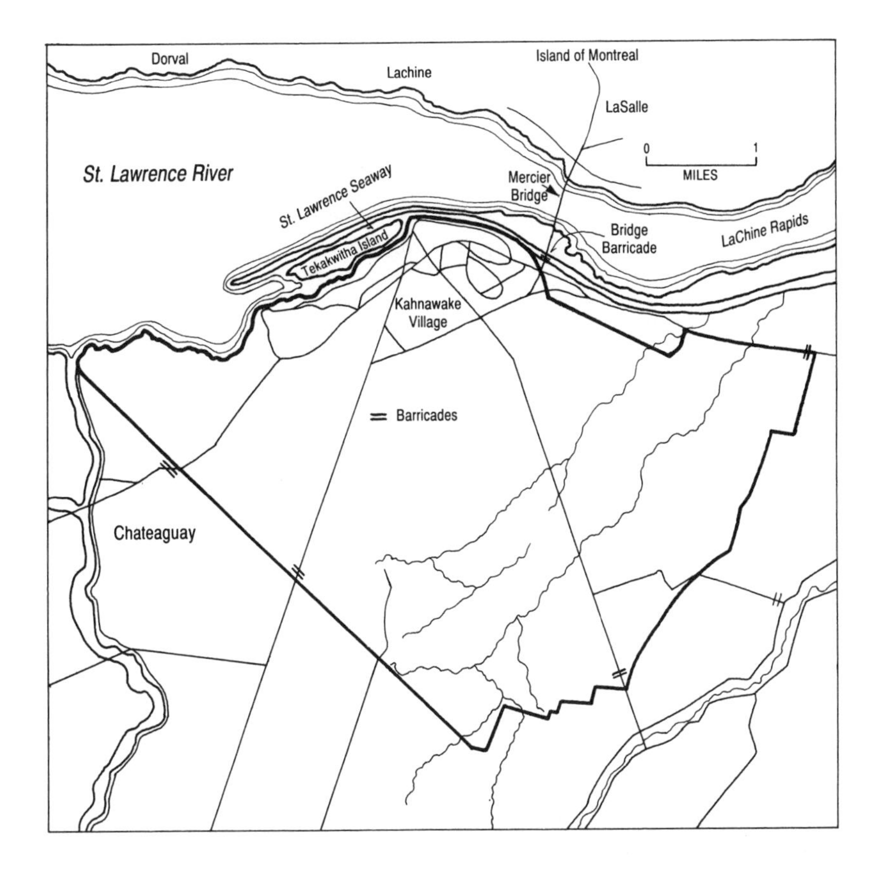

Broadcasting Corporation that their dissent was answered with threats of being shot.

In Châteauguay, a town of 40,000 near Kahnawake, local residents called for military action to end the blockade of the Mercier Bridge within a day of its erection. Crowds of several hundred townspeople who use the bridge to commute to Montreal chanted "We want the Army! We want the Army!" By night, residents of the town carried cameras, binoculars, and snacks to the bridge's on-ramps behind the police blockades to watch the confrontation. Vendors sold food to people in the crowd, some of whom carried signs urging police to "give the Indians what they want—a war."

After the bridge blockade began, impromptu marches of 1,000 to 2,000 people wound through streets lined with fast-food restaurants and muffler shops, burning Mohawks in effigy.

At one point, the Mohawks on the bridge answered the Châteauguay residents' effigies, signs, and slurs by setting a pile of old tires on fire, sending a large plume of smoke over the town where Indian-hating had become the thing to do.

Before the Mercier bridge had been blockaded a week, a crowd of angry French Canadians strung up a life-sized effigy of a native man clad in army fatigues. They had painted a large red target on its chest and stuffed a pack of cigarettes into the pocket of its shirt. As one man slipped a noose around the strawman's head, another hoisted the rope around a traffic light. The growing mob cheered and chanted, "Fuck the Warriors. The damned savages!"[10] One observer wrote:

> The saddest part, in Châteauguay, was seeing the children laugh. Children like the beautiful little blonde girl, four or five years old, who giggled when the mob jammed the burning brand into the crotch of a Mohawk effigy. Children like the dark-haired, big-eyed boy, maybe seven years old, who grasped his father's hand, smiling up in his father's face, as flames ripped another Mohawk effigy apart. ... Children who stand in the streets of this town every night, wearing amusement-park grins, watching fire consume symbols of human beings.[11]

The hatred was so visceral one could feel it in the air. The same day that the first effigy was burned, a non-Indian woman was attacked by a mob because she was wearing an Indian-style necklace.

Obstruction of ambulances became a common tactic of the mobs. An ambulance taking a sick Indian boy to an off-reservation hospital was blocked by an angry crowd that police had to disperse. On another occasion, a Mohawk woman who was bleeding badly after giving birth was transported from the reserve into Montreal in an ambulance, only to have a chanting crowd obstruct its passage. Instead of clearing away the crowd and allowing the ambulance to pass without delay, the SQ allowed a man from the mob into the ambulance to determine to his satisfaction whether the woman was really bleeding. She was forced to open her legs for him! According to one account, "When women negotiators inquired how a government negotiator would feel if she were a female relative of his, he appeared temporarily affected."[12]

At Kahnawake, the offices of the Warrior longhouse turned into a sort of command central with several persons on a telephone bank passing information and contacting international organizations for support. The Kahnawake Warriors also broadened the scope of the controversy by criticizing the Canadian government for asking Nelson Mandela, leader of the African National Congress, to renounce violence at the same time police surrounded the two Mohawk settlements. Mandela had visited Canada a few days before Quebec police stormed the barricade at Oka.

Kahnawake also prepared to host a meeting of elected native officials from across Canada a week after the shootout at Oka. Joe Norton, band council chief at Kahnawake, said that he hoped such nationwide support would "kick the federal government in the pants and get them moving ... to do something positive."[13] Because the Kahnawake reserve had been sealed off by more than 500 provincial police as well as about

300 Royal Canadian Mounted Police, the 150 tribal representatives and members of the press were ferried to the meeting by boat.

As the police encircled the Mohawks at Kahnawake blocking the Mercier bridge, other people from on the reserve tried their hand at an unaccustomed diversion. Like the Mohawks of Oka, the people of Kahnawake also occupied a golf course, the exclusive Kanawaki Golf Club. This course, unlike the one at Oka, was located on leased land belonging to the Mohawks. The club charged wealthy businessmen from Montreal a $15,000 initiation fee, and excluded the few native people who could afford membership. The police blockades stopped the businessmen from coming to the club, and local Mohawks tried the course. "We don't get to play there much," Arnold Goodleaf, a chief in the band council said. Then, grinning, Goodleaf added: "But, for the past few days, we have."[14] One local resident reported that on one balmy summer afternoon, six Mohawk foursomes were lined up at the first tee. Warriors also stormed the freezer of the clubhouse during the Mercier Bridge blockade, making off with lobster tails, steaks, and other gourmet foods.

Indian Affairs Minister Thomas Siddon proposed a solution to the crisis: The Canadian Government would buy the land at Oka and give it to the Indians. Despite criticism from both sides, Siddon nevertheless continued to press his solution. On July 27, a few days after the first proposal, Siddon announced that the federal government was negotiating to buy 60 residential lots (about 30 acres) from Maxime Rousseau, a citizen of France, for $1.2 million. Reports circulated from Siddon's office that the government was prepared to spend up to $5 million for a total of 54 acres that would be added to the land base of the Kanesatake Mohawks. The Mohawks continued to oppose the proposal as "a drop in the bucket" and an invalid commercial exchange of land that they already owned by right of original occupancy.

On July 31 the Oka village council met to consider the proposal that would deed the land to the Mohawks. Two days before citizens with placards reading "Savages Go Home" and "What About Rights for Whites?" had marched outside the same building during the council's regular business meeting. Mayor Ouelette drew cheers by refusing to negotiate until the barricades came down, and a long list of speakers criticized the proposed deal. Later, opposition softened significantly as the size of the payments the government was offering began to sink in.

On July 25 the standoff at Oka entered its third week. Many grocery store shelves had emptied at Kanesatake, but the Mohawks seemed to be getting some food that was being smuggled past police barricades. Reports circulated that the Quebec Native Women's Association was secretly ferrying food onto the reserve by boat. Louis LeClaire, a Mohawk and a resident of Queens, New York was in communication with relatives at Oka. He complained that newspaper reports were not describing the full impact of the siege on residents of Kanesatake.

> My relatives have not been able to leave the reservation in more than three weeks. The milkman who serves our community has been arrested every time he has attempted to deliver much-needed dairy products. His truck has been abandoned just outside the town limits, with the milk left to rot rather than being delivered. People who need medical attention are told to go to Montreal General Hospital and are given a pass to get off the reservation with the promise that they will be able to return. But those who leave find themselves stranded. No mail has been delivered in or out of town, except for a couple of bags brought in a few days ago filled with telephone, light and water bills. With the inability to get the mail, how will these bills get paid?
>
> Sections of the town [have] had telephone service disrupted for hours, even days. Last week, electric outages forced people who still had meat in their freezers to find friends and relatives with electricity to store their perishables. Is this coincidence?[15]

At the end of July, Quebec Superior Court Judge John Gormery rejected a request for a court order that would have forced police to remove the barricades. Ronald Bonspille, Kanesatake's director of ambulance services, one of the people who had filed the request for a temporary injunction, argued that after three weeks the barricades were no longer necessary and a hazard to people's health and safety. Judge Gormery said that the blockades were justified because the Mohawks who set up the initial barricade had broken the law by obstructing a public road. As for public safety, the judge asked Bonspille if the woman in the delayed ambulance had died. After Bonspille said she hadn't died, Gormery told him to "come back and see me" after someone did. Bonspille was very angry. "You heard him. He said: 'Come back to me when someone dies.' You heard him. It's the typical white man's justice. ... It's always like this, and then they say the Mohawks are bad people. Well, when we come to court and hear garbage like this, what do you think we should do?"

More than 3,000 people from across Canada and several other countries came together in Oka's Parc Paul Sauve during the afternoon of Sunday, July 29, to support the Mohawks and to pray for a peaceful settlement of the confrontation. Some of the people at the peace rally, organized by Canada's Assembly of First Nations, offered flowers to police. The people at the rally also had planned to deliver truckloads of food to the besieged Mohawks during a procession, but they canceled the public event after angry Oka residents threw up a protest blockade along their route. The SQ immediately dispatched a few of the 1,500 men encircling the Indians and their supporters to erect checkpoints in front and behind two non-Indian blockades on Route 344.[16] The donated food was delivered later by what organizers called "an alternate route" with the implied consent of the police.

At about the same time, Quebec provincial officials ordered the 1,500 police who still ringed Kanesatake not to impede the flow of food and medicine into the blockaded area. Canada dispatched an official of its Indian Affairs ministry to Geneva to answer inquiries by the United Nations into human-rights abuses at Kanesatake.

As debates over human rights continued, two Mohawks returned to Kanesatake to bury their son, who had recently died. Provincial police removed the body so that they could search the boy's coffin. Such tactics tended to support Mohawks' allegations that the SQ were deliberately humiliating Mohawks to avenge the still-unsolved death of Lemay.[17]

Within days of the shootout at Kanesatake and the blockading of the Mercier Bridge, Canada's summer of Mohawk discontent tapped a large number of long-smoldering grievances among native people across the country. Sympathy blockades rose across the sparsely settled plains and mountains of this vast country. There was a wave of fear that summer among some white Canadians that if Canada's natives got organized and angry enough, they could cripple the country's infrastructure. They could block train tracks hobbling commerce, blockade bridges, and topple power lines from remote regions to urban areas. All through the summer, Hall's warning that the Warriors could shut down Canada spread through the nation's communication media.

Natives already had thrown a political monkey wrench into the works of the Meech Lake Accord in 1990. The accord was meant to satisfy Quebec's demands for autonomy within the Canadian federation. Konrad Sioui, a chief from Quebec and regional representative with the Assembly of First Nations, indicated that the raid at Oka had been in direct retaliation for the fact that Elijah Harper, the only native member of Manitoba's legislature, had led an effort against ratification of the Meech Lake Accord. Harper's vote started a chain of procedural circumstances that kept the accord from going into effect.

If it had been ratified, the accord would have given Quebec a "special status" designation in the Canadian confederation, but would have refused to acknowledge native peoples' original occupancy of Quebec and the rest of Canada. Harper obstructed the accord precisely because Canadian natives were angered by their omission from it. Sioui's position was that the entire Canadian governmental system for negotiating land claims ought to be revamped.

Eighty-five percent of Quebec never has been signed away by treaty. While leaders of the Quebec independence movement had at least paid lip service to the idea that any constitution for an independent Quebec should respect native land claims as an issue of minority-group justice, very few French Canadians were probably prepared to meet the natives' assertion that nonnative claims to the province did not extend much beyond the Montreal and Quebec City urban areas.

Many native people believed that they had been treated less unfairly by the English-speaking people of Canada than the French. The 10,000 Crees, one-fifth of Quebec's native population, had actively opposed the massive hydroelectric projects that Quebec planned to construct on their homeland around James Bay.

The Union of British Columbia Indian Chiefs asked all native bands in Canada's west to block roads and bridges in their territories. One woman stood in the midst of Vancouver's Lion's Gate Bridge carrying a sign urging support of land claims while rush-hour traffic streamed around her. In British Columbia virtually none of the 77,000 "recognized" Indians (who live on 1,650 reserves, some only a few acres in size) have treaties with the government. In a situation similar to that of Quebec, most of the province had never been legally ceded by the natives.

Blockades of rarely traveled roads in sparsely populated areas of British Columbia and other provinces attracted little attention, so natives decided to stop railroad traffic instead. Several railroad blockades sprang up on the Canadian prairies and in British Columbia assembled by native people who sympathized with the Mohawks at Oka and who also wanted to advance their own long-neglected land claims. On August 20 negotiations brought down a blockade on one of Canada's main cross-continent rail lines established by the Long Lake and Pic Mobert bands in northern Ontario.

At the same time, the railway link between Vancouver and Prince George, British Columbia, remained blocked despite a court order. That railroad forms the main link between the urban areas of the southwest coast and the resource-rich interior. A few days later, the Royal Canadian Mounted Police swept into the area, breaking the protest by setting

***(Photo: Sam McLeod,* London Free Press)**

German shepherds on the Indians at the blockade. More than 100 people were arrested.

Native people in British Columbia were dealing with a provincial government that didn't even recognize the legitimacy of aboriginal title, claiming it had been entirely extinguished when British Columbia joined Canada in 1871. Nineteen of 24 land-claims cases accepted for consideration by the Canadian federal government to September 1990 were from British Columbia. Even so, with the government accepting only six new land-claim cases for consideration each year, the whole process seemed to be more of a delaying tactic than an attempt to do justice to natives across Canada. Bill Wilson, an attorney who chaired the First Nations Congress (which represents 95 percent of British Columbia's natives), said that at six a year it would take three and a half centuries to review all outstanding land-claim cases in the province. Some citizens' groups estimated that the total cost of settlements in that province of Canada alone could run $2 billion to $4 billion.

Mike Myers, a self-proclaimed official of the Iroquois Confederacy, (Onondaga's council disavowed him) said that if Mohawks were injured at Kahnawake or Kanesatake, natives across Canada would strike at hydroelectric power lines and railway tracks. "They'll get hit right across the country. Gas lines, railway lines, telephone lines, hydro lines, you name it. They can't guard it all."[18]

The confrontation at Oka also provoked the airing of issues affecting indigenous peoples the world over. In Geneva, about 200 aboriginal people took part in a prayer for peace addressed at Oka, after Swiss officials had refused them permission to march in protest at the Canadian mission, under a law that prohibits public demonstrations aimed at embarrassing the diplomatic offices of another country. On August 9 more than 400 people attending the sixth annual conference of native peoples at Tromsoe, Norway, above the arctic circle, heard a statement from Alwyn Morris, a Mohawk delegate.

Jonathon Mazower, Survival International's director for America, said that the confrontation at Oka was getting more press coverage in London than any other indigenous struggle in the world. Demonstrations in support of the Mohawks were held at points as diverse as Sydney, Berlin, and Rome.

Press reports throughout the crisis exhibited considerable confusion over just who was speaking for the Iroquois Confederacy and for the communities at Kanesatake and Kahnawake. The confusion was often fed by the Warriors' use of the Iroquois Confederacy's name (and even bootlegged letterhead) during its high-profile media campaign. While the Warriors held no portfolio from the Iroquois Council at Onondaga nor its Canadian counterpart at Grand River, its members were able at times to create an impression that they were, indeed, speaking for all Iroquois on both sides of the international border. One picture of a masked Indian toting an AK-47 seemed to many in the non-Indian media worth at least 1,000 peace-seeking words from the team of negotiators actually appointed by the chiefs at Onondaga. Profits from the tobacco trade allowed the Warriors to purchase their headline-grabbing arsenal, rent expensive hotel rooms, and cover the landscape with press releases while the Iroquois Confederacy's negotiating team operated without an adequate budget, with borrowed cars.[19]

Despite their lack of a funding base, the Confederacy's negotiators came to occupy a crucial middle ground between the Warriors and Canadian officials during the months of negotiations that preceded the use of armed force by the Canadian Army and police at Kanesatake and Kahnawake. With little fanfare (and often less press coverage), the team of Harvey Longboat (Cayuga), Bernie Parker (Seneca), Oren Lyons (Onondaga), Samson Gabriel (Mohawk), Leo Henry (Tuscarora), John Mohawk (Seneca), Arnold General (Onondaga), Paul Williams (Onondaga), Tom Deer (Mohawk), Allen Gabriel (Mohawk), and Curtis Nelson (Mohawk) urged both sides to concentrate on long-term solutions to problems brought to light by the summer's violence. They recommended a fair land-rights process, the creation of viable economic bases for the communities involved in the crisis, and the recognition of long-standing (but often ignored) treaty rights, including border rights.

The Confederacy team's position sought to achieve a land base for the Mohawks at Kanesatake, but did not endorse the Warriors' demands for complete international sovereignty, a seat at the United Nations, and adjudication of disputes by the World Court at The Hague. The Confederacy's negotiators thought that many of the Warriors' demands were just posturing. The Warriors accused the Confederacy of selling out. These themes echoed time and again during the course of the summer as negotiations between government officials, Warriors, and the Confederacy team collapsed several times on both sides of the barricades and in crowded hotel meeting rooms.

While the issues of land rights and respect for native burial grounds gained a degree of respect at Kanesatake that the Warrior did not enjoy at Akwesasne, support for their tactics was hardly universal. As days stretched into weeks and the daily lives of many people were devastated, resentment of the Warriors' role in the confrontation intensified. The settlement's elected grand chief George Martin led the opposition. At about 8 P.M. on August 1, by Martin's account, a group of Warriors responded to his demand that they get off the reserve by breaking down the door of his house. They assaulted fellow band council member Jerry Etienne, then pointed submachine guns at both men and threatened their lives. "As they left, they fired about twenty shots in the air. We warned them there were children in the house ... but there was no reasoning with them."[20] A growing number of people at Kanesatake were ready to settle for the federal government's offer of 54 acres, so that they could resume their daily lives.

Martin said that he had telephoned Loran Thompson, a Warrior spokesman and told him, "Get your Warriors out of my reserve. This is not your reserve. I'm the grand chief. This is my reserve. ... Let us do our business and get back to normal."[21] Many Mohawks at Kanesatake, disturbed at the degree to which the Warriors were using Kanesatake's crisis to advance their own agenda, had sent messengers to Onondaga, via Akwesasne, as early as the second week in August in the traditional fashion—bearing wampum, asking for assistance.

At about the same time, the Warriors alienated the press who had been covering the standoff by restricting reporters, photographers, and camera operators to an area "the size of a postage stamp." The Warriors singled out the Montreal *Gazette,* calling its coverage unfavorable and expelled two of its reporters from the blockaded area.

About two dozen other reporters walked out in sympathy for a short time. Within a day the *Gazette* was playing Martin's confrontation with the Warriors on page one and blasting the Warriors editorially.

As the standoffs at Oka and Kahnawake began their sixth week another attempt was made to start negotiations in mid-August. Formal talks had stopped a month earlier. During the next two weeks, both sides stuck to their original positions. During the third week, roughly 2,500 Canadian Army troops began to replace some of the provincial and national police at both sites.

Also, by the middle of August, a coalition of Mohawks inside Kanesatake appealed to Canadian native leaders to help stop the Warriors from "hijacking" negotiations. The Mohawks' statement was addressed to the First Nations of Canada.

> We have made repeated attempts to co-operate [sic] with the "Mohawk Nation" [Warriors'] negotiators to ensure that the voice of the majority of the Mohawk people of Kanesatake is clearly heard and understood—only to be rebuffed, insulted, and abused. ... This situation is intolerable. Issues of concern to the community in the areas of land and jurisdiction were not being addressed by Warrior negotiators.[22]

During the late summer of 1990, many residents of Kahnawake who favored neither the Warriors' tactics nor agenda, tacitly supported their actions in the face of outside authority. Inside the reserve, however, opposition to the Warriors continued to grow. On August 23, a group of Kahnawake women circulated an open letter to the community.

> Many people in Kahnawake, Kanesatake & Akwesasne believe that the present blockade crisis is out of hand and is, indeed[,] in the wrong hands. [The elected Council] should not assume that the majority of the community has accepted the Warriors nation office as leaders/spokespeople for the Confederacy. What is indicated is the people's disgust as the Mohawk Council of Kahnawake continues to abdicate responsibility & authority to a self-interested, small but aggressive faction in Mohawk communities.[23]

On August 25 Ciaccia telephoned Iroquois Confederacy negotiator John Mohawk to tell him that negotiations had again collapsed and that negotiators for the Canadian federal government and Quebec had resigned. Ciaccia then told Mohawk that Quebec's premier Robert Bourassa had set a deadline. After 48 hours he would order troops to take "appropriate action" to end the blockade of the Mercier Bridge by force. Ciaccia also requested a meeting with the Confederacy's negotiating team the next day in Toronto.

Indian Affairs minister Siddon called the Warriors' demands:

> Utterly unacceptable ... [requiring] nothing less than the setting up of an autonomous nation-state or territory to be ceded by Canada. ... The Warriors do not have a just cause; their goals are not legitimate; their tactics are not in keeping with the honoured and peaceful traditions of the first citizens of Canada.[24]

Mulroney went on nationwide television on August 29 in an attempt to explain to Canadians why he had just ordered the Canadian Army to prepare to disassemble the Mohawks' blockades by force of arms. Mulroney said that federal and Quebec officials had dealt with the Mohawks "in good faith," but Mohawk negotiators had pressed "unrealistic conditions." "We cannot overlook the illegal activities of an extremist minority," said Mulroney.[25]

Georges Erasmus, national chief of the Assembly of First Nations representing 593,000 native people across Canada, said that the governments of Canada and Quebec had declared war on the Mohawks.

The spate of deadlines from high Canadian officials came as French Canadians along Montreal's south shore began to organize blockades of all bridges linking the central city with its southern suburbs. This was an attempt to bring commerce in the area to a standstill, a threat meant to force the government to order the army to end the Kahnawake Mohawks' 49-day siege of the two highways leading to the Mercier bridge.

The French-Canadian anger boiled over into another riot on August 28. More than 500 angry residents on Montreal's south shore stoned a caravan of 60 automobiles carrying Mohawk families, including many children and old people, out of the besieged Kahnawake reserve. The mob pounded the Mohawks' automobiles relentlessly with rocks and construction materials. One police officer described the attack. "It was a rain of rocks; it was terrible. there were windshields broken and lots of people hurt. Those cars were full of old folks. It was really ugly." One of the refugees was Joe Armstrong, a 71-year-old Mohawk man with a history of heart trouble. He died of a heart attack five days afterward.

A few hours after the Kahnawake convoy was stoned, John Mohawk and Oren Lyons arrived at Kahnawake's Warrior longhouse about 8 P.M. in a last-ditch attempt to secure an agreement. Intense debate followed with Paul Delaronde and Selma Delisle. They both said that the community was not willing to dismantle the barricades, give up its weapons, or to have any of its members face government prosecution for their actions. Mohawk strongly urged the people in the packed Warrior longhouse not to fight the army. The meeting broke up around 3 A.M. at an impasse.

Within hours, an unexpected settlement averted a potentially violent showdown at the barricades near the Mercier Bridge. The men at the barricades decided to cooperate with the army in dismantling them. "The decision was taken to avoid bloodshed. We have reached an honorable settlement between the military and the community of Kahnawake," said Mohawk spokesman Jack LeClaire.[26]

When soldiers began dismantling the Mohawk blockade of the Mercier Bridge they were taking no chances. More than 1,400 troops swarmed onto the sites that the Mohawks had been maintaining, backed by an equal number of provincial police, a show of force that probably exceeded the number of protesters by at least 10 to 1. The soldiers also were backed by heavy artillery, including howitzers capable of firing smoke bombs and explosives as well as earth-moving machinery and armored personnel carriers.[27]

On August 30, only a day after the barricades on the Mercier bridge had been dismantled, Kahnawake Grand Chief Joseph Norton said that the Mohawks might stop cooperating with the government. Police and troops were still impeding the flow of much-needed food and medicine onto the reserve, thereby acting in bad faith.

On September 3, as if taunting Norton, Canadian Army troops invaded the reserve, stomping through the Warrior longhouse, looking for hidden weapons. The soldiers did find a few weapons in the Longhouse, including an M-50 machine gun, several AK-47s, and perhaps a half-dozen types of ammunition.

As word spread that the troops had invaded the Warrior longhouse—the symbolic heart of the reserve—Mohawks rushed to it. Arriving at the longhouse as the troops were about to enter it, some of the Mohawk women jumped at the soldiers, pounding them with their fists. About 30 of the women lined up across the road. Canadian Army soldiers pushed them back. A number of children had joined the women at this point, running about, hugging their mothers' legs, as the soldiers fixed them in gunsights. Agnes Robertson, one of the women, said:

> When I turned around, [I saw] in the bushes, there were twenty to twenty-five [soldiers] that came toward us on the road, They started pushing us around. There was a pregnant woman and an older woman, and they just pushed us. [The soldiers] all started going toward the Longhouse, and the women thought they were going to shoot the people there. We started pulling on them and holding onto them. They started hurting the women. My sister got hit in the ribs. We called the Kateri Hospital, and they sent out an ambulance. Another woman got hit in the head, and we called the ambulance again.[28]

After the soldiers shoved through the double line of women and children, Robertson said they smashed the longhouse's windows and surrounded the building with so many soldiers that the women could not see or hear what was happening inside.

An Army spokesman rather sheepishly acknowledged that one soldier had smashed his rifle butt into a woman's ribs during the melee. The women had used their bodies to shield the men out of fear that the soldiers would shoot to kill them.

The injury toll might have been higher if cooler heads had not prevailed during some moments of that incendiary day when angry Mohawks reached for weapons the Army had not seized, and squared off against the heavily armed troops. At one point, after one shot had been fired the Army tightened its physical vise on defenders of the longhouse. Both sides raised their weapons, cocked, and began to press triggers. One soldier fired before his commander ordered, "Do not lock and load!" A few seconds passed in incredibly tense silence, and then both sides stepped back.[29]

At Oka, troops continued to methodically tighten a circle of barbed wire on three blockades there. Canadian fighter jets occasionally zoomed overhead as negotiators struggled to reach agreement on a peaceful solution. The main sticking point in the negotiations was whether participants in the blockades should have amnesty from prosecution.

On September 2, at about 8:30 A.M., two dozen troops backed by two armored personnel carriers moved onto Highway 344 in Oka. They approached the main barricade on a hilltop. None of the Warriors at the blockade made an effort to stop the soldiers who strung barbed wire around the barricade and inspected it for booby traps.

The army continued to close its ragged circle of barbed wire around 50 people who did not leave, sealing them into 2 acres surrounding the settlement's alcohol and drug treatment center. As they closed the circle, the soldiers passed through two other blockade sites that had been abandoned days earlier, one at the north side of Kanesatake and another at the western edge of the territory.

By early September the federal government had already spent $5.2 million to buy 39 hectares of the disputed land. By that time, all but about 300 of Kanesatake's roughly 1,500 residents had left the settlement. About 60 people, half of them Warriors, were living inside the besieged treatment center along with roughly a dozen journalists who were camping in the basement.

On September 5, Mike Myers issued a press release on Iroquois Confederacy letterhead that was a virtual declaration of war.

> The Confederacy can no longer tolerate the continuing manipulations of the Governments of Canada and Quebec. The delegation has decided to move ahead with our solution to the war being waged against our people in Kanesatake. ...[30]

The next day, Warrior representatives, calling themselves the Haudenosaunee Delegates, sent a letter to George Erasmus, president of the Assembly of First Nations, calling on him to retract his call to cease civil disobedience throughout Canada. The Warriors urged Erasmus to call for renewed action throughout the country.

On September 18 the army invaded Kahnawake looking for weapons a second time. This time, the soldiers concentrated their search on Tekakwitha Island.

Roughly 300 Mohawks gathered on the Tekakwitha Bridge after the soldiers had been dropped onto the island by helicopter. "It's ass-kicking time!" shouted one native man as the Indians poured over the bridge. "Tell them to get the hell off our land," yelled another. One soldier was dragged to the ground, punched and kicked, then pounded on the head with his own helmet. The soldiers then fired several volleys into the air and shot tear gas point-blank into the crowd.

More than 80 people were injured, 19 of them soldiers. Many Mohawks on the bridge spared themselves serious injury and escaped the stinging tear gas by jumping off the bridge connecting Tekakwitha Island to the mainland. One Mohawk woman fell off the bridge and broke a hip. Once the Indians had been dispersed, the large Huey helicopters that had brought the troops and police to the island returned to retrieve them. After the raid, the military staged a press conference during which the roughly 50 weapons seized during the raid were displayed. Major Rusty Bassarab, a military spokesman, said that the army had found an assortment of AK-47s, shotguns, handguns, and hunting rifles. The weapons were found under rocks in the forest, wrapped in plastic.

Reporters who had camped with other media representatives and free-lance journalists in the basement of the occupied treatment center at Kanesatake provided a picture of the people inside. They were a small rag-tag band of guerrilla fighters from a number of reservations, armed with a collection of modern weaponry, bows and arrows, homemade bombs, road flares, and other makeshift devices, including at least one large slingshot made from the tire of a child's bicycle. The Warriors went by aliases such as Mad Jap, Noriega, Lasagna, the General, and Boltpin. The General was a Micmac poet and writer from the Eskasoni Reserve in Nova Scotia. Boltpin was a 51-year-old grandfather and former construction worker who said he did not believe in guns. Kahn-tineta Horn, a 50-year-old Mohawk activist and former fashion model, had been called "the Indian Princess" 30 years earlier by fashion magazines across Canada. She had fought for aboriginal rights and land claims most of her life; her father had been among the last holdouts when the Mohawks fought the construction of the Saint Lawrence Seaway. Not all of the people inside the treatment center were natives. "Blondie" was a 15-year-old white Quebecker who wanted to protect the pine forests.

At Oka, tensions between the army and the occupants of the detoxification center rose after soldiers on an intelligence mission behind Warrior lines allegedly beat up an Indian sentry during the early morning of September 8. The 40-year-old man, nicknamed Spud Wrench, was taken to the intensive care ward of a Montreal hospital. Two soldiers were slightly injured by knives in the scuffle.

A few minutes after the incident, reporters inside the detoxification center watched Spud Wrench shiver from shock as Mohawk women dressed his bloody wounds. Once he had partially recovered, Spud Wrench said soldiers had jumped him after he fell asleep at his sentry post. The soldiers told their commander that Spud Wrench had jumped them. The Army refused to let a doctor into the compound to inspect Spud Wrench for several hours after he was injured. Dr. David Gorman was finally allowed to cross the razor wire, after which he applied 25 stitches to close deep gashes in Spud Wrench's face. He also suffered a concussion.

During mid-September, the army again tried to cut off food supplies to the people barricaded inside the detox center. The army relented after public criticism alleged that they were trying to starve women and children into submission. The Army also tried to cut communications by obtaining a court order to have cellular phones inside the building disconnected, severing the Warriors' only communication link with the outside.

When reporters inside the building complained that the troops were preventing them from filing dispatches on the mobile phones, the army told some of them to use its hotline. The press corps refused because such use implied censorship. Photographers inside the compound tried to throw film to colleagues across the army's razor-wire barriers; soldiers dove for the film and scuffled with news media employees, seizing some of the cannisters. A few hours later, the Warriors managed to silence the Army's hotline itself in retaliation.

Negotiations continued at Oka. On September 18 a group of about 40 people paraded in front of the Canadian Embassy in Washington, D.C., in support of the Mohawks at Oka. They carried signs reading "Golf on Your Mother, Not Ours" and "No Indian Blood on Canadian Hands." The situation at Oka had become a public embarrassment to the Canadian government the world over. At one point, an official of the South African foreign affairs department upbraided Canada for criticizing human-rights abuses in his country, citing "problems with their native peoples."[31]

On September 24, hope rose that a peaceful solution might finally be at hand. Ciaccia said he had drawn up a 13-point plan that Mike Myers, speaking for the people inside the detox center, said "is really worth looking at."[32] After rejecting a very similar proposal three weeks earlier, weariness, dissent inside Kanesatake, and the intercession of negotiators for the Iroquois Confederacy had softened the Warriors' hard line. Myers indicated that many of the people inside the drug treatment center thought it was time for the confrontation to end. On the crucial issue of amnesty, the agreement appeased the police by not promising it to anyone, but soothed Indian fears of retaliation by saying that all charges would be brought before a specially appointed Crown attorney.

The agreement called for the Indians to surrender their arms to the Canadian Forces, who would then turn them over to the peace chiefs of the Iroquois Confederacy for destruction. The Mohawks of Kanesatake would get title to 49 hectares of land while the federal and provincial governments would agree to the creation of a native-controlled police force for the settlement, removing the provincial police from local enforcement. The agreement also included money for social and economic development programs at Kanesatake.

By September 25, the Warriors and others inside the treatment center were visibly tired of living under siege for two and a half months. They were tired of constant confrontation, going without food, and dealing with an overflowing septic tank they called "the monster."

On September 26, at 6:53 P.M., after 78 days, the 50 men, women, and children occupying the treatment center surrendered. Most of them emerged wearing camouflage clothing, waving a Warrior flag. Some of those who had walked out of the treatment center complained that Loran Thompson, who had urged everyone to wear their camouflage uniforms and "walk out proud," had slipped past troops earlier in street clothes, with a woman and a baby.[33] The dehorned chief later turned himself in to police. The number of people occupying the treatment center had dwindled by at least half its original number since being encircled on September 2.

During the following days, troops and police began rolling up razor-wire fences and removing sandbags before they rolled away in their armored personnel carriers and other vehicles. Residents of both the Mohawk settlement and the town began to trickle back into their homes. Most of the Mohawks were not happy with the outcome. "We were traumatized. We were brutalized by our own government. I don't think people understand how deeply angry we feel," said Dan David, who grew up at Kanesatake.[34] Forty of those who surrendered were charged with obstruction of justice, firearms violations, or participating in a riot. They were arraigned two days later.

Through the fall, the list of people charged with crimes related to the Oka standoff by Canadian prosecutors grew to more than 70. Some of the Warriors collected four-figure speakers' fees to help offset mounting legal bills. Mike Myers, who had shed his alias as an official of the Iroquois Confederacy to become a Warrior spokesman, quipped that his compatriots had become "the biggest thing since Rice Krispies." Dan Gaspe, a Kanesatake Mohawk, summed up the situation.

> Non-natives continue to romanticize about the poor Indian who has been treated unfairly. Sure, there have been a lot of wrongs done to us,

> but you can't use that guilt to close your eyes to wrongdoings, whether they are wrong under our [Iroquois] law, or Canadian law.[35]

The results of background checks into 260 people known or suspected of being affiliated with the Warriors were published in the Toronto *Star* in November 1990. Of that number, 50 had been convicted of "serious criminal offences" in Canada and New York state while charges were pending against another 30.

In an attempt to defray rising legal costs, the Warriors increasingly took their cause on the road across Canada after forming a fund-raising arm called the Haudenosaunee Liberation Group. The Liberation Group appealed for local organizers to donate food and time and announced plans to sell T-shirts. On CKRK radio, Dale Deom advocated a bottle drive to pay Warriors' legal fees. Some observers wondered whether this was a public-relations ploy. Had the cigarette kingpins of Kahnawake and Akwesasne found the Warriors' protection unnecessary, to the point that they were now reduced to selling T-shirts and scavenging bottles?

Tensions remained high between police and residents of Kahnawake for several months after the blockade of the Mercier Bridge came down. On January 8, 1991, 19 people, 13 of them police officers, were injured after a vehicle check on a service road near Highway 132. The driver of the four-wheel truck that Royal Canadian Mounted Police had stopped fled into a nearby lumberyard as a group of Mohawks emerged, arguing that the Royal Canadian Mounted Police had no jurisdiction on the reserve. The Mohawks said that an officer started a fight with one of the Mohawk men. As a woman tried to break it up, other officers pushed her to the ground, igniting a larger melee in which the 19 people were hurt. Most of the injuries were minor, although one officer required 20 stitches to close a wound on his face.

Two hours after the initial face-off at 2:30 P.M., the fight had grown such that police had to close the Mercier Bridge just as rush-hour traffic was building.

Following the confrontation, Kahnawake Grand Chief Joe Norton said that police harassment had been constant on the reserve. "As far as we are concerned, this may be the last straw. We aren't going to take it anymore. The people of the community will defend themselves in any way they can."[36] Three days later, the Royal Canadian Mounted Police announced plans to establish its own "aboriginal affairs" unit. Provincial officers continued to patrol Kahnawake as negotiations began on recognizing the Mohawk police force by Quebec authorities. In Kanesatake, where the previous summer's confrontation had begun, the treatment center that had become the center of the standoff reopened to treat alcoholics on January 14, 1991.

During June 1991, a delegation of three Warriors traveled to the Libyan capital of Tripoli to collect a $250,000 "human-rights" award "for the Red Race of the Americas." "We stand before you knowing that we are amongst such kindred spirits," the Warriors told the Libyans in their acceptance speech. "We understand that all of you and your peoples have faced much of what we have, and that you have struggled the noble struggle of survival."[37]

Platitudes about common struggle aside, the Warriors anticipated criticism for accepting a "human-rights" award from a leader whose human-rights record was far from spotless. The acceptance speech, released by the pro-Warrior Mohawk Nation office at Kahnawake, said,

> Some from the West[ern] world actually tell us we should not be here. ... They would say ... that we are betrayers. We ask simply, who killed our 100 million people? Was it not the West in Canada and the United States who did this? How do you betray governments that betrayed our people for centuries?[38]

Tom Porter, the Akwesasne Bear Clan subchief who had spoken out against the Warriors so often, said "Gadhafi is a known terrorist and that's what people are saying about the Warrior Society. It seems like they may go together."[39] Darren Bonaparte, an Akwesasne Mohawk, and also an opponent of the Warriors, agreed. "All they care about is money," he said. "They will even take money from a government that supports terrorists. Now, all they need is an award from Saddam Hussein." Bonaparte said that the Warriors' world travels as spokespeople for all Native Americans saddened him: "They present themselves as defenders of our history, language, and culture. But they are not defenders of our people. They're killing our people."[40]

Notes

[1] Peter Hamel, "Aboriginal Land Rights: A National Crisis," Background paper prepared for Archbishop Desmond Tutu and Archbishop Michael Peers (July 30–August 3, 1990): 2.

[2] Ibid., 4.

[3] *Sun* (Ottawa, Ont.), July 12, 1990.

[4] *Post-Standard* (Syracuse, NY), July 12, 1990.

[5] *Sun* (Ottawa, Ont.), July 12, 1990.

[6] Ibid.

[7] *Post-Standard* (Syracuse, NY), July 13, 1990. Jacobson was elected to the Kanesatake band council the following June.

[8] *Globe and Mail* (Toronto, Ont.), July 13, 1990.

[9] *Gazette* (Montreal, Ont.), July 13, 1990.

[10] *Globe and Mail* (Toronto, Ont.), July 16, 1991. Within a few hours of Lemay's death, the SQ had arrested two Mohawk men at an Oka bar as suspects in his death. One of the men, Allister Nicholas, told the Montreal *Gazette* (July 12) that he was let go for lack of evidence the next day. The two men were drinking beer in the bar when the officers arrived at about 5 P.M. "They pulled us by the hair and threw us against the wall," Nicholas said.

[11] *Sunday Citizen* (Ottawa, Ont.), July 22, 1990.

[12] Greta Hofmann Nemiroff, "*Kaien'keha:ka:* Mohawk Women," Ms. (May–June 1991): 20.
[13] *Post-Standard* (Syracuse, NY), July 18, 1990.
[14] Peeter Kopvillem, "Fury in the Ranks," *Maclean's* (August 6, 1990).
[15] Letter to the Editor, *New York Times* (New York, NY), August 14, 1990.
[16] At the end of July the SQ surrounded Kanesatake with three officers for every two Mohawks living in the settlement and 10 for every active participant in the confrontation. The operation was costing Quebec $1 million a day by July 31.
[17] Deborah DeBois, *Post-Standard* (Syracuse, NY), August 31, 1990.
[18] *Star* (Toronto, Ont.), September 14 , 1990.
[19] Canadian estimates of the revenue that the illegal tobacco trade cost governments illustrate the size of those profits. In 1990 Canada estimated that the tobacco trade was costing its federal and provincial governments $324 million (Canadian) a year in lost revenue. A year later, as social pressure against smoking and the government's search for expedient sources of tax revenue caused already stiff tobacco taxes to rise even further, the estimates of the revenue loss approached $400 million a year. With Canadian taxes on cigarettes rising, the appeal of cut-rate smuggled cigarettes rose, along with the profit margins of smoke-shop operators.
[20] *Gazette* (Montreal, Ont.), August 3, 1990.
[21] *Gazette* (Montreal, Ont.), August 3, 1990.
[22] *Gazette* (Montreal, Ont.), August 19, 1990.
[23] Gerald Alfred, "From Bad to Worse: Internal Politics in the 1990 Crisis at Kahnawake," *Northeast Indian Quarterly* (Spring 1991): 28–29.
[24] "Report of the Committee on Aboriginal Affairs: Summer of 1990," Report of Iroquois Confederacy negotiators to Canadian House of Commons (May 7, 1991): 12.
[25] Ibid.
[26] *Post-Standard* (Syracuse, NY), August 30, 1990.
[27] On September 4 a number of Warriors drove their cars onto the Cornwall International Bridge, which crosses the U.S.–Canada border at Akwesasne, and stopped for one and a half hours, snarling traffic to show their support for the people barricaded inside the treatment center at Oka. Some of the people who stopped their cars on the Cornwall bridge had just fled the army's advance at the Mercier Bridge; about 50 Warriors vanished at the first rumble of army tanks, personnel carriers, and front-loaders, taking a sizable number of weapons with them. After 90 minutes, police told the Warriors on the bridge to move along, and they did. Ontario provincial police said 25 to 30 cars took part in the short blockade; the Warriors claimed that 75 to 100 people took part.
[28] *Press-Republican* (Plattsburgh, NY), September 5, 1990.
[29] *The Guardian* (New York, NY), September 19, 1990.
[30] Iroquois Confederacy, "Summer of 1990," p. 19.
[31] *Maclean's,* August 8, 1990.
[32] *Globe and Mail* (Toronto, Ont.), September 25, 1990.
[33] *Gazette* (Montreal, Ont.), September 29, 1990.
[34] *Post-Standard* (Syracuse, NY), September 28, 1990.
[35] *Star* (Toronto, Ont.), November 24, 1990.
[36] *Gazette* (Montreal, Ont.), January 9, 1991.
[37] Warrior Society press release, n.d., in files of *Akwesasne Notes.*
[38] Ibid.
[39] Tom Porter. Interview with author. Akwesasne, August 4, 1991.
[40] Darren Bonaparte. Interview with author. Akwesasne, August 5, 1991.

CHAPTER 7

▼▼▼

A Time for Healing

A year after the Mohawks' spring and summer of iron, fire, and death, Akwesasne felt like an overwound spring. A year of enforced but shaky peace had given people on all sides time to reflect, step back, and ask themselves how their battles had gotten so violent the year before. A year's time had not addressed the root causes of the violence in this place with a tradition of peace, this wonderful natural setting so violated by industry and greed. After a year the healing had only begun between fractured families; however the police could not withdraw without the danger of renewed traumatic nights of fire and death.

Despite the continuing occupation of Akwesasne by outside police forces from the United States and Canada, violence continued to flare. Two Quebec police were injured and seven police cruisers damaged during an hour-and-a-half rampage on Halloween night 1991. About 30 people, most of them teenagers, massed outside the Akwesasne Mohawk Police Station in St. Regis Village, throwing rocks, Molotov cocktails, and eggs. Two police officers were injured by rocks. As the riot intensified, the police donned riot gear and waded into it while 100 people watched the melee. Eyewitnesses said that the youths attacking the police station were wearing camouflage gear and carrying flags used by the Warrior Society. New York state police briefly sealed off roads at the border while older people in the community urged the rioters to disperse. Police made no arrests.

Along Route 37, the reservation's two bingo halls, the Mohawk Bingo Palace, and Billy's Bingo Hall had reopened, but the casinos remained closed. Billy's was decorated with two large posters commemorating the events at Kahnawake and Kanesatake the summer before, with complete Warrior regalia—fatigues, rifles, and flags. Warrior flags flapped in the summer breeze atop a few houses around the reserve, one of them across the street from the offices of the Mohawk Council of Akwesasne in St. Regis Village. Many of the casinos along Route 37 were boarded up, their parking lots all but empty. A forest of signs had sprouted along the highway, advertising cigarettes for about $1.40 a pack (or $12 a carton). They drew small swarms of automobiles with Ontario and Quebec plates, their drivers buying the two cartons that Canadian law allows them to take home duty free, or a few more on the chance that Canadian customs would not find them.

The three Mohawk communities continued to be a center of controversy a year after Mathew Pyke and J. R. "Junior" Edwards died at Akwesasne and Corporal Lemay at Oka. None of the three murders had been solved and no one had even been charged with the exception of Quebec's groundless prosecution of Doug George on charges of killing J. R. Edwards. The unsolved murders symbolized the many other problems that had been argued and fought over but not resolved.

A week after Mathew Pyke's funeral, his father said:

> Two SQ detectives came to my house. ... They said they had two slugs and a gun. Now I'm not stupid. I served in the [U. S.] Army. I know that if you have a gun, you can find the name of the person you got it from. If he says he didn't do the shooting, you ask who had it before him. Yet, there has been no prosecution ... no followup. There are a lot of unanswered questions from the police.[1]

Pyke wondered aloud why Quebec police are so frustrated that they can't find out who killed Corporal Lemay, "When they can't tell me anything about my son. There's two standards here—white, and Indian. If you're an Indian, you get the shaft."[2]

The crises at Akwesasne, Kahnawake, and Kanesatake caused the Iroquois Grand Council to examine its procedures and the way it was perceived. A year after the two deaths at Akwesasne, the Grand Council issued a complex report on its own operations authored by Seneca historian John Mohawk. It advocated the establishment of full-time administrative offices at Onondaga and Grand River, Ontario, the site of the Canadian Grand Council. Representatives of other native nations as well as non-Indian officials and journalists would have greater access to council chiefs who often had been difficult to locate. Mohawk's report also recommended combining the two councils into one. The report called on the confederacy to adopt an official position on the Warriors.

Louis Hall continued to assert that the Grand Council's reliance on the Code of Handsome Lake made it illegitimate. By mid-1991, however, Hall seemed to have backed off his earlier statements that the Grand Council's members should be exterminated in cold blood. "We want to get rid of them, but we're working to do it peacefully."[3]

The crises also caused many in New York state to take a closer look at their relationship with the Iroquois. By the summer of 1991, proposals were circulating within the New York Assembly that would establish a nonvoting member from the confederacy in the statehouse.

The struggle over gambling and smuggling continued. "Buttlegging" increased following a 60-cents-a-pack rise in Canadian cigarette taxes on February 26, 1991. More than two-thirds of the cost of a legal pack of smokes in Canada was going to taxes. A pack sold for $2 in Massena and for $6 in Cornwall across the international bridge; most smokers were commuting internationally to purchase their tobacco. For those who didn't care to commute, the smuggling pipeline was pumping cigarettes over the border in greater numbers than ever. A standard 12-ounce tin of pipe tobacco that sold for $8 in Massena was priced at $25 in Cornwall. Gilles Bourdon, owner of Ti-Gilles Smoke Shop in Cornwall, said he had quit carrying pipe tobacco because it simply was not selling at the legal price. The Royal Canadian Mounted Police estimated that $26 million worth of smuggled smokes (a million cartons) was entering Quebec each month in 1991. This represented roughly $12 million a month in gross profit.[4]

With increased "buttlegging" came increased vigilance by the Royal Canadian Mounted Police. On April 15, 1991, at 8 P.M., Kenny Lazore was quietly sitting at his dining room table having coffee with two friends on the Canadian side of Akwesasne. The Lazore children were playing with their friends in the living room. Five minutes later all of them were spread-eagle on the floor. Mounties from the Valleyfield, Quebec, division pointed 9 mm. automatic rifles at their heads.

The Mounties had obtained a search warrant; they shouted that they were searching for contraband cigarettes on a tip. Perhaps not coincidentally, Ken Lazore had been the man whose recantation busted Quebec's case against Doug George in the murder of J. R. "Junior" Edwards. The police found no smuggled cigarettes.

By March 1991, New York Assemblyman Steven Sanders made good on a promise made during the assembly's hearings on the crisis at Akwesasne the previous summer. With six cosponsors (including assembly members Eve, Hinchey, and Ortloff who had taken part in the hearings) Sanders introduced a bill in the state house that would allow the Mohawks to choose the form of governance on the U.S. side of Akwesasne. Sanders' rationale for dissolving the elected council rested on Mohawk sovereignty. "We unequivocally reject the idea that the state has the legal or moral authority to dictate conditions by which the Mohawk people will conduct their internal affairs."[5] If enacted, the new law would end the St. Regis Tribal Council's nearly two-century tenure under New York state sponsorship.

Subchief Jake Swamp of the Mohawk Nation Council said, "It's about time. ... It's only about two hundred years too late."[6] However, the chiefs of the St. Regis Tribal Council promptly issued a press release defending its governance. Spokesman Joseph Gray said the elected chiefs would lobby the Assembly heavily against the bill.

Elected chiefs Jacobs, White, and Tarbell called the bill condescending and paternalistic.

> Governor Cuomo and the assemblymen are sadly mistaken if they expect the majority of the Mohawk people to sit idly by while the reservation's truly legitimate government is destroyed and replaced with a submissive and complacent government, which caters to the state's every whim."[7]

To the elected chiefs, their government represented "one of the last vestiges of stability on the reservation at this time."[8]

The elected chiefs and their supporters asserted that "history proves that the Mohawks who settled at what is now St. Regis chose a form of government where chiefs were elected rather than chosen by clan mothers." In so doing, they ignored the continued existence of the Mohawk Nation Council. Up to two-thirds of eligible voters routinely refused to participate in the St. Regis Tribal Council's elections. The elected chiefs argued that if the state repealed legislation supporting the Tribal Council, "the federal government will recognize the Tribal Council under federal Indian law, and the federal government makes the rules."[9]

On April 22, the New York State Assembly voted 141 to 4 in support of the bill to repeal the 1802 law. Despite such overwhelming support, the proposal died, at least for that session of the legislature because no one in the state senate had offered to support it. According to senatorial courtesy, that decision fell to Senator Ronald Stafford, Plattsburgh Republican, whose district includes Akwesasne. Senator Stafford's role was all the more crucial in a senate dominated by Republicans among whom he served as deputy majority leader. The assembly had a Democratic majority.

On May 2, a delegation of Mohawks met with Senator Stafford in Albany to request his support of the measure. The group included current elected subchief James Ransom as well as Rosemarie Bonaparte, who served as an elected chief between 1985 and 1988. Ransom and Bonaparte said that the elected council is essentially undemocratic because it has no written constitution, no criminal justice system, and no bill of rights. "We have no civil rights. There is no appeal from any of the decisions of the tribal chiefs," said Bonaparte.[10] Julius Cook, who served as an elected chief between 1981 and 1984, said that the current chiefs "have been bought, body and soul. They learned to make money through illegal gambling and smuggling."[11]

In late May, New York State Supreme Court Judge Jan H. Plumadore ruled that the four St. Regis Tribal Council staff members who had been "purged" by Chief Jacobs almost a year earlier had not gotten a proper hearing and should be reinstated. The judge ruled that they were also entitled to back pay: Jim Ransom, environmental director for the tribe; Sakakohe Pembleton, an administrator; Wesley Laughing economic director; and Brian Cole, an economic planner. The ruling came at a time when Ransom was running against Jacobs for tribal chief in the June 1 tribal council elections. Jacobs won by only 24 votes. Ransom again assumed his role as environmental advocate for the council and pressed for a Superfund plan that would force General Motors to permanently clean up its waste dumps. To underscore the Mohawks' disaffection with the St. Regis Council, 25 percent fewer Mohawks turned out to vote than in the previous year.

As spring turned to summer along the Saint Lawrence River, the Mohawks on the Canadian side of Akwesasne were also debating their own future, which had become entwined with Quebec's proposed secession from Canada. Akwesasne could find itself divided not between two nations but three: the United States, independent Quebec, and English-speaking Canada.

On June 22, 1991, Mike Mitchell was reelected as grand chief on Akwesasne's Canadian side. Gambling supporters turned out six "antis," however, splitting the council down the middle. Francis Boots, Warrior spokesman, made a brief run for the office of grand chief but withdrew.

Guilford D. White, one of the partners in the Mohawk Bingo Palace, said he and other business owners on the U.S. side were preparing to sue the Mohawk Council of Akwesasne for disrupting their operations "in any court, in any jurisdiction we can."

> It's rather difficult for one little Indian businessman, or a couple, to take on the federal government of Canada. ... People suffered a lot. There are still people from Canada who are afraid to come over here. And now we find that the federal government of Canada funded it![12]

The St. Regis Tribal Council asserted collusion between the Mohawk Council of Akwesasne and the Black and Puerto Rican Caucus of the New York State Assembly on ways to stack the hearings held the previous summer. Sniffing what it regarded as a major international scandal, the chiefs of the St. Regis Council produced a memo written by Timothy Thompson, composed at a time when he was a chief on the Mohawk Council of Akwesasne, describing how the Canadian-recognized council had spent nearly $16,000 to aid the antigambling blockades in the spring of 1990. Using the catchwords of international espionage, the St. Regis Tribal Council asserted that the funding amounted to a "covert operation in a foreign country." The St. Regis Tribal Council called this disclosure "a major story with international implications."[13] The St. Regis Tribal Council also characterized attempts by the Mohawk Council of Akwesasne to start a unified police force for Akwesasne and hold a reservationwide referendum on gambling as foreign interference in the affairs of the United States.

Charles Webb, director of Band Governance and Indian Estates Directorate, said that the Canadian government did not control how native governments spend their money. He said that government funding must be accounted for but that the Mohawk Council of Akwesasne also had other sources of income to use as it pleased. The Mohawk Council of Akwesasne's internal documents displayed at the St. Regis Tribal Council press conference had been obtained after pro-gambling chiefs took office on the Canadian council and went though its files. It was also alleged that the Mohawk Council of Akwesasne paid $30,000 or more to aid the defense of Doug George against charges that he murdered "Junior" Edwards. Speaking for the Mohawk Nation Council, Barbara Barnes said that the money spent on George's defense was a loan and that it was being repaid. Barnes said that the Mohawk Council of Akwesasne had acted in the best interests of all people at Akwesasne by aiding the blockade defenders. Also speaking for the Mohawk Council of Akwesasne, Darren Bonaparte said that the allegations of the St. Regis Tribal Council were groundless, and solely an attempt to create more discord on the reserve.

At the same time the St. Regis Tribal Council squared off against the Mohawk Council of Akwesasne, Warrior legal representative Stanley Cohen found it convenient to recognize New York state jurisdiction over Akwesasne, which the Warriors had rejected during the spring of 1990. The denial of state jurisdiction had been the crux of the Warriors' ideological argument in support of gambling and smuggling. In an attempt to win a dismissal of charges against 21 Warrior Society members accused of firing weapons, issuing threats, throwing gasoline bombs, setting fires, and damaging vehicles at the antigamblers' roadblocks, Cohen argued that the barricades themselves were illegal under the New York state law. Cohen said, "My clients were not the criminals. The criminals were the people who shut down the territory and held Akwesasne hostage."[14]

Cohen also argued that Warriors who brought down the blockades should not be in the dock at all. The Mohawk Council of Akwesasne had helped staff and finance the barricades. He contended that the Canadian council's aid to the blockades was an illegal aid from a foreign country. Now the international border was convenient to the Warriors' defense.

Under U.S. law the boundary does exist, and Cohen's arguments won the support of Franklin County district attorney Richard H. Edwards. He said that the Canadian council had spent at least $16,000 on the blockades "and other activities," and that the employees of the council had stood at the blockades during working hours. Canadian law defines native band councils as agents of the federal government. Edwards argued that by extension the council's aid to the blockades on the U.S. side of the reservation could constitute interference by a foreign government.[15]

The Mohawk Council of Akwesasne argued that a single Mohawk territory should take precedence over the international line that splits Akwesasne. Their press release also pointed out that seven of the eight people charged with riot and arson were also enrolled members of the Mohawk Council on the Canadian side and that many other people who live on the U.S. side were also similarly enrolled. The Mohawk Council of Akwesasne provided a number of social services on both sides of the border as well.

> People who participated in what were called the 'roadblocks' were residents of both sides of the community, including [St. Regis] Tribal Council officials, supporters and employees [as well as] traditional people, supporters of the Mohawk Council of Akwesasne, and many others who are not included in any of these categories.[16]

The barricades were "a very brave grass-roots effort by community people to block illegal gambling from taking root in their community," the statement concluded.[17]

On November 29, 1991, charges were dropped against all but three of the defendants. Warrior Society spokeswoman Minnie Garrow maintained that the dismissals were a vindication of the Warriors' allegations that the Mohawk Council of Akwesasne had been behind the blockades all along. She insisted that the people who built the roadblocks ought to be indicted instead. "Another roadblock of this type will never happen in this territory," Garrow said.[18]

Art Kakwirakeron Montour walked out of Allenwood Federal Prison after a 10-month sentence, one year to the day after Mathew Pyke and J. R. "Junior" Edwards had died by gunfire. The two murders had remained unsolved. Back home in Akwesasne Kakwirakeron said that the Warriors would continue to be "emblems of sovereignty and independence. Lies and prison sentences ... will not stop the movement. My imprisonment will help to increase the movement across the country."[19]

As Kakwirakeron was released from prison, Leigh Hunt, the former Syracuse police chief who had vouched for Kakwirakeron's character during his trial, was hired by Cuomo to head the new state Office of Indian Relations created by the State Assembly following the two deaths at Akwesasne. Hunt's appointment met with support across the political spectrum at Akwesasne, a rare event. From Mohawk Nation Council subchief Ron LaFrance to Joe Gray, speaking for the St. Regis Tribal Council, plaudits rang out for Hunt.[20]

In July 1990 a Franklin County grand jury indicted Bill Sears for perjury, carrying a maximum five years in prison and a $250,000 fine. Found not guilty for possession of gambling devices in 1987, Sears was indicted for lying during the trial about his military service in Vietnam. The U.S. attorney charged that he had never served in Vietnam nor received any of the decorations described during his earlier trial. On November 27, 1991, Sears was sentenced to eight months in prison and fined $10,000 for perjury. In addition, U.S. District Court in Syracuse also assessed Sears $12,000, the expected cost of the time he would spend in prison.

Sears had stirred animosity among some people at Akwesasne as he built his grocery, bingo hall, and smoke shop. Glen Lazore, who lives east of Billy's Bingo along Route 37, provided legal papers indicating that Sears had constructed his smoke shop over a right-of-way owned by his uncle Francis Laughing without compensation. Sears maintained that Laughing had sold him all the land, including the right-of-way in 1981.

At the end of May 1991, the U.S. Supreme Court refused to consider an appeal by the casino owners convicted of illegal gambling activities in 1990 on the grounds of sovereignty, a popular but unsuccessful Warrior defense strategy. Many Mohawks worried that these attempts to apply the sovereignty rationale on an individual basis to support gambling operations eroded judicial support for more fundamental collective sovereignty rights that the Mohawks needed to argue land claims and other issues facing them. The Supreme Court's refusal opened the path to jail for Tony Laughing, Eli Tarbell, Pete Burns, and Roderick Cook along with Paul A. Tatlock, James Burns, David Mainville, and Hattie Rene Hart, all of whom had been free on bail after conviction on similar charges while the appeal was pending.

As the casino owners began serving their terms July 12, Massena resident Karen St. Hilaire said that she had gathered 860 signatures on a petition asking President Bush to pardon them. The petition argued that the jail sentences were invalid because of Mohawk sovereignty. St. Hilaire, not a Mohawk herself, said a majority of the signatures on the petition came from whites. Some of them acted in support of business interests that could benefit from reservation gambling. St. Regis Tribal Council spokesman Joseph Gray said that the elected chiefs also would call for pardon of the casino owners.

Meanwhile, in Canada during the summer of 1990, native peoples were on the verge of gaining some measure of genuine self-government, due in part to the upheaval at Kanesatake and Kahnawake the previous summer. At Akwesasne, a host of questions not only remained unresolved but also reached a degree of crisis rarely known elsewhere. For all the violence and death, they were no closer to attaining self-government, resolving land claims, deterring pollution, and stopping illegal gambling than before.

Would people at Akwesasne be able to overcome the acrimony of violence? Would the multitude of bureaucracies allow the formulation of a government under Mohawk control suited to a single community? Would the people of Akwesasne be able to call upon the traditions of the Great Law of Peace to become of one mind on the issue of gambling? Could such enterprises be tribally owned? Could their profits benefit everyone?

Subchiefs Jake Swamp and Tom Porter held out hope during the summer of 1991 that a time of healing could begin. Swamp said that while most of the Mohawk Nation Council chiefs were personally inclined against commercial gambling at Akwesasne, "the council has not taken a stand on the issue." Its members were waiting for a genuine community consensus..

> A unity has to occur. It may be a few years ... but such a unity of people is important. We have been under colonization for so long, but we have never been completely colonized. That's remarkable in itself. No matter what ... the Mohawk people succeeded for the people. Today is the first time that Canada and the United States have designed the disruption of the Mohawk among themselves, through entrepreneurship. It's caused Mohawk people to forsake their dignity and their principles. ... Now, everything is for money, whether it is honestly done, or deceitfully done. It's very sad.[21]

Porter and other Mohawks at Akwesasne sometimes wavered between a desire to bring their homeland back to sanity and a hope to escape it and begin over in another place. Proposals for a migration to the Mohawk Valley that were aired when the violence hit its height in 1990 had assumed more concrete proportions a year later. Porter and others circulated a proposal for the purchase of a tract of land in the Mohawk Valley, a traditional Mohawk homeland before the establishment of Akwesasne. The Mohawks were negotiating with the Mennonite church for financial support that could amount to $1 million. The proposal called the settlement Kanatshiohare, Mohawk for "the clean pot." The proponents envisioned it as an agriculturally based settlement that would also offer traditional spiritual teaching and combine the old ways with modern energy conservation technology.

> [The] events at Akwesasne [that] have rapidly deteriorated the ability of traditionally minded Mohawks to practice their lifestyle [and] to pass these practices on to their children and grandchildren. ... Gambling and the smuggling of guns, liquor, [and] cigarettes have become rampant ... [a]long with the development of a paramilitary force, alcohol and substance abuse, violent acts and intimidation [that] have become a way of life for many Mohawk people at Akwesasne ... and no end appears in sight.[22]

Many Mohawks said that they could no longer raise their children under conditions like those at Akwesasne. Tom Porter commented:

> [Native American ways of thinking and acting] can be a handicap ... because the native mind is not an aggressive mind. The native mind tends to think about the community. Because of that, we have been unable to counteract all the propaganda meant to discredit our council. In a way, therefore, we are handicapped by the dictates of our tradition. ... All across North America, the hearts of the native people have always been too big for their own good.[23]
>
> If you are not spiritually or historically briefed, in order to survive ... the chances are so great that you will become one of them. That is the

> saddest thing of all. That is heartbreaking. It leads people to a sense of hopelessness.[24]

To Porter, the "civil war" at Akwesasne also assumed the shape of a battle between two ways of looking at the world—of spirit and of flesh. Even though the Warriors donned the language and symbols of Iroquois tradition, they practiced the ways of the shark. "We continue to try to give it our best shot, to act as examples of peace. We have to heal. ... I don't want to hurt anyone."[25]

As 1991 drew to a close, there were hints that the healing Porter sought had begun to occur. In late November Mike Mitchell, grand chief of the Canadian council, ended a speech before the Assembly of First Nations in Ottawa by calling on his opponent Francis Boots to stand and recognize a new unity in pursuit of peace at Akwesasne. "We felt we had to make a statement [that] we no longer wanted to fight each other and we should instead fight together not only for Mohawks, but for all natives across Canada. Sometimes your enemy is not really your enemy," Boots said.[26]

However, many people greeted rumors that the state police would withdraw with the fear that the shooting might start again. Even under police occupation some people reported hearing rounds being shot off in the night. A Mohawk group led by Minnie Garrow marched in Albany to protest police brutality while officers on the scene retorted that the demonstration was a ploy to allow the Warriors to regain control of the reservation by armed force.

Nearly two years to the day after Mathew Pyke and "Junior" Edwards were killed at Akwesasne, gambling opponents filed two multimillion dollar, class-action lawsuits against Cuomo, State Police Superintendent Constantine, and the casino operators. They sought compensation for damages suffered during the conflict leading up to the two shooting deaths May 1, 1990. The lawsuits were filed in U.S. District Court at Albany. "This level of violence—a virtual state of terror—would not have been tolerated in any other community in this state. For six weeks in 1990, the state allowed a state of warfare to exist," said David Barrett, attorney for the Mohawks, at a press conference in Albany.[27]

One suit charged Cuomo, Constantine, and the others with violating the civil rights of Akwesasne residents by failing to use state troopers to restore order at Akwesasne as violence escalated in March 1990. "Defendants refused to provide police protection even though they knew that gambling, smuggling, and other illegal racketeering activity was rampant at Akwesasne," stated the complaint.[28] The suit attributed the erection of blockades by gambling opponents to "the defendants' refusal to enforce the law," and enumerated the hundreds of appeals for protection made by reservation residents to authorities in the United States and Canada as "casino operators conspired with and incited

Warriors to commit literally hundreds of criminal acts, including attempted murder, extortion, and arson." The suit contended that police protection was withheld "from the New York portion of Akwesasne on the basis of the race and national origin of its residents."[29]

The second suit charged 45 Akwesasne residents with operating and defending illegal high-stakes gambling operations. Brought under the federal Racketeer Influenced and Corrupt Organizations Act (RICO), the second suit sought to recover gambling revenues and distribute them to the community. "The money was stolen from the community by a few greedy and unscrupulous individuals. The money they have gotten was obtained criminally."[30] The 51-page legal brief contained allegations regarding not only racketeering but also several dozen incidences of attempted murder, arson, and other violations of law on the part of gaming supporters. Barrett estimated that awards under the two lawsuits could range from $100 million to $500 million.

The filing of the two lawsuits stirred memories of the brutal spring two years earlier at Akwesasne, but gambling opponents needed to seek the legal redress even if it reopened old wounds. Selena Smoke, one of several people who brought the suits, recalled at the press conference "I lived right on the border, and I watched the gunfire from the American side into the Canadian side all the time, constantly. That's what I lived in, a war zone. I mean every night [and] every day."[31]

Although Mohawks on both sides of the conflict cannot forget that they live in a community still racked by acute turmoil, there is little doubt in their minds that the Mohawks will survive spiritually, culturally, economically, and environmentally. The Great Law of Peace is too much a part of the Mohawks' psyche and soul to be abandoned; the roots of the symbolic Tree of Peace run deep and secure. This belief was illustrated by the reaction to my first working title, *The White Roots Torn Asunder*. The Mohawk people who did so much to gather information for the book also critiqued its early drafts, and their judgement was that the working title was too harsh, too final. As John Kahionhes Fadden wrote me: "Some branches of the tree have been broken, and there definitely have been diggings beneath the roots with graspings for the weapons buried underneath ... but the roots are still secure."

The roots referred to by Fadden were those of the Iroquois symbolic tree of peace. "Looking at it historically," Fadden continued, "the White Roots have put up with more devastating events ... [such as] ... population-depleting diseases of enormous magnitude, French and Indian wars, the Revolutionary War, the War of 1812, New York and federal legislation, alien religions, et al., and they have survived."[32] As this book was being written, I watched the first tentative attempts to heal the wounds that death had brought to Mohawk Country, to a community that still struggles, and still survives, against very steep environmental and social odds.

Notes

[1] Harry Pyke and Gus Pyke. Interview with author. Akwesasne, August 5, 1991.
[2] Ibid.
[3] Ibid.
[4] *Daily Times* (Watertown, NY), August 4, 1991; *Akwesasne Notes* (Akwesasne), Late Summer 1991.
[5] St. Regis Tribal Council press release, April 24, 1991. In files of *Akwesasne Notes*.
[6] Jake Swamp. Interview with author. Akwesasne Freedom School, August 4, 1991.
[7] St. Regis Tribal Council press release, April 24, 1991.
[8] Ibid.
[9] Ibid. Joesph Gray, St. Regis Tribal Council spokesman and former Massena *Courier-Observer* newspaper editor, traces his ancestry to William Gray, one of the first three trustees appointed by New York state in 1802 to act as liaison with the Mohawk Nation Council. The statement asserted that the elective tradition dated from 1670 when historical accounts related that permanent settlement did not even begin at St. Regis until around 1750.
[10] Ottaway News Service, *Press-Republican* (Plattsburgh, NY), May 3, 1991.
[11] Ibid.
[12] *Daily Times* (Watertown, NY), August 8, 1991.
[13] *Daily Times* (Watertown, NY), August 8, 1991 and August 10, 1991.
[14] *Press-Republican* (Plattsburgh, NY), July 25, 1991.
[15] *Daily Times* (Watertown, NY), October 17, 1991.
[16] *Indian Time* (Akwesasne), October 18, 1991.
[17] Ibid.
[18] *Press-Republican* (Plattsburgh, NY), December 11, 1991.
[19] *Press-Republican* (Plattsburgh, NY), May 7, 1991.
[20] Ottaway News Service, *Press-Republican* (Plattsburgh, NY), n.d. Hunt resigned his position with the Law Enforcement Television Network of Dallas, Texas to take the job; he had been fired from the Syracuse post in December, 1990, by Mayor Tom Young, who cited "policy conflicts." Several community groups in Syracuse protested the firing, as their leaders praised Hunt for dealing effectively with law-enforcement problems in the inner city.
[21] Tom Porter. Interview with author. Akwesasne, August 4, 1991.
[22] "Kanatsiohare: The Clean Pot. A Proposal for the Mohawk Valley for a 1,000-acre Community." Submitted by the Mohawk Community of Akwesasne, January 1990, p. 1.
[23] Tom Porter. Interview with author. Akwesasne, August 4, 1991.
[24] Ibid.
[25] Ibid.
[26] *Daily Times* (Watertown, NY), November 27, 1991. Boots had taken a job with the Mohawk Council of Akwesasne as part of the Community Reconciliation Project begun shortly after the deaths of Mathew Pyke and "Junior" Edwards on May 1, 1990.
[27] *Press-Republican* (Plattsburgh, NY), May 1, 1992.
[28] Complaint number 92-CV-0554, U.S. District Court, Northern District of New York (April 30, 1992): 1–2.
[29] Ibid. pp. 16, 20.
[30] Ibid.
[31] *Times-Union* (Albany, NY), May 1, 1992.
[32] Personal communication, John Kahionhes Fadden to author, December 31, 1990. Copy in files of author and John Kahionhes Fadden.

▼▼▼

Bibliography

For those who wish to delve more deeply into the history and archaeology of the Mohawks, I recommend the following selective bibliography. Once into these titles, a diligent reader will discover many more.

Alfred, Gerald. "From Bad to Worse: Internal Politics in the 1990 Crisis at Kahnawake." *Northeast Indian Quarterly* (Spring 1991).

Beauchamp, William M. *History of the New York Iroquois*. Albany: New York State Education Department, 1905.

Blanchard, David. *Seven Generations: A History of the Kanienkenhaka*. Kahnawake, Quebec: Center for Curriculum Development, Kahnawake Survival School, 1980.

Chalmers, Harvey. *Joseph Brant*. East Lansing: University of Michigan Press, 1955.

Course, M. R. "The Mohawk Iroquois." In *Archaeological Society of Connecticut Bulletin* XXII (1949).

Fenton, William N., ed. *Parker on the Iroquois*. Syracuse, NY: Syracuse University Press, 1968.

Fenton, William N., and Elisabeth Tooker. "Mohawks." In *Handbook of North American Indians: Northeast*, vol. 15. Washington, D.C.: Smithsonian Institution, 1978.

Flexner, James T. *Sir William Johnson: Mohawk Baronet*. New York: Harper's, 1959.

Grassman, Thomas. *The Mohawk Indians and Their Valley*. New York: Fonda, 1969.

Grinde, Donald A., Jr. *The Iroquois and the Founding of the American Nation*. San Francisco: Indian Historian Press, 1977.

Grinde, Donald A., Jr., and Bruce E. Johansen. *Exemplar of Liberty: Native America and the Evolution of Democracy.* Los Angeles: UCLA American Indian Studies Center, 1991.

Hamilton, Milton. *Sir William Johnson: Colonial American, 1715–1763.* Port Washington, NY: Kennikat Press, 1976.

Hauptman, Laurence M. *Formulating American Indian Policy in New York State, 1970–1986.* Albany: State University of New York Press, 1988.

Johansen, Bruce E. *The Forgotten Founders: Benjamin Franklin, the Iroquois and the Rationale for the American Revolution.* Boston and Ipswich, MA: Gambit/Harvard Common Press, 1982 and 1987.

Johnston, Charles M. *The Valley of the Six Nations.* Toronto, Canada: The Champlain Society, 1964.

Lydekker, John W. *The Faithful Mohawk.* Cambridge, UK: Cambridge University Press, 1938.

Mitchell, Mike, ed. *Traditional Teachings.* Cornwall, Ontario: North American Indian Traveling College, 1984.

Newell, William B. *Crime and Justice Among the Iroquois.* Montreal, Quebec: Caughnawage Historical Society, 1965.

Norton, Thomas Eliot. *The Fur Trade in Colonial New York, 1686–1776.* Madison: University of Wisconsin Press, 1974.

Rarihokwats. "How Democracy Came to St. Regis." Rooseveltown, NY: *Akwesasne Notes,* n.d.

Reid, Gerald F. *Mohawk Territory: A Cultural Geography.* Kahnawake, Quebec: Center for Curriculum Development, Kahnawake Survival School, 1981.

Starna, William A., and Charles T. Gehring. *A Journey into Mohawk and Oneida Country, 1634-1635: The Journey of Harmen Mayndertsz Van den Bogaert.* Syracuse, NY: Syracuse University Press, 1988.

Wilson, Edmund. *Apologies to the Iroquois.* New York: Farrar, Straus & Cudahy, 1960.

▼▼▼

Index